THE BEST TEST PREPARATION FOR THE

CLEP

Natural Sciences

With REA's TestWare® on CD-ROM

Laurie Ann Callihan

University Fellow
Florida State University
Tallahassee, Florida

David Callihan

Bishop Hall Charter School
Thomasville, Georgia

Research & Education Association
Visit our website at
www.rea.com

Planet Friendly Publishing
✔ Made in the United States
✔ Printed on Recycled Paper
Text: 10%   Cover: 10%
Learn more: www.greenedition.org

GREEN
EDITION

At REA we're committed to producing books in an Earth-friendly manner and to helping our customers make greener choices.

Manufacturing books in the United States ensures compliance with strict environmental laws and eliminates the need for international freight shipping, a major contributor to global air pollution.

And printing on recycled paper helps minimize our consumption of trees, water and fossil fuels. This book was printed on paper made with **10% post-consumer waste**. According to Environmental Defense's Paper Calculator, by using this innovative paper instead of conventional papers, we achieved the following environmental benefits:

Trees Saved: 4 • Air Emissions Eliminated: 745 pounds
Water Saved: 716 gallons • Solid Waste Eliminated: 220 pounds

For more information on our environmental practices, please visit us online at **www.rea.com/green**

Research & Education Association
61 Ethel Road West
Piscataway, New Jersey 08854
E-mail: info@rea.com

The Best Test Preparation for the
CLEP NATURAL SCIENCES EXAM
With TestWare® on CD-ROM

Printed in the United States of America

Library of Congress Control Number 2009925860

ISBN 13: 978-0-7386-0465-7
ISBN 10: 0-7386-0465-8

Windows® is a registered trademark of Microsoft Corporation.

REA® and TestWare® are registered trademarks of
Research & Education Association, Inc.

CONTENTS

Chapter 4   Structure and Function of Plants and Animals; Genetics

Chapter 5   Ecology and Population Biology

PART II—PHYSICAL SCIENCE

Chapter 6   Atomic Chemistry

Chapter 7   Chemistry of Reactions

Chapter 8   Physics

Chapter 9   Energy

About Research & Education Association

Founded in 1959, Research & Education Association (REA) is dedicated to publishing the finest and most effective educational materials—including software, study guides, and test preps—for students in elementary school, middle school, high school, college, graduate school, and beyond.

Today, REA's wide-ranging catalog is a leading resource for teachers, students, and professionals.

We invite you to visit us at *www.rea.com* to find out how "REA is making the world smarter."

Acknowledgments

In addition to our author, we would like to thank Larry B. Kling, Vice President, Editorial, for his overall guidance, which brought this publication to completion; Pam Weston, Vice President, Publishing, for setting the quality standards for production integrity and managing the publication to completion; John Cording, Vice President, Technology, for coordinating the design and development of REA's TestWare®; Diane Goldschmidt, Senior Editor, for editorial project management; Alice Leonard, Senior Editor, for preflight editorial review; Heena Patel and Amy Jamison, Technology Project Managers, for their design contributions and software testing efforts; and Christine Saul, Senior Graphic Designer, for designing our cover.

We also extend our thanks to Christina Alex for copyediting, Ellen Gong for proofreading, Terry Casey for indexing, and Kathy Caratozzolo of Caragraphics for typesetting this edition.

About Our Authors

Laurie Ann Callihan received her Bachelor of Science in Biology from San Diego Christian College in El Cajon, California. She is currently pursuing her Ph.D. in Science Education as a University Fellow at Florida State University. She has extensive writing, speaking, and teaching experience. Her authorship includes *The Best Test Preparation for the CLEP Biology Exam* and other REA titles and journal articles currently in press. She is an internationally known speaker on education, having been the keynote speaker at state and local education conventions throughout the U.S., Canada, and Mexico. In addition to years of study, curriculum development, and teaching Biology and Physical Science, her current research focuses on development of effective teaching methods and tools for conceptual understanding.

David Callihan earned a Bachelor of Science in Geophysics from San Diego Christian College in El Cajon, California. He currently teaches physical science and mathematics at Bishop Hall Charter School in Thomasville (Thomas County), Georgia. He began his teaching career at DeSoto Middle School in Arcadia, Florida, where he was recognized as the top performing teacher based on AYP results. Prior to becoming a teacher, Mr. Callihan had a successful career in manufacturing, oil exploration, and high technology sales. Mr. Callihan is a Zero-G teacher coach, and has worked with the Florida Space Grant Consortium, the Center for Oceanic Studies in Educational Excellence, and the Florida Institute of Phosphate Research. He is currently working on his Master's in Science Education at Florida State University.

CLEP NATURAL SCIENCES
Independent Study Schedule

The following study schedule allows for thorough preparation for the CLEP Natural Sciences exam. Although it is designed for four weeks, it can be condensed to a two-week course by collapsing each two-week period into one. Be sure to set aside enough time—at least two hours each day—to study. No matter which study schedule works best for you, the more time you spend sudying, the more prepared and relaxed you will feel on the day of the exam.

Week	Activity
1	Read and study Chapter 1 of this book, which will introduce you to the CLEP Natural Sciences exam. Take Practice Test 1 on CD-ROM to determine your strengths and weaknesses. Assess your results by using our raw score conversion table. You can then determine the areas in which you need to strengthen you skills.
2	Carefully read and study the review material for Biological Science found in Chapters 2 through 5 in this book.
3	Read and study the review material for Physical Science found in Chapters 6 through 11 in this book.
4	Take Practice Test 2 on CD-ROM and carefully review the explanations for all of the questions you answered incorrectly. Take Practice Test 3 printed in this book and again review the explanations for the questions you answered incorrectly. If there are any types of questions or particular subjects that still seem difficult to you, review those subjects by again studying the appropriate sections of the CLEP Natural Sciences review chapters.

Note: If you care to, and time allows, retake the Practice Tests. This will help strengthen the areas in which your performance may still be lagging and build your overall confidence.

Chapter 1

Passing the CLEP Natural Sciences Exam

ABOUT THIS BOOK AND TESTWARE®

This book provides you with complete preparation for the CLEP Natural Sciences exam. Inside you will find a targeted review of the subject matter, as well as tips and strategies for test taking. We also give you three practice tests, featuring content and formatting based on the official CLEP Natural Sciences exam. Our practice tests contain every type of question that you can expect to encounter on the actual exam. Following each practice test you will find an answer key with detailed explanations designed to help you more completely understand the test material.

Practice tests 1 and 2 are included in two formats: in printed format in this book, and in TestWare® format on the enclosed CD. **We strongly recommend that you begin your preparation with the TestWare® practice exams.** The software provides the added benefits of instant scoring and enforced time conditions. Practice test 3 is included in printed format only.

All CLEP exams are computer-based. As you can see, the practice tests in our book are presented as paper-and-pencil exams. The content and format of the actual CLEP subject exams are faithfully mirrored. Later in this chapter you'll find a detailed outline of the format and content of the CLEP Natural Sciences exam.

ABOUT THE EXAM

Who takes CLEP exams and what are they used for?

CLEP examinations are typically taken by people who have acquired knowledge outside the classroom and wish to bypass certain college courses and earn college credit. The CLEP is designed to reward students for learning—no matter where or how that knowledge was acquired. The CLEP is the most widely accepted credit-by-examination program in the country, with more than 2,900 colleges and universities granting credit for satisfactory scores on CLEP exams.

Although most CLEP examinees are adults returning to college, many graduating high school seniors, enrolled college students, military personnel, and international students also take the exams to earn college credit or to demonstrate their ability to perform at the college level. There are no prerequisites, such as age or educational status, for taking CLEP examinations. However, because policies on granting credits vary among colleges, you should contact the particular institution from which you wish to receive CLEP credit.

There are two categories of CLEP examinations:

1. **CLEP General Examinations**, which are five separate tests that cover material usually taken as requirements during the first two years of college. CLEP General Examinations are available for English Composition (with or without essay), Humanities, College Mathematics, Natural Sciences, and Social Sciences and History.

2. **CLEP Subject Examinations** include material usually covered in an undergraduate course with a similar title. For a complete list of the subject examinations offered, visit the College Board website.

Who administers the exam?

The CLEP exams are developed by the College Board, administered by Educational Testing Service (ETS), and involve the assistance of educators throughout the United States. The test development process is designed and implemented to ensure that the content and difficulty level of the test are appropriate.

When and where is the exam given?

CLEP exams are administered each month throughout the year at more than 1,300 test centers in the United States and can be arranged for candidates abroad on request. To find the test center nearest you and to register for the exam, you should obtain a copy of the free booklets *CLEP Colleges* and *CLEP Information for Candidates and Registration Form*. They are available at most colleges where CLEP credit is granted, or by contacting:

CLEP Services
P.O. Box 6600
Princeton, NJ 08541-6600
Phone: (800) 257-9558 (8 A.M. to 6 P.M. ET)
Fax: (609) 771-7088
Website: *www.collegeboard.com/clep*

CLEP Options for Military Personnel and Veterans

CLEP exams are available free of charge to eligible military personnel and eligible civilian employees. All the CLEP exams are available at test centers on college campuses and military bases. In addition, the College Board has developed a paper-based version of 14 high-volume/high-pass-rate CLEP tests for DANTES Test Centers. Contact the Educational Services Officer or Navy College Education Specialist for more information. Visit the College Board website for details about CLEP opportunities for military personnel.

Eligible U.S. veterans can claim reimbursement for CLEP exams and administration fees pursuant to provisions of the Veterans Benefits Improvement Act of 2004. For details on eligibility and submitting a claim for reimbursement, visit the U.S. Department of Veterans Affairs website at *www.gibill. va.gov/pamphlets/testing.htm*.

SSD Accommodations for Students with Disabilities

Many students qualify for extra time to take the CLEP Natural Sciences exam, but you must make these arrangements in advance. For information, contact:

College Board Services for Students with Disabilities
P.O. Box 6226
Princeton, NJ 08541-6226
Phone: (609) 771-7137 (Monday through Friday, 8 A.M. to 6 P.M. ET)
TTY: (609) 882-4118
Fax: (609) 771-7944
E-mail: ssd@info.collegeboard.org

Our TestWare® can be adapted to accommodate your time extension. This allows you to practice under the same extended-time accommodations that you will receive on the actual test day. To customize your TestWare® to suit the most common extensions, visit our website at *http://www.rea.com/ssd*.

HOW TO USE THIS BOOK AND TESTWARE®

What do I study first?

To begin your studies, read over the introduction and the suggestions for test taking. Take Practice Exam 1 on CD-ROM to determine your strengths and weaknesses, and then study the course review material, focusing on your specific problem areas. The course review includes the information you need to know when taking the exam. Make sure to follow up your diagnostic work by taking the remaining practice exam on CD-ROM to become familiar with the format and feel of the CLEP Natural Sciences exam.

To best utilize your study time, follow our Independent Study Schedule, which you'll find in the front of this book. The schedule is based on a four-week program, but can be condensed to two weeks if necessary by collapsing each two-week period into one.

When should I start studying?

It is never too early to start studying for the CLEP Natural Sciences exam. The earlier you begin, the more time you will have to sharpen your skills. Do not procrastinate! Cramming is not an effective way to study, since it does not allow you the time needed to learn the test material. The sooner you learn the format of the exam, the more time you will have to familiarize yourself with it.

FORMAT AND CONTENT OF THE EXAM

The CLEP Natural Sciences exam covers the material one would find in a freshman or sophomore general science survey course covering biology and physical science. It is meant for students who are non-science majors. The exam stresses basic facts and principles, as well as general theoretical approaches used by scientists.

There are 120 multiple-choice questions on the exam, each with five possible answer choices, to be answered in 90 minutes.

The approximate breakdown of topics is as follows:

50% Biological Science

    10% Origin, evolution, and classification of life (Chapter 2)

    10% Cell organization and division, gene regulation, bioenergetics,biosynthesis (Chapter 3)

    20% Structure, function, and development of organisms; heredity (Chapter 4)

    10% Concepts of population biology, ecology (Chapter 5)

50% Physical Science

7% Atomic and nuclear structure, properties, and reactions, elementary particles (Chapter 6)

10% Chemical elements, compounds, reactions, molecular structure and bonding (Chapter 7)

12% Heat, thermodynamics, states of matter; classical mechanics; relativity (Chapter 8)

4% Electricity and magnetism, waves, light, and sound (Chapter 9)

7% The universe: galaxies, stars, the solar system (Chapter 10)

10% Earth: atmosphere, hydrosphere, structure features, geologic processes and history (Chapter 11)

ABOUT OUR COURSE REVIEW

The review in this book provides you with a complete background of all the important natural sciences principles and theories relevant to the exam. It will help reinforce the facts you have already learned while better shaping your understanding of the discipline as a whole. By using the review in conjunction with the practice tests, you should be well prepared to take the CLEP Natural Sciences exam.

SCORING YOUR PRACTICE TESTS

How do I score my practice tests?

The CLEP Natural Sciences exam is scored on a scale of 20 to 80. To score your practice tests, count up the number of correct answers. This is your total raw score. Convert your raw score to a scaled score using the conversion table on the following page. (*Note:* The conversion table provides only an estimate of your scaled score. Scaled scores can and do vary over time, and in no case should a sample test be taken as a precise predictor of test performance. Nonetheless, our scoring table allows you to judge your level of performance within a reasonable scoring range.)

When will I receive my score report?

The test administrator will print out a full Candidate Score Report for you immediately upon your completion of the exam (except for CLEP English

PRACTICE-TEST RAW SCORE CONVERSION TABLE*

Raw Score	Scaled Score	Course Grade		Raw Score	Scaled Score	Course Grade
120	80	A		60	55	B
119	80	A		59	54	B
118	80	A		58	54	B
117	80	A		57	53	B
116	80	A		56	53	B
115	80	A		55	52	B
114	79	A		54	52	B
113	79	A		53	51	B
112	79	A		52	51	C
111	79	A		51	50	C
110	78	A		50	50	C
109	78	A		49	50	C
108	78	A		48	49	C
107	77	A		47	49	C
106	77	A		46	48	C
105	77	A		45	48	C
104	77	A		44	47	C
103	76	A		43	47	C
102	76	A		42	47	C
101	75	A		41	47	C
100	75	A		40	46	D
99	75	A		39	46	D
98	74	A		38	45	D
97	74	A		37	45	D
96	73	A		36	44	D
95	73	A		35	44	D
94	73	B		34	43	D
93	72	B		33	43	D
92	72	B		32	42	D
91	71	B		31	41	D
90	71	B		30	40	D
89	70	B		29	39	D
88	69	B		28	38	D
87	69	B		27	37	D
86	68	B		26	36	D
85	68	B		25	35	D
84	67	B		24	34	F
83	67	B		23	34	F
82	67	B		22	33	F
81	66	B		21	33	F
80	66	B		20	32	F
79	65	B		19	32	F
78	65	B		18	31	F
77	65	B		17	31	F
76	64	B		16	30	F
75	64	B		15	29	F
74	63	B		14	28	F
73	63	B		13	28	F
72	62	B		12	27	F
71	62	B		11	27	F
70	61	B		10	26	F
69	61	B		9	25	F
68	60	B		8	24	F
67	59	B		7	23	F
66	59	B		6	22	F
65	58	B		5	21	F
64	57	B		4	20	F
63	57	B		3	20	F
62	56	B		2	20	F
61	56	B		1	20	F
				0	20	F

* This table is provided for scoring REA practice tests only. The American Council on Education recommends that colleges use a single across-the-board credit-granting score of 50 for all CLEP computer-based exams. Nonetheless, on account of the different skills being measured and the unique content requirements of each test, the actual number of correct answers needed to reach 50 will vary. A 50 is calibrated to equate with performance that would warrant the grade C in the corresponding introductory college course.

Composition with Essay). Your scores are reported only to you, unless you ask to have them sent elsewhere. If you want your scores reported to a college or other institution, you must say so when you take the examination. Since your scores are kept on file for 20 years, you can also request transcripts from Educational Testing Service at a later date.

STUDYING FOR THE EXAM

It is very important for you to choose the time and place for studying that works best for you. Some students may set aside a certain number of hours every morning, while others may choose to study at night before going to sleep. Other students may study during the day, while waiting on a line, or even while eating lunch. Only you can determine when and where your study time will be most effective. But be consistent and use your time wisely. Work out a study routine and stick to it!

When you take the practice tests, try to make your testing conditions as much like the actual test as possible. Turn your television and radio off, and sit down at a quiet table free from distraction. Make sure to time yourself. Start off by setting a timer for the time that is allotted for each section, and be sure to reset the timer for the appropriate amount of time when you start a new section.

As you complete each practice test, score your test and thoroughly review the explanations to the questions you answered incorrectly; however, do not review too much at one time. Concentrate on one problem area at a time by reviewing the question and explanation, and by studying our review until you are confident that you completely understand the material.

TEST-TAKING TIPS

Although you may not be familiar with computer-based standardized tests such as the CLEP Natural Sciences exam, there are many ways to acquaint yourself with this type of examination and to help alleviate your test-taking anxieties. Listed below are ways to help you become accustomed to the CLEP, some of which may be applied to other standardized tests as well.

Know the format of the test. CLEP computer-based tests are not adaptive but rather fixed-length tests. In a sense, this makes them kin to the familiar paper-and-pencil exam in that you have the same flexibility to go back and review your work in each section. Moreover, the format isn't a great deal different from the paper-and-pencil CLEP.

Read all of the possible answers. Just because you think you have found the correct response, do not automatically assume that it is the best answer. Read through each choice to be sure that you are not making a mistake by jumping to conclusions.

Use the process of elimination. Go through each answer to a question and eliminate as many of the answer choices as possible. By eliminating just two answer choices, you give yourself a better chance of getting the item correct, since there will only be three choices left from which to make your guess. Remember, your score is based only on the number of questions you answer correctly.

Work quickly and steadily. You will have only 90 minutes to work on 120 questions, so work quickly and steadily to avoid focusing on any one question too long. Taking the practice tests in this book will help you learn to budget your time.

Acquaint yourself with the computer screen. Familiarize yourself with the CLEP computer screen beforehand by logging on to the College Board website. Waiting until test day to see what it looks like in the pretest tutorial risks injecting needless anxiety into your testing experience. Also, familiarizing yourself with the directions and format of the exam will save you valuable time on the day of the actual test.

Be sure that your answer registers before you go to the next item. Look at the screen to see that your mouse-click causes the pointer to darken the proper oval. This takes less effort than darkening an oval on paper, but don't lull yourself into taking less care!

THE DAY OF THE EXAM

On the day of the test, you should wake up early (hopefully after a decent night's rest) and have a good breakfast. Make sure to dress comfortably, so that you are not distracted by being too hot or too cold while taking the test. Also plan to arrive at the test center early. This will allow you to collect your thoughts and relax before the test, and will also spare you the anxiety that comes with being late. As an added incentive to make sure you arrive early, keep in mind that no one will be allowed into the test session after the test has begun.

Before you leave for the test center, make sure that you have your admission form and another form of identification, which must contain a recent photograph, your name, and signature (i.e., driver's license, student identification card, or current alien registration card). You will not be admitted to the test center if you do not have proper identification.

If you would like, you may wear a watch to the test center. However, you may not wear one that makes noise, because it may disturb the other test-takers. No dictionaries, textbooks, notebooks, briefcases, or packages will be permitted and drinking, smoking, and eating are prohibited.

Good luck on your CLEP Natural Sciences exam!

PART I
Biological Science

Chapter 2

Evolution

HISTORY OF EVOLUTIONARY CONCEPTS

Evolutionary concepts are the foundation of much of the current study in biology. The term **evolution** refers to the gradual change of characteristics within a population, producing a change in species over time. Evolution is driven by the process of **natural selection**, a feature of population genetics first articulated by Charles Darwin in his book *The Origin of Species by Means of Natural Selection, or The Preservation of Favoured Races in the Struggle for Life* (published in 1859). Darwin was the first to explain natural selection as a driving force, and the first to lay out the full range of evidence for evolution. However, scientists before Darwin had already promoted some of the ideas inherent in evolutionary biology.

Carolus Linnaeus, the well-known botanist (who is credited with developing the classification system for organisms still used widely today) speculated on the origin of and relationships between groups of species in the mid-1700s. The French scientist Lamarck proposed that organisms acquire traits over their lifespan that equip them to survive within

ORIGIN OF SPECIES.

INTRODUCTION.

When on board H.M.S. 'Beagle,' as naturalist, I was much struck with certain facts in the distribution of the organic beings inhabiting South America, and in the geological relations of the present to the past inhabitants of that continent. These facts, as will be seen in the latter chapters of this volume, seemed to throw some light on the origin of species—that mystery of mysteries, as it has been called by one of our greatest philosophers. On my return home, it occurred to me, in 1837, that something might perhaps be made out on this question by patiently accumulating and reflecting on all sorts of facts which could possibly have any bearing on it. After five years' work I allowed myself to speculate on the subject, and drew up some short notes ; these I enlarged in 1844 into a sketch of the conclusions, which then seemed to me probable : from that period to the present day I have steadily pursued the same object. I hope that I may be excused for entering on these personal details, as I give them to show that I have not been hasty in coming to a decision.

My work is now (1859) nearly finished; but as it will take me many more years to complete it, and as my health is far from strong, I have been urged to publish this Abstract. I have more especially been induced to do this, as Mr. Wallace, who is now studying the natural history of the Malay archipelago, has arrived at almost exactly the same general conclusions that I have on the origin of species. In 1858 he sent me a memoir on this subject, with a request that I would forward it to Sir Charles Lyell, who sent it to the Linnean Society, and it is published in the third volume of the Journal of that Society. Sir C. Lyell and Dr. Hooker, who both knew of my work—the latter having read my sketch of 1844—honoured me by thinking it advisable to publish, with Mr. Wallace's excellent memoir, some brief extracts from my manuscripts.

This Abstract, which I now publish, must necessarily be imperfect. I cannot here give references and authorities for my

Introduction to the 1859 edition of Charles Darwin's *Origin of Species.*

their environment and pass those traits on to their offspring. He presented the idea that, for example, giraffes developed longer necks during their lifetime from their efforts to reach food high on tree branches. The children, born with longer necks would then further lengthen their necks reaching for high branches, passing these even longer necks on to their children. This Lamarckian theory of acquired characteristics has since been discredited.

Darwinian Concept of Natural Selection

Current theories of evolution have their basis in the work of Charles Darwin and one of his contemporaries, Alfred Russell Wallace. Darwin's book, however, served to catalyze the study of evolution across scientific disciplines. A synopsis of Darwin's ideas follows.

From a study of populations, we know that population growth and maintenance of a species is dependent on limiting factors. Individuals within the species that are unable to acquire the minimum requirement of resources are unable to reproduce. The ecosystem can support only a limited number of organisms—known as the carrying capacity (usually designated by the letter K).

Once the carrying capacity (K) is reached, a competition for resources ensues. Darwin considered this competition to be the basic *struggle for existence*. Some of the competitors will fail to survive. Within every population, there is variation among traits. Darwin proposed that those individuals who win the competition for resources pass those successful traits on to their children. Only the surviving competitors reproduce successfully generation after generation. Therefore, traits providing the competitive edge will be represented most often in succeeding generations.

Modern Concept of Natural Selection

Although the concepts of natural selection put forth by Darwin still form the basis of evolutionary theory today, Darwin had no real knowledge of genetics when he put forth his ideas.

Several years after Darwin's writings, Mendel's work (on experimental genetics) was rediscovered independently by three scientists. The laws of genetics served to support the suppositions Darwin had made. Over the next 40 years, the study of genetics included not only individual organisms but also population genetics (how traits are preserved, changed, or introduced within a population of organisms). Progress in the studies of biogeography and paleontology of the early 1900s also served to reinforce Darwin's basic observations.

The modern concept of natural selection emerged from Darwin's original ideas, with additions and confirmations of genetics, population studies, and paleontology. This **modern synthesis** focused on the concept that evolution was a process of gradual (over thousands or hundreds of thousands of generations) adaptive change in traits among populations.

Mechanisms of Evolution

Modern understanding of the process of natural selection recognizes that there are some basic mechanisms that support evolutionary change. Mutations happen only in individuals, and natural selection happens to individuals. However, modern theories focus on the change that occurs among populations, not in individuals.

All evolution is dependent upon genetic change. The entire collection of genes within a given population is known as its **gene pool.** Individuals in the population will have only one pair of alleles for a particular single-gene trait. Yet, the gene pool may contain dozens or hundreds of alleles for this trait. Evolution does not occur through changes from individual to individual, but rather as the gene pool changes through one of a number of possible mechanisms.

One mechanism that drives the changing of traits over time in a population is **differential reproduction.** Natural selection assumes some individuals within a population are more suited for survival, given environmental conditions. Differential reproduction takes this supposition one step further by proposing that those individuals within a population that are most adapted to the environment are also the most likely individuals to reproduce successfully. Therefore, the reproductive processes tend to strengthen the frequency of expression of desirable traits across the population. Differential reproduction increases the number of alleles for desirable traits in the gene pool. This trend will be established and strengthen gradually over time, eventually producing a population where the desirable trait is dominant, if environmental conditions remain the same.

Another mechanism of genetic change is mutation. A **mutation** is a change of the DNA sequence of a gene, resulting in a change of the trait. Although a mutation can cause a very swift change in the genotype (genetic code) and possibly phenotype (expressed trait) of the offspring, mutations do not necessarily produce a trait desirable for a particular environment. Mutation is a much more random occurrence than differential reproduction.

Although mutations occur quickly, the change in the gene pool is minimal, so change in the population occurs very slowly (over multiple generations). Mutation does provide a vehicle of introducing new genetic possibilities; genetic traits, which did not exist in the original gene pool, can be introduced through mutation.

A third mechanism recognized to influence the evolution of new traits is known as **genetic drift.** Over time, a gene pool (particularly in a small population) may experience a change in frequency of particular genes simply due to chance fluctuations. In a finite population, the gene pool may not reflect the entire number of genetic possibilities of the larger genetic pool of the species population. Over time, the genetic pool within this finite population changes, and evolution has occurred. Genetic drift has no particular tie to environmental conditions, and thus the random change in gene frequency is unpredictable. The change of gene frequency may produce a small or a large change, depending on what traits are affected. The process of genetic drift, as opposed to mutation, actually causes a reduction in genetic variety.

Genetic drift occurs within finite separated populations, allowing that population to develop its own distinct gene pool. However, occasionally an individual from an adjacent population of the same species may immigrate and breed with a member of the previously locally isolated group. The introduction of new genes from the immigrant results in a change of the gene pool, known as **gene migration.** Gene migration is also occasionally successful between members of different, but related, species. The resultant hybrids succeed in adding increased variability to the gene pool.

The study of genetics shows that in a situation where random mating is occurring within a population (which is in equilibrium with its environment), gene frequencies and genotype ratios will remain constant from generation to generation. This law is known as the **Hardy-Weinberg Law of Equilibrium,** named after the two men (G.H. Hardy and Wilhelm Weinberg, c. 1909) who first studied this principle in mathematical studies of genetics. The Hardy-Weinberg Law is a mathematical formula that shows why recessive genes do not disappear over time from a population.

According to the Hardy-Weinberg Law, the sum of the frequencies of all possible alleles for a particular trait is 1. That is,

$$p + q = 1$$

where the frequency of one allele is represented by **p** and the frequency of another is **q**. It then follows mathematically that the frequency of genotypes within a population can be represented by the equation:

$$p^2 + 2pq + q^2 = 1$$

where the frequency of homozygous dominant genotypes is represented by p^2, the homozygous recessive by q^2, and the heterozygous genotype by $2pq$.

For instance, in humans the ability to taste the chemical phenylthiocarbamide (PTC) is a dominant inherited trait. If **T** represents the allele for tasting PTC and **t** represents the recessive trait (inability to taste PTC) then the possible genotypes in a population would by **TT**, **Tt**, and **tt**. If the frequency of non-tasters in a particular population is 4% or 0.04 (that is, $q^2 = 0.04$), then the frequency of the allele **t** equals the square root of 0.04 or 0.2. It is then possible to calculate the frequency of the dominant allele, **T**, in the population using the equation:

$$p + 0.2 = 1 \text{ so, } p = 0.8$$

The frequency of the allele for tasting PTC is 0.8. The frequency of the various possible genotypes (**TT**, **Tt**, and **tt**) in the population can also be calculated since the frequency of the homozygous dominant is p^2 or 0.64 or 64%. The frequency of the heterozygous genotype is 2pq.

$$2pq = 2(0.8)(0.2) = 0.32 = 32\%.$$

Frequency of TT = 64%, Tt = 32%, tt is 4% . . . totaling 100%
or 0.64 + 0.32 + 0.04 = 1

In order for Hardy-Weinberg equilibrium to occur, the population in question must meet the following conditions, random mating (no differential reproduction) must be taking place and no migration, mutation, selection, or genetic drift can be occurring. When these conditions are met, Hardy-Weinberg equilibrium can occur, and there will be no changes in the gene pool over time. Hardy-Weinberg is important to the evolutionary process because it shows that alleles that have no current selective value will be retained in a population over time.

Speciation

A species is an interbreeding population that shares a common gene pool and produces viable offspring. Up to this point we have been considering mechanisms that produce variation within species. It is apparent that to explain evolution on a broad scale we must understand how genetic change produces new species. There are two mechanisms that produce separate species: allopatric speciation and sympatric speciation.

In order for a new species to develop, substantial genetic changes must occur between populations, which prohibit them from interbreeding. These genetic changes may result from genetic drift or from mutation that take place separately in the two populations. **Allopatric speciation** occurs when two populations are geographically isolated from each other. For instance, a population of squirrels may be geographically separated by a catastrophic event such as a volcanic eruption. Two populations (separated by the volcanic flow) continue to reproduce and experience genetic drift and/or mutation over time. This limits each population's gene pool and produces changes in expressed traits. Later, the geographical separation may be eliminated as the volcanic flow subsides; even so, the two populations have now experienced too much change to allow them to successfully interbreed again. The result is the production of two separate species.

Speciation may also occur without a geographic separation when a population develops members with a genetic difference, which prevents successful reproduction with the original species. The genetically different members reproduce with each other, producing a population, which is separate from the original species. This process is called **sympatric speciation**.

As populations of an organism in a given area grow, some will move into new geographic areas looking for new resources or to escape predators. (In this case, a natural event does not separate the population; instead, part of the population moves.) Some of these adventurers will discover new niches and advantageous conditions. Traits possessed by this traveling population will grow more common over several generations through the process of natural selection. Over time the species will specially adapt to live more effectively in the new environment. Through this process, known as **adaptive radiation,** a single species can develop into several diverse species over time. If the separated populations merge again and are able to successfully interbreed, then by definition new species have not been developed. Adaptive radiation is proven to have occurred when the species remerge and do not interbreed successfully.

All of the above evolutionary mechanisms are dependent upon reproduction of organisms over a long period of time, a very gradual process. **Punctuated equilibrium** is an entirely different method of explaining speciation. Punctuated equilibrium is a scientific model that proposes that adaptations of species arise suddenly and rapidly. Punctuated equilibrium states that species undergo a long period of equilibrium, which at some point is upset by environmental forces causing a short period of quick mutation and change.

Punctuated equilibrium was first proposed as paleontologists studied the fossil record. Gradualism would produce slowly changing and adapting species over many generations. However, the fossil record seems to show that organisms in general survive many generations in many areas with very little change over long periods of geologic time. New species appear in the fossils suddenly, without transitional forms, though "sudden" in this context needs to be understood on a geologic time scale.

Scientists still do not agree on the degree to which gradualism, punctuated equilibrium, or a combination of these processes is responsible for speciation.

There are also beliefs about origins (e.g., intelligent design, scientific creationism, and theistic evolution) involving neither of these ideas that depend instead on faith in an intelligent creator. These beliefs have survived in spite of scientific investigators having concluded that, as the National Academy of Sciences has put it, "the same forces responsible for the evolution of all other life forms on Earth can account for the evolution of human beings."

PLANT AND ANIMAL EVOLUTION

Evolution of the First Cells

The modern theory of the evolution of life on Earth assumes the earliest forms of life began approximately four billion years ago. It is presumed that conditions on Earth were very different from conditions today. The pre-life Earth environment would have been rich in water, ammonia, and methane, all compounds rich in hydrogen. In order for life to arise on Earth, organic molecules such as amino acids (the building blocks of proteins), sugars, acids, and bases would need to have formed from the available chemicals.

Over the last century there has been much research into plausible mechanisms for the origin of life. The **Oparin Hypothesis** is one theory regarding origin of life, developed by a Russian scientist (A.I. Oparin) in 1924. Oparin proposed that the Earth was formed approximately 4.6 billion years old and that the early Earth had a reducing atmosphere, meaning there was very little free oxygen present. Instead, there was an abundance of ammonia, hydrogen, methane, and steam (H_2O), all escaping from volcanoes. The Earth was in the process of cooling down, so there was a great deal of heat energy available, as well as a pattern of recurring violent lightening storms providing another source of energy. During this cooling of the Earth, much of the steam surrounding the Earth would condense, forming hot seas. In the presence of abundant energy, the synthesis of simple organic molecules from the available chemicals became possible. These organic substances then collected in the hot, turbulent seas (sometimes referred to as the "primordial soup").

As the concentration of organic molecules became very high, they began forming into larger, charged, complex molecules. Oparin called these highly absorptive molecules "coacervates." Coacervates were also able to divide.

Oparin's research involved experimental findings of evidence to support his ideas that amino acids could combine to form proteins under early Earth conditions. Oparin knew proteins were catalysts, so they could encourage further change and development of early cells.

Stanley Miller provided support for Oparin's hypotheses in experiments where he exposed simple inorganic molecules to electrical charges similar to lightning. Miller recreated conditions as they were supposed to exist in early Earth history, and was successful in his attempts to produce complex organic molecules including amino acids under these conditions. Miller's experiments served to support Oparin's hypotheses.

Sidney Fox, a major evolution researcher of the 1960s, conducted experiments that proved ultraviolet light may induce the formation of dipeptides from amino acids. Under conditions of moderate dry heat, Fox showed formation of proteinoids, polypeptides of up to 18 amino acids. He also showed that poly-phosphoric acid could increase the yield of these polymers, a process that simulates the modern role of ATP in protein synthesis. These proteins formed small spheres known as microspheres; these showed similarities to living cells.

Further strides were made by researcher Cyril Ponnamperuma who demonstrated that small amounts of guanine formed from the thermal polymerization of amino acids. He also proved the synthesis of adenine and ribose from long-term treatment of reducing atmospheric gases with electrical current.

Once organic compounds had been synthesized, primitive cells most likely developed that contained genetic material in the form of RNA, and that used energy derived from ATP. These primitive cells were prokaryotic and similar to some bacteria now found on Earth.

The endosymbiont theory suggests that original prokaryotic cells took in other cells that performed various tasks. For instance, an original cell could absorb several symbiotic bacteria that then evolve into mitochondria. Several cells that lived in symbiosis would have combined and evolved to form a single eukaryotic cell.

Plant Evolution

The evolution of plant species is considered to have begun with heterotrophic prokaryotic cells. Since it is presumed that the early Earth's atmosphere was lacking in oxygen, early cells were anaerobic. Over time, some bacteria evolved the ability to carry on photosynthesis (cyano-bacteria), thus becoming autotrophic, which in turn introduced significant amounts of oxygen into the atmosphere. As oxygen is poisonous to most anaerobic cells, a new niche opened up: cells able not only to survive in the presence of oxygen, but also to use it in metabolism.

Cyanobacteria were incorporated into larger aerobic cells, which then evolved into photosynthetic eukaryotic cells. Cellular organization increased, nuclei and membranes formed, and cell specialization occurred, leading to multicellular photosynthetic organisms, that is, plants.

The earliest plants were aquatic, but as niches filled in marine and freshwater environments, plants began to move onto land. Anatomical changes occurred over time allowing plants to survive in a non-aqueous environment. Cell walls thickened, and tissues to carry water and nutrients developed. As plants continued to adapt to land conditions, differentiation of tissues continued, resulting in the evolution of stems, leaves, roots, and seeds. The development of the seed was a key factor in the survival of land plants. Asexual reproduction dominated in early species, but sexual reproduction developed over time, increasing the possibilities of diversity.

Processes of adaptive radiation, genetic drift, and natural selection continued over long periods of time to produce the incredible diversity seen in the plant world today.

Animal Evolution

The evolution of animals is thought to have begun with marine protists. Although there is no fossil record, going back to the protist level, animal cells bear the most similarity to marine protist cells. Fossilized burrows from multicellular organisms begin to appear in the geological record approximately 700 million years ago, during the Precambrian period. These multicellular animals had only soft parts—no hard parts, which could be fossilized.

During the Cambrian period (the first period of the Paleozoic Era), beginning about 570 million years ago, the fossil record begins to show multicellular organisms with hard parts, namely exoskeletons. The fossil record at this time includes fossil representations from all modern day (and some extinct) phyla. This sudden appearance of multitudes of differentiated animal forms is known as the **Cambrian explosion**.

At the end of the Paleozoic Era, the fossil record attests to several mass extinction events. These combined events resulted in the extinction of about 95% of animal species developed to that point. Fossils indicate that many organisms, such as Trilobites, that were numerous in the Cambrian era, did not survive the end of the Paleozoic Era.

Approximately 505 million years ago was the beginning of the Ordovician period, which lasted until about 440 million years ago. The Ordovician period was marked by diversification among species that survived past the Cambrian extinctions. The Ordovician is also known for the development of land plants. Early forms of fish arose in the Cambrian, but developed during the Ordovician, these being the first vertebrates to be seen in the fossil record. Again, the end of the Ordovician is marked by vast extinctions, but these extinctions allowed the opening of ecological situations, which in turn encouraged adaptive radiation.

Adaptive radiation is the mechanism credited with the development of new species in the next period, the Silurian, from 440 to 410 million years ago. The Silurian period is marked by widespread colonization of landmasses by plants and animals. Large numbers of insect fossils are recognizable in Silurian geologic sediments, as well as fish and early amphibians. The mass movement onto land by formerly marine animals required adaptation in numerous areas including gas exchange, support (skeletal), water conservation, circulatory systems, and reproduction.

In the study of animal evolution, attention is paid to two concepts, homology, and analogy. Structures that exist in two different species because they share a common ancestry are called **homologous**. For instance, the forelimbs of a salamander and an opossum are similar in structure because of common ancestry. **Analogous** structures are similar because of their common function, although they do not share a common ancestry. Analogous structures are the product of **convergent evolution**. For instance, birds and insects both have wings, although they are not relatives. Rather the wings evolved as a result of convergence. Convergence occurs when a particular characteristic evolves in two unrelated populations. Wings of insects and birds are analogous structures (they are similar in function regardless of the lack of common ancestors).

The process of **extinction** has played a large part in the direction evolution has taken. Extinctions occur at a generally low rate at all times. It is presumed that species that face extinction have not been able to adapt appropriately to environmental changes. However, there have also been several "extinction events" that have wiped out up to 95% of the species of their time. These events served to open up massive ecological niches, encouraging evolution of multitudes of new species.

Approximately 400 million years ago, the first amphibians gave rise to early reptiles that then diversified into birds, then mammals. One branch of mammals developed into the tree dwelling primates, considered the ancestors of humans.

Human Evolution

Humans are thought to have evolved from primates who over time developed larger brains. A branch of bipedal primates gave rise to the first true hominids about 4.5 million years ago. The earliest known hominid fossils were found in Africa in the 1970s. The well-known "Lucy" skeleton was named *Australopithecus afarensis*. It was determined from the skeleton of *Australopithecus*

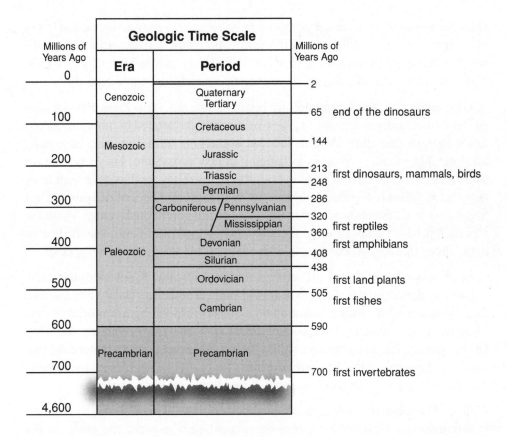

that it was a biped. It had a human-like jaw and teeth, but a skull that was more similar to that of a small ape. The arms were proportionately longer than humans, indicating the ability to still be motile in trees.

The fossilized skull of *Homo erectus*, who is considered the oldest known fossil of the human genus, is thought to be about 1.8 million years old. The skull of *Homo erectus* was quite a lot larger than *Australopithecus*, about the size of a modern human brain. *Homo erectus* was thought to walk upright and had facial features more closely resembling humans than apes. The oldest fossils to be designated *Homo sapiens* are also called Cro-Magnon man, with brain size and facial features essentially the same as modern humans. Cro-Magnon *Homo sapiens* are thought to have evolved in Africa and migrated to Europe and Asia approximately 100,000 years ago.

Evolutionary Ecology

Organisms evolve within ecosystems; therefore, the ecological circumstances affect (if not determine) the course of evolution of species in a particular area. Some organisms are better suited to develop in a new ecosystem. Others only thrive in an established equilibrium. The characteristics that differentiate these types of organisms are known collectively as **life history strategies**. There are two types of life history strategies: opportunistic and equilibreal.

Organisms with **opportunistic** life history strategies (also known as r-selected) tend to be pioneer species in a new or recently devastated community. In addition to traits that allow them to succeed in the long term, they also have traits that help make them succeed in a changing or new ecosystem. They tend to have short maturation times and short overall life spans. They tend to have high mortality rates. Often reproduction is asexual, with high numbers of offspring. They find it easy to disperse over large areas. They do not parent their young. These are rapidly reproducing species that are also easily wiped out by more sophisticated populations that follow. For example, dandelions are an opportunistic species.

Species with **equilibreal** life strategies (also known as K-selected) are those organisms that overtake the opportunistic pioneer species. These tend to have long life spans with a long maturation time and corresponding low mortality rate. They reproduce sexually and produce fewer (longer-living) offspring that they tend to parent. They tend to stay within their established borders rather than dispersing. These characteristics form the basis for particular species to dominate in varying ecosystems. For example, an oak tree is an equilibreal species.

One of the most interesting ecological behaviors to explain through evolution is **altruism** (social behavior where organisms seem to place the needs of the community over their own need). An altruistic trait may actually decrease the fitness of the individual with the trait (known as the cost of altruism), while it increases the fitness of the community (the benefit of altruism). When you look at altruism in terms of the individual, it would not have been an evolved trait since it decreases the individual's fitness. However, when looked at in terms of the community, an altruistic trait has value. In order for the traits of altruism to evolve it would be necessary for some other factor to influence the preservation and proliferation of those traits. This is thought to occur in nature through a process known as **kin selection**.

Kin selection is the tendency of an individual to be altruistic toward a close relative, resulting in the preservation of its genetic traits. Close relatives have a greater likelihood of passing on identical traits to their offspring. For instance, kin selection for a gene that causes an animal to share food with its close relatives would result in this altruistic trait being spread throughout the gene pool and passed on to future generations. Thus, those relatives are more likely to survive, and their genes are passed on to the offspring, thus preserving the altruistic trait in future generations.

Since the communities that have altruistic individuals are more likely to persevere, natural selection will work to maintain those communities, while the weaker communities die out. It is widely accepted that those communities containing altruistic individuals are made up of close relatives that have been able to preserve the altruism through kin selection.

Classification of Living Organisms

The study of **taxonomy** seeks to organize living things into groups based on morphology, or more recently, genetics. Scientists have sought to categorize the great diversity of life on Earth for hundreds of years.

Carolus Linnaeus, who published his book *Systema Naturae* in 1735, first developed our current methods of taxonomy. Linnaeus based his taxonomic keys on the morphological (outward anatomical) differences seen among species. Linnaeus designed a system of classification for all known and unknown organisms according to their anatomical similarities and differences. Although Linnaeus was a Biblical creationist who sought to show the great diversity of creation, and although he devised his system over 100 years before Darwin's *Origin of Species*, his system remains as the basis of our classification system today.

Linnaeus used two Latin-based categories—*genus* and *species*—to name each organism. Every genus name could include one or more types of species. We refer to this two-word naming of species as **binomial nomenclature** (literally meaning "two names" in Latin). For example, Linnaeus named humans *Homo sapiens* (literally "man who is wise"). *Homo* is the genus name and *sapiens* the species name. *Homo sapiens* is the only extant species left from the genus *Homo*.

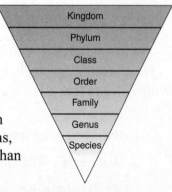

Beyond genus and species, Linnaeus further categorized organisms in a total of seven levels. Every **species** also belongs to a **genus**, **family**, **order**, **class**, **phylum**, and **kingdom**. *Kingdom* is the most general category, *species* the most limited. Taxonomists now also add "sub" and "super" categories to give even more opportunity for grouping similar organisms, and have added categories even more general than kingdom (that is, **domains**).

Although Linnaeus's system was designed before evolution was understood, the system he designed remains in use because it is based on similarities of species. An evolutionary classification system would use these same criteria. However, today, the classification system also serves to show relationships between organisms. When one constructs a **phylogenetic tree** (an evolutionary family tree of species) the result will generally show the same relationships represented with Linnaeus's taxonomy.

The most modern classification system contains three domains: the **Archaea,** the **Eubacteria**, and the **Eukaryota**. The organisms of the domain Archaea are prokaryotic, have unique RNA, and are able to live in the extreme ecosystems on Earth. The domain Archaea includes methane-producing organisms, and organisms able to withstand extreme temperatures and high salinity. The domain Eubacteria contains the prokaryotic organisms we call bacteria.

[Note: Some taxonomists still use a system including five kingdoms and no domains. In this case, the kingdom Monera would include organisms that are considered by other taxonomists to be included within the domains Archaea and Eubacteria.]

The domain Eukaryota includes all organisms that possess eukaryotic cells. The domain Eukaryota includes the four kingdoms: **Kingdom Protista, Kingdom Fungi, Kingdom Animalia,** and **Kingdom Plantae**. The following chart gives the major features of the four kingdoms of the Eukaryota:

Kingdom	No. of Known Phyla/Species	Nutrition	Structure	Included Organisms
Protista	27/250,000 +	photosynthesis, some ingestion and absorption	large eukaryotic cells	algae & protozoa
Fungi	5/100,000 +	absorption	multicellular (eukaryotic) filaments	mold, mushrooms, yeast, smuts, mildew
Animalia	33/1,000,000 +	ingestion	multicellular, specialized eukaryotic motile cells	various worms, sponges, fish, insects, reptiles, amphibians, birds, and mammals
Plantae	10/250,000 +	photosynthesis	multicellular, specialized eukaryotic nonmotile cells	ferns, mosses, woody and non-woody flowering plants

There are nine major phyla within the **Kingdom Animalia**. (Each phylum is further broken down, but the focus here will be on the phylum Chordata.) The Phyla are as follows:

1. **Porifera**—the sponges

2. **Cnidaria**—jellyfish, sea anemones, hydra, etc.

3. **Platyhelminthes**—flat worms

4. **Nematoda**—round worms

5. **Mollusca**—snails, clams, squid, etc.

6. **Annelida**—segmented worms (earthworms, leeches, etc.)

7. **Arthropoda**—crabs, spiders, lobster, millipedes, insects

8. **Echinodermata**—sea stars, sand dollars, etc.

9. **Chordata**—fish, amphibians, reptiles, birds, mammals, lampreys

Vertebrates are within the phylum Chordata, which is split into three sub-phyla, the **Urochordata** (animals with a tail cord such as tunicates), the **Cephalochordata** (animals with a head cord, such as lampreys), and **Vertebrata** (animals with a backbone).

The subphylum Vertebrata is divided into two **superclasses**, the **Aganatha** (animals with no jaws), and the **Gnathostomata** (animals with jaws). The Gnathostomata includes six classes with the following major characteristics:

a. **Chondrichthyes**—fish with a cartilaginous endoskeleton, two-chambered heart, 5–7 gill pairs, no swim bladder or lung, and internal fertilization (sharks, rays, etc.).

b. **Osteichthyes**—fish with a bony skeleton, numerous vertebrae, swim bladder (usually), two-chambered heart, gills with bony gill arches, and external fertilization (herring, carp, tuna).

c. **Amphibia**—animals with a bony skeleton, usually with four limbs having webbed feet with four toes, cold-blooded (ectothermic), large mouth with small teeth, three-chambered heart, separate sexes, internal or external fertilization, amniotic egg (salamanders, frogs, etc.).

d. **Reptilia**—horny epidermal scales, usually have paired limbs with five toes (except limbless snakes), bony skeleton, lungs, no gills, most have three-chambered heart, cold-blooded (ecothermic), internal fertilization, separate sexes, mostly egg-laying (oviparous), eggs contain extraembryonic membranes (snakes, lizards, alligators).

e. **Aves**—spindle shaped body (with head, neck, trunk, and tail), long neck, paired limbs, most have wings for flying, four-toed foot, feathers, leg scales, bony skeleton, bones with air cavities, beak, no teeth, four-chambered heart, warm blooded (endothermic), lungs with thin air sacs, separate sexes, egg-laying, eggs have hard calcified shell (birds - ducks, sparrows, etc.).

f. **Mammalia**—body covered with hair, glands (sweat, scent, sebaceous, mammary), teeth, fleshy external ears, usually four limbs, four-chambered heart, lungs, larynx, highly developed brain, warm-blooded, internal fertilization, live birth (except for the egg-laying monotremes), milk producing (cows, humans, platypus, apes, etc.).

Chapter 3

Cellular and Molecular Biology

THE STRUCTURE AND FUNCTION OF CELLS

The **cell** is the smallest and most basic unit of most living things (**organisms**). Many species have only a single cell, others are multicellular. (Although viruses are sometimes considered to be living, they are non-cellular and cannot fulfill the characteristics of life without invading the cell of another organism.) Cell structure varies according to the function of the cell and the type of living thing.

There are two main types of cells: prokaryotic and eukaryotic. **Prokaryotes** have no nucleus or any other membrane-bound **organelles** (cell components that perform particular functions). The DNA in prokaryotic cells usually forms a single chromosome, which floats within the cytoplasm. Prokaryotic organisms have only one cell and include all bacteria. Plant, fungi, and animal cells, as well as protozoa, are **eukaryotic**. Eukaryotic cells contain membrane-bound intracellular organelles, including a nucleus. The DNA within eukaryotes is organized into chromosomes.

A single organism can be *unicellular* (consisting of just one cell), or *multicellular* (consisting of many cells). A multicellular organism may have many different types of cells that differ in structure to serve different functions. Individual cells may contain organelles that assist them with specialized functions. For example, muscle cells tend to contain more mitochondria (organelles that make energy available to the cells) since muscle requires the use of extra energy.

Animal cells differ in structure and function from photosynthetic cells, which are found in plants, some bacteria, and some protists. Photosynthetic cells have the added job of producing food, so they are equipped with specialized photosynthetic organelles. Plant cells also have a central vacuole and cell walls, structures not found in animal cells.

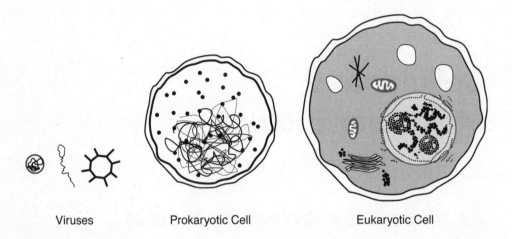

Viruses   Prokaryotic Cell   Eukaryotic Cell

Fig. 3-1: Viruses and Cells. Viruses are much smaller than cells, ranging from approximately 0.05 - 0.1 micrometers. The prokaryotic cell has no nucleus or other membrane-bound organelles and is approximately 1-10 micrometers in diameter. The eukaryotic cell has membrane-bound organelles, including a nucleus containing the chromosomes. Eukaryotic cells are approximately 10-100 micrometers in diameter.

Viruses

Viruses are much smaller than even the smallest cells. Scientists do not agree as to whether viruses are actually alive. Although they can reproduce, they do not have the ability to conduct metabolic functions on their own. Virus structure consists of only a protein capsule, DNA, or RNA, and sometimes enzymes. Viruses survive and replicate by invading a living cell. The virus then utilizes the cell's mechanisms to reproduce itself, sometimes destroying the cell in the process.

Cell Organelles of Plants and Animals

The light microscope is useful in examining most cells and some cell organelles (such as the nucleus). However, many cell organelles are very small and require the magnification and resolution power of an **electron microscope.**

All cells are enclosed within the **cell membrane** (or plasma membrane). Near the center of each eukaryotic cell is the **nucleus**, which contains the chromosomes. Between the nucleus and the cell membrane, the cell contains a region called the **cytoplasm**. Since all of the organelles outside the nucleus but within the cell membrane exist within the cytoplasm, they are all called **cytoplasmic organelles**.

The shape and size of cells can vary widely. The longest nerve cells (neurons) may extend over a meter in length with an approximate diameter of only 4-100 micrometers (1 millimeter = 1,000 micrometers, μm). A human egg cell may be 100 micrometers in diameter. The average size of a bacterium is 0.5 to 2.0 micrometers. However, most cells are between 0.5 and 100 micrometers in diameter. The size of a cell is limited by the ratio of its volume to its surface area. In the illustration below, note the variation of shape of cells within the human body:

| egg cell (ovum) | epithelial cell (cheek) | muscle cell | red blood cell (no nucleus) | sperm cell | nerve cell (neuron) |

Fig. 3-2: Varying Cell Types. The six sketches of human cell types show some of the diversity in shape and size among cells with varying functions. The sketches are not sized to scale.

Animal Cells

1.   The **cell membrane (1a)** encloses the cell and separates it from the environment. It may also be called a plasma membrane. This membrane is composed of a double layer (bilayer) of phospholipids with globular proteins embedded within the layers. The membrane is extremely thin (about 80 angstroms; 10 million angstroms = 1 millimeter) and elastic. The combination of the lipid bilayer and the proteins embedded within it allow the cell to determine what molecules and ions can enter and leave the cell, and regulate the rate at which they enter and leave.

Endocytic vesicles (1b) form when the plasma membrane of a cell surrounds a molecule outside the membrane, then releases a membrane-bound sack containing the desired molecule or substance into the cytoplasm. This process allows the cell to absorb larger molecules than would be able to pass through the cell membrane, or that need to remain packaged within the cell.

2.   **Microvilli** are projections of the cell extending from the cell membrane. Microvilli are found in certain types of cells, for example, those involved in absorption (such as the cells lining the intestine). These filaments

Fig. 3-3: Cell Membrane. A phospholipid bilayer with embedded globular proteins.

Fig. 3-4: A Generalized Animal Cell (cross-section). Since there are many types of animal cells, this diagram is generalized. In other words, some animal cells will have all of these organelles, others will not. However, this illustration will give you a composite picture of the organelles within the typical animal cell. It is also important to note the function of each organelle. Each labeled component above is explained by the corresponding text below.

increase the surface area of the cell membrane, increasing the area available to absorb nutrients. They also contain enzymes involved in digesting certain types of nutrients.

3.   The **cytoskeleton** provides structural support to a cell. **Microtubules (3a)** are long, hollow, cylindrical protein filaments, which give structure to the cell. These filaments are scattered around the edges of a cell and form a sort of loose skeleton or framework for the cytoplasm. Microtubules also are found at the base of cilia or flagella (organelles which allow some cells to move on their own) and give these organelles the ability to move. **Microfilaments (3b)** are double-stranded chains of proteins, which serve to give structure to the cell. Together with the larger microtubules, microfilaments form the cytoskeleton,

providing stability and structure. **Centrioles (3c)** are structural components of many cells, and are particularly common in animal cells. Centrioles are tubes constructed of a geometrical arrangement of microtubules in a pinwheel shape. Their function includes the formation of new microtubules, but is primarily the formation of structural skeleton around which cells split during mitosis and meiosis. Basal bodies are structurally similar to centrioles, but their function is to anchor and aid in the movement of flagella or cilia.

Fig. 3-5: Cross-section of a Centriole. Centrioles are tubes constructed of a geometrical arrangement of microtubules in a pinwheel shape.

4.   **Ribosomes** are the site of protein synthesis within cells. Ribosomes are composed of certain protein molecules and RNA molecules (ribosomal RNAs, or rRNAs). **Free ribosomes (4a)** float unattached within the cytoplasm. The proteins synthesized by free ribosomes are made for use in the cytoplasm, not within membrane-bound organelles. **Attached ribosomes (4b)** are attached to the ER (see No. 5). Proteins made at the site of attached ribosomes are destined for use within the membrane-bound organelles.

5.   The **endoplasmic reticulum,** a large organization of folded membranes, is responsible for the delivery of lipids and proteins to certain areas within the cytoplasm (a sort of cellular highway). **Rough endoplasmic reticulum** or **RER (5a)** has attached ribosomes. In addition to packaging and transport of materials within the cell, the RER is instrumental to protein synthesis. **Smooth endoplasmic reticulum** or **SER (5b)** is a network of membranous channels. Smooth endoplasmic reticulum does not have attached ribosomes. The endoplasmic reticulum is responsible for processing lipids, fats, and steroids, which are then packaged and dispersed by the Golgi apparatus.

6.   The **Golgi apparatus** (also known as Golgi bodies, or the Golgi complex) is instrumental in the storing, packaging, and shipping of proteins. The Golgi apparatus looks much like stacks of hollow pancakes and is constructed of folded membranes. Within these membranes, cellular products are stored, or packaged by closing off a bubble of membrane with the proteins or lipids inside. These packages are shipped (via the endoplasmic reticulum) to the part of the cell where they will be used, or to the cell membrane for secretion from the cell.

7.   **Secretory vesicles** are packets of material packaged by either the Golgi apparatus or the endoplasmic reticulum. Secretory vesicles carry substances produced within the cell (a protein, for example) to the cell membrane. The vesicle membrane fuses with the cell membrane in a process called **exocytosis**, allowing the substance to escape the cell.

8.   **Lysosomes** are membrane-bound organelles containing digestive enzymes. Lysosomes digest unused material within the cell, damaged organelles, or materials absorbed by the cell for use.

9.   **Mitochondria** are centers of cellular respiration (the process of breaking up covalent bonds within sugar molecules with the intake of oxygen and release of ATP, adenosine tri-phosphate). ATP molecules store energy that is later used in cell processes. Mitochondria (plural of mitochondrion) are more numerous in cells requiring more energy (muscle, etc.). Mitochondria are self-replicating, containing their own DNA, RNA, and ribosomes. Mitochondria have a double membrane; the internal membrane is folded. Cellular respiration reactions occur along the folds of the internal membrane (called **cristae**). Mitochondria are thought to be an evolved form of primitive bacteria (prokaryotic cells) that lived in a symbiotic relationship with eukaryotic cells more than 2 billion years ago. This concept, known as the **endosymbiont hypothesis,** is a plausible explanation of how mitochondria, which have many of the necessary components for life on their own, became an integral part of eukaryotic cells.

10.   The **nucleus** is an organelle surrounded by two lipid bilayer membranes. The nucleus contains chromosomes, nuclear pores, nucleoplasm, and nucleoli. The **nucleolus (10a)** is a rounded area within the nucleus of the cell where ribosomal RNA is synthesized. This rRNA is incorporated into ribosomes after exiting the nucleus. Several nucleoli (plural of nucleolus) can exist within a nucleus. The **nuclear membrane (10b)** is the boundary between the nucleus and the cytoplasm. The nuclear membrane is actually a double membrane, which allows for the entrance and exit of certain molecules through the nuclear pores. **Nuclear pores (10c)** are points at which the double nuclear membrane fuses together, forming a passageway between the inside of the nucleus and the cytoplasm outside the nucleus. Nuclear pores allow the cell to selectively move molecules in and out of the nucleus. There are many pores scattered about the surface of the nuclear membrane.

Plant Cells

The structure of plant cells differs noticeably from animal cells with the addition of three organelles: the cell wall, the chloroplasts, and the central vacu-

Fig. 3-6: A Typical Plant Cell.

ole. In Figure 3-6, the organelles numbered 1 to 7 function the same way in plant cells as in animal cells (see above).

1. **Golgi apparatus**

2. **Mitochondria**

3. **Rough endoplasmic reticulum**

4. **Ribosome**

5. **Nucleus**

6. **Nucleolus**

7. **Smooth endoplasmic reticulum**

8. **Cell walls** surround plant cells. (Bacteria also have cell walls.) Cell walls are made of cellulose and lignin, making them strong and rigid (whereas the cell membrane is relatively weak and flexible). The cell wall encloses the cell membrane providing strength and protection for the cell. The cell wall allows plant cells to store water under relatively high concentration. The combined strength of a plant's cell walls provides support for the whole organism. Dry wood and cork are essentially the cell walls of dead plants. The structure of the cell wall allows substances to pass through it readily, so transport in and out of the cell is still regulated by the cell membrane.

9. The **cell membrane** (or plasma membrane) functions in plant and animal cells in the same way. However, in some plant tissues, channels connect the cytoplasm of adjacent cells.

10. **Chloroplasts** are found in plant cells (and also in some protists). Chloroplasts are the site of photosynthesis within plant cells. **Chlorophyll** pigment molecules give the chloroplast their green color, although the chloroplasts also contain yellow and red carotenoid pigments. In the fall, as chloroplasts lose chlorophyll, these pigments are revealed, giving leaves their red and yellow colors. The body (or **stroma**) of the chloroplast contains embedded stacked, disk-like plates (called **grana**), which are the site of photosynthetic reactions.

11. The **central vacuole** takes up much of the volume of plant cells. It is a membrane-bound (this particular membrane is called the **tonoplast**), fluid-filled space, which stores water and soluble nutrients for the plant's use. The tendency of the central vacuole to absorb water provides for the rigid shape (turgidity) of some plant cells. (Animal cells may also contain vacuoles for varying purposes, and these too are membrane-bound, fluid-filled spaces. For instance, contractile vacuoles perform the specific function of expelling waste and excess water from single-celled organisms.)

Properties of Cell Membranes

The cell membrane is an especially important cell organelle with a unique structure, which allows it to control movement of substances into and out of the cell. Made up of a fluid phospholipid bilayer, proteins, and carbohydrates, this extremely thin (approximately 80 angstroms) membrane can only be seen clearly with an electron microscope. The selective permeability of the cell membrane serves to manage the concentration of substances within the cell. Substances can cross the cell membrane by passive transport, facilitated diffusion, and active transport. During **passive transport,** substances freely pass across the membrane without the cell expending any energy. **Facilitated diffusion** does not require added energy, but it cannot occur without the help of specialized proteins. Transport requiring energy output from the cell is called **active transport**.

Simple diffusion is one type of passive transport. **Diffusion** is the process whereby molecules and ions flow through the cell membrane from an area of higher concentration to an area of lower concentration (thus tending to equalize concentrations). Where the substance exists in higher concentration, collisions occur, which tend to propel them away toward lower concentrations. Diffusion generally is the means of transport for ions and molecules that can slip between the lipid molecules of the membrane. Diffusion requires no added energy to propel substances through a membrane.

$\square = CO_2$ $\blacktriangledown = O_2$

Fig. 3-7: Diffusion. CO_2 diffuses out of the cell since its
concentration is higher inside the cell. O_2 diffuses into
the cell because its concentration is higher outside.
Molecules diffuse from areas of high concentration to
areas of lower concentration.

Another type of passive transport is **osmosis,** a special process of diffusion
occurring only with water molecules. Osmosis does not require the addition
of any energy, but occurs when the water concentration inside the cell differs
from the concentration outside the cell. The water on the side of the membrane
with the highest water concentration will move through the membrane until
the concentration is equalized on both sides. When the water concentration is
equal inside and outside the cell, it is called isomotic or isotonic. For instance,
a cell placed in a salty solution will tend to lose water until the solution outside
the cell has the same concentration of water molecules as the cytoplasm (the
solution inside the cell).

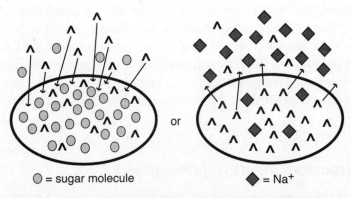

O = sugar molecule   ◆ = Na^+

∧ = water molecule

Fig. 3-8: Osmosis. Water crosses the membrane into a cell that has a higher
concentration of sugar molecules than the surrounding solution. Water crosses the membrane to leave the cell when there is a higher concentration of Na^+
ions outside the cell than inside the cell.

Facilitated diffusion is another method of transport across the cell membrane. Facilitated diffusion allows for transfer of substances across the cell membrane with the help of specialized proteins. These proteins, which are embedded in the cell membrane, are able to pick up specific molecules or ions and transport them through the membrane. The special protein molecules allow the diffusion of molecules and ions that cannot otherwise pass through the lipid bilayer.

Fig. 3-9: Facilitated Diffusion. Specialized proteins embedded in the cell membrane permit passage of substances of a particular shape and size.

Active transport, like facilitated diffusion, requires membrane-bound proteins. Unlike facilitated diffusion, active transport uses energy to move molecules across a cell membrane against a concentration gradient (in the opposite direction than they would go under normal diffusion circumstances). With the addition of the energy obtained from ATP, a protein molecule embedded in the membrane changes shape and moves a molecule across the membrane against the concentration gradient.

Large molecules are not able to pass through the cell membrane, but may be engulfed by the cell membrane. **Endocytosis** is the process whereby large molecules (i.e. some sugars or proteins) are taken up into a pocket of membrane. The pocket pinches off, delivering the molecules, still inside a membrane sack, into the cytoplasm. This process, for instance, is used by white blood cells to engulf bacteria. **Exocytosis** is the reverse process, exporting substances from the cell.

Energy Transformations (Bioenergetics)

All living things require energy. Ultimately, the source of most energy for life on Earth is the sun. Photosynthetic organisms (plants, some protists, and some bacteria) are able to harvest solar energy and transform it into chemical energy eventually stored within covalent bonds of molecules (such as carbohydrates, fats, and proteins). These organisms are called primary producers. Consumers eat producers and utilize the chemical energy stored in them to carry on the functions of life. Other organisms then consume the consumers. In each of these steps along the food chain, some energy is lost as heat (see discussion of thermodynamic laws in Chapter 7).

Cellular metabolism is a general term, which includes all types of energy transformation processes, including photosynthesis, respiration, growth, movement, etc. Energy transformations occur as chemicals are broken apart or synthesized within the cell. The process whereby cells build molecules and store energy (in the form of chemical bonds) is called **anabolism**. **Catabolism** is the process of breaking down molecules and releasing stored energy.

ATP

Energy from the sun is transformed by photosynthetic organisms into chemical energy in the form of ATP. ATP (adenosine triphosphate) is known as the energy currency of cellular activity. While energy is stored in the form of carbohydrates, fats, and proteins, the amount of energy contained within the bonds of any of these substances would overwhelm (and thus kill) a cell if released at once. In order for the energy to be released in small packets usable to a cell, large molecules need to be broken down in steps. ATP is an efficient storage molecule for the energy needed for cellular processes. ATP consists of a nitrogenous base (adenine), a simple sugar (ribose), and three phosphate groups. When a cellular process requires energy, a molecule of ATP can be broken down into ADP (adenosine diphosphate) plus a phosphate group. Even more energy is released when ATP is decomposed into AMP (adenosine monophosphate) and two phosphate groups. These energy-releasing reactions are then coupled with energy-absorbing reactions.

Photosynthesis

The process of **photosynthesis** includes a crucial set of reactions. These reactions convert the light energy of the sun into chemical energy usable by living things. Photosynthetic organisms carry out photosynthesis. They use the converted energy for their own life processes, and also store energy that may be used by organisms that consume them.

Although the process of photosynthesis actually occurs through many small steps, the entire process can be summed up with the following equation:

$$6CO_2 + 6H_2O + \text{light energy} \rightarrow C_6H_{12}O_6 + 6O_2$$

(carbon dioxide + water $\rightarrow$ glucose + oxygen)

Chlorophyll is a green pigment (a pigment is a substance that absorbs light energy). Photosynthesis occurs in the presence of chlorophyll, as the chlorophyll is able to absorb a photon of light. Chlorophyll is contained in the grana of the chloroplast (see discussion of plant cells earlier in this chapter). Photo-synthesis can only occur where chlorophyll is present. It is not used up in the photosynthetic process, but must be present for the reactions to occur.

There are two phases of the photosynthetic process, the light reaction, or **photolysis,** and the dark reaction, or **CO_2 fixation**. During photolysis, the chlorophyll pigment absorbs a photon of light, leaving the chlorophyll in an excited (higher energy) state. The light reaction is a decomposition re-action, which separates water molecules into hydrogen and oxygen atoms utilizing the energy from the excited chlorophyll pigment. Oxygen, which is not needed by the cell, combines to form O_2 (gas) and is released into the environment. The free hydrogen is grabbed and held by a particular molecule (called the hydrogen acceptor) until it is needed. The excited chlorophyll also supplies energy to a series of reactions that produce ATP from ADP and in-organic phosphate (Pi).

The dark reaction (CO_2 fixation) then occurs in the stroma of the chloroplast. This second phase of photosynthesis does not require light; however, it does require the use of the products (hydrogen and ATP) of photolysis. In this phase, six CO_2 molecules are linked with hydrogen (produced in photolysis) forming glucose (a six-carbon sugar). This is a multi-step process, which requires the ATP produced in the photolysis phase. Glucose molecules can link to form polysaccharides (starch or sugar), which are then stored in the cell.

Cellular Respiration

Unlike photosynthesis (which only occurs in photosynthetic cells), respira-tion occurs in all cells. Respiration is the process that releases energy for use by the cell. There are several steps involved in cellular respiration. Some require oxygen (that is, they are **aerobic**) and some do not (that is, they are **anaerobic** reactions).

Glycolysis is the breaking down of the six-carbon sugar (glucose) into small-er carbon-containing molecules yielding ATP (glyco = sugar, lysis = break-down). It is the first step in all respiration pathways and occurs in the cytoplasm of all living cells. Each molecule of glucose (six carbons) is broken down into two molecules of pyruvic acid (or pyruvate with three carbons each), two ATP molecules, and two hydrogen atoms (attached to NADH, nicotinamide adenine dinucleotide). This is an **anaerobic reaction** (no oxygen is required). After glycolysis has occurred, respiration will continue on one of two pathways, de-pending upon whether oxygen is present or not. The process of glycolysis is summarized by the following chemical equation:

glucose (6 C) + 2 ADP + 2 Pi + 2 NAD^+ → 2 pyruvic acid (3 C each) + 2 ATP + 2 NADH + 2H^+

Aerobic Pathways

Aerobic respiration (in the presence of oxygen) begins with glycolysis and proceeds through two major steps, the **Krebs cycle** (also known as the citric acid cycle) and **electron transport**. The first step, the Krebs cycle, occurs in the matrix of a cell's mitochondria and breaks down pyruvic acid molecules (three carbons each) into CO_2 molecules, H^+ (protons), and 2 ATP molecules. The Krebs cycle also liberates electrons, which then enter the next step.

The second step occurs along the electron transport system, or ETS, which captures the energy (in the form of electrons) released by the Krebs cycle. The ETS is a series of **cytochromes**, which exist on the cristae of the mitochondria. Cytochromes are pigment molecules, which include a protein and a **heme** (iron containing) group. The iron in heme groups may be either oxidized (loses electron to form Fe^{+3}) or reduced (gains electron to form Fe^{+2}) as electrons are passed along the ETS. As electrons pass from one cytochrome to another, energy is given off. Some of this energy is lost as heat; the rest is stored in molecules of ATP. This process can produce the most ATP molecules per cycle, 32 ATPs per glucose molecule. The final step of the electron transport chain occurs when the last electron carrier transfers two electrons to an oxygen atom that simultaneously combines with two protons from the surrounding medium to produce water.

Anaerobic Pathways

If no oxygen is present within the cell, respiration will proceed anaerobically after glycolysis. Anaerobic respiration is also called **fermentation**. Anaerobic respiration breaks down the two pyruvic acid molecules (three carbons each) into end products (such as ethyl alcohol, C_2H_6O or lactic acid $C_3H_6O_3$), plus carbon dioxide (CO_2). The net gain from anaerobic respiration is two ATP molecules per glucose molecule. Fermentation is not as efficient as aerobic respiration; it uses only a small part of the energy available in a glucose molecule.

CHEMICAL NATURE OF THE GENE

Watson and Crick were responsible for explaining the structure of the DNA molecule, research that laid the foundation of our current understanding of the function of chromosomes and genes. Today, through the discoveries of these two scientists, and through the collaborative work of scientists worldwide, the study of chromosomes and genetic inheritance has proceeded to discover the intricacies of the **genomes** (sum total of genetic information) of many organisms, including humans.

A **gene** is a length of DNA that encodes a particular protein. Each protein the cell synthesizes performs a specific function in the cell. The function of one protein, or the function of a group of proteins, is called a trait.

DNA Replication

In order to replicate, a portion of a DNA molecule unwinds, separating the two halves of the double helix. (This separation is aided by the enzyme helicase.) Another enzyme (DNA polymerase) binds to each strand and moves along them as it collects nucleotides using the original DNA strands as templates. The new strand is complementary to the original template and forms a new double helix with one of the parent strands. If no errors occur during DNA synthesis, the result is two identical double helix molecules of DNA.

The process of DNA replication, however, is occasionally subject to a mistake known as a **mutation.** All the DNA of every cell of every organism is copied repeatedly to form new cells for growth, repair, and reproduction. A mutation can result from an error that randomly occurs during replication. Mutations can also result from damage to DNA caused by exposure to certain chemicals, such as some solvents or the chemicals in cigarette smoke, or by radiation, such as ultraviolet radiation in sunlight or x-rays. Cells have built-in mechanisms for finding and repairing most DNA errors, however, they do not fix them all. The result of a DNA error, a mutation, expresses itself in a change (small or large) in the cell structure and function.

DNA carries the information for making all the proteins a cell can make. The DNA information for making a particular protein can be called the gene for that protein. Genetic traits are expressed, and specialization of cells occurs, as a result of the combination of proteins encoded by the DNA of a cell. Protein synthesis occurs in two steps called transcription and translation.

Transcription refers to the formation of an RNA molecule, which corresponds to a gene. The DNA strand "unzips" and replicates; individual RNA nucleotides are strung together to match the DNA sequence by the enzyme RNA polymerase. The new RNA strand (known as messenger RNA or **mRNA)** migrates from the nucleus to the cytoplasm, where it is modified in a process known as **post-transcriptional processing**. This processing prepares the mRNA for protein synthesis by removing the non-coding sequences. In the processed RNA, each unit of three nucleotides or **codon** encodes a particular amino acid.

The next phase of protein synthesis is called **translation**. In order for the protein synthesis process to continue, a second type of RNA is required, transfer RNA or **tRNA**. Transfer RNA is the link between the "language" of nucleotides (codon and anticodon) and the "language" of amino acids (hence the word "translation"). Transfer RNA is a chain of about 80 nucleotides. At one point along the tRNA chain, there are three unattached bases, which are called the anticodon. This anticodon will line up with a corresponding codon during translation. Each tRNA molecule also has an attached, specific amino acid.

Translation occurs at the ribosomes. A ribosome is a structure composed of proteins and ribosomal RNA (rRNA). A ribosome attaches to the mRNA strand at a particular codon known as the start codon. This codon is only recognized by a particular initiator tRNA. The ribosome continues to add tRNA whose anticodons make complementary bonds with the next codon on the mRNA string, forming a peptide bond between amino acids as each amino acid is held in place by a tRNA. At the end of the translation process, a terminating codon stops the synthesis process and the protein is released.

Structural and Regulatory Genes

Genes encode proteins of two varieties. **Structural genes** code proteins that form organs and structural characteristics. **Regulatory genes** code proteins that determine functional or physiological events, such as growth. These proteins regulate when other genes start or stop encoding proteins, which in turn produce specific traits.

Transduction and Transformation

In most organisms, DNA replication preserves a continuity of traits throughout the organism's lifespan. However, the genetic makeup of bacteria can be changed through one of two processes, transduction or transformation. **Transduction** is the transfer of genetic material (portions of a bacterial chromosome) from one bacterial cell to another. The transfer is mediated by a bacteriophage (a virus that targets bacteria). Bacteria may also absorb and incorporate pieces of DNA from their environment (usually from dead bacterial cells), a process called **transformation**.

Cell Division

The process of cell reproduction is called **cell division**. The process of cell division centers on the replication and separation of strands of **DNA**.

Structure of Chromosomes

Chromosomes are long chains of subunits called **nucleosomes**. Each nucleosome is composed of a short length of DNA wrapped around a core of small proteins called **histones**. The combination of DNA with histones is called **chromatin**. Each nucleosome is about 11 nm in diameter (a nanometer is one billionth of a meter) and contains a central core of eight histones with the DNA double helix wrapped around them. Each gene spans dozens of nucleosomes. The DNA plus histone strings are then tightly packed and coiled, forming chromatin.

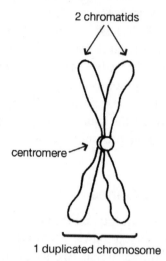

Fig. 3-10: A Chromosome.

In a cell that is getting ready to divide, each strand of chromatin is duplicated. The two identical strands (called **chromatids**) remain attached to each other at a point called the **centromere**. During cell division, the chromatin strands become more tightly coiled and packed, forming a chromosome, which is visible in a light microscope. At this stage, a chromosome consists of two identical chromatids, held together at the centromere, giving each chromosome an **X** shape.

Within the nucleus, each chromosome pairs with another of similar size and shape. These pairs are called **homologs**. Each set of homologous chromosomes has a similar genetic constitution, but the genes are not necessarily identical. Different forms of corresponding genes are called **alleles.**

Fig. 3-11: Paired Homologous Chromosomes.

Restriction Enzymes

The study of DNA has been greatly aided by the discovery of restriction enzymes (restriction endonucleases). Restriction enzymes cut sections of DNA molecules by cleaving the sugar-phosphate backbone at a particular nucleotide sequence.

Scientists have isolated hundreds of different restriction endonucleases that act on a few hundred different DNA sequences. Restriction enzymes are made by bacteria and act to destroy foreign DNA (for example, viral DNA) that has entered the bacterial cell.

In the laboratory, restriction enzymes are used to cut DNA into small strands of DNA for study. Restriction enzymes are generally named after their host of origin, rather than the substrate upon which they act. For example, EcoRI is from the host *Escherichia coli*, Hind II and Hind III from *Haemophilus influenzae*, XhoI from *Xanthomonas holcicola*, etc.

The Cell Cycle

A cell that is going to divide progresses through a particular sequence of events ending in cell division, which produces two daughter cells. This is known as the **cell cycle** (see Fig. 3-12). The time taken to progress through the cell cycle differs with different types of cells, but the sequence is the same. Cells in many tissues never divide.

The Cell Cycle

Fig. 3-12: The Cell Cycle. Interphase includes the G1, S, and G2 phases. The cell division phase includes mitosis and cytokinesis.

There are two major periods within the cell cycle: interphase and mitosis (also called the M phase or cell division phase). **Interphase** is the period when the cell is active in carrying on its function. Interphase is divided into three phases. During the first phase, the G_1 **phase**, metabolism and protein synthesis are occurring at a high rate, and most of the growth of the cell occurs at this time. The cell organelles are produced (as necessary) and undergo growth during this phase. During the second phase, the **S phase**, the cell begins to prepare for cell division by replicating the DNA and proteins necessary to form a new set of chromosomes. In the final phase, the G_2 phase, more proteins are produced, which will be necessary for cell division, and the centrioles (which are integral to the division process) are replicated as well. Cell growth and function occur through all the stages of interphase.

Mitosis

Mitosis is the process by which a cell distributes its duplicated chromosomes so that each daughter cell has a full set of chromosomes. Mitosis progresses through four phases: prophase, metaphase, anaphase, and telophase (see Fig. 3-13).

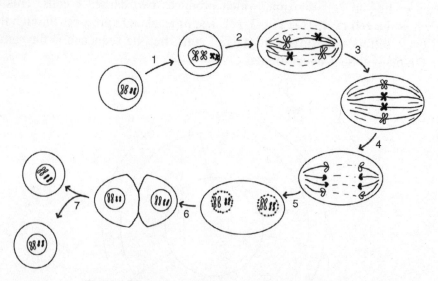

Fig. 3-13: Mitosis. See explanations of numbered steps below.

During **prophase (1, 2)**, the first stage of mitosis, the chromatin condenses into chromosomes within the nucleus and becomes visible through a light microscope. The centrioles move to opposite ends of the cell, and **spindle fibers** begin to extend from the centromeres of each chromosome toward the center of the cell. At this point, although the chromosomes become visible, the nucleolus no longer is. During the second part of prophase, the nuclear membrane dissolves and the spindle fibers attach to the centromeres forming a junction called a **kinetochore**. The chromosomes then begin moving in preparation for the next step, metaphase.

During **metaphase (3)**, the spindle fibers pull the chromosomes into alignment along the equatorial plane of the cell, creating the metaphase plate. This arrangement insures that one copy of each chromosome is distributed to each daughter cell.

During **anaphase (4)**, the chromatids are separated from each other when the centromere divides. Each former chromatid is now called a chromosome. The two identical chromosomes move along the spindle fibers to opposite ends of the cell. **Telophase (5)** occurs as nuclear membranes form around the chromosomes. The chromosomes disperse through the new nucleoplasm, and are no longer visible as chromosomes under a standard microscope. The spindle fibers disappear. After telophase, the process of **cytokinesis (6)** produces two separate cells **(7)**.

Cytokinesis differs somewhat in plants and animals. In animal cells, a ring made of the protein actin surrounds the center of the cell and contracts. As the actin ring contracts, it pinches the cytoplasm into two separate compartments. Each cell's plasma membrane seals, making two distinct daughter cells. In plant cells, a cell plate forms across the center of the cell and extends out towards the edges of the cell. When this plate reaches the edges, a cell wall forms on either side of the plate, and the original cell then splits into two.

Mitosis, then, produces two nearly identical daughter cells. (Cells may differ in distribution of mitochondria or because of DNA replication errors, for example.) Organisms (such as bacteria) that reproduce asexually, do so through the process of mitosis.

Meiosis

Meiosis is the process of producing four daughter cells, each with single unduplicated chromosomes (**haploid**). The parent cell is **diploid**, that is, it has a normal set of paired chromosomes. Meiosis goes through a two-stage process resulting in four new cells, rather than two (as in mitosis). Each cell has half the chromosomes of the parent. Meiosis occurs in reproductive organs, and the resultant four haploid cells are called **gametes** (egg and sperm). When two haploid gametes fuse during the process of fertilization, the resultant cell has one chromosome set from each parent, and is diploid. This process allows for the huge genetic diversity available among species.

Two distinct nuclear divisions occur during meiosis, reduction (or meiosis 1, steps **1 to 5** in Fig. 3-14), and division (or meiosis 2, steps **6 to 10**). **Reduction** affects the **ploidy** (referring to haploid or diploid) level, reducing it from 2n to n (i.e., diploid to haploid). **Division** then distributes the remaining set of chromosomes in a mitosis-like process.

Fig. 3-14: Meiosis. See explanations of numbered steps, above and below.

The phases of meiosis 1 are similar to the phases of mitosis, with some notable differences. As in mitosis, chromosome replication (**1**) occurs before prophase; then during prophase 1 (**2**), homologous chromosomes pair up and join at a point called a **synapse** (this happens only in meiosis). The attached chromosomes are now termed a tetrad, a dense four-stranded structure composed of the four chromatids from the original chromosomes. At this point, some portions of the chromatid may break off and reattach to another chromatid in the tetrad. This process, known as **crossing over**, results in an even wider array of final genetic possibilities.

The nuclear membrane disappears during late prophase (or prometaphase). Each chromosome (rather than each chromatid) develops a kinetochore, and as the spindle fibers attach to each chromosome, they begin to move.

In metaphase 1 (**3**), the two chromosomes (a total of four chromatids per pair) align themselves along the equatorial plane of the cell. Each homologous pair of chromosomes contains one chromosome from the mother and one from the father from the original sexual production of that organism. When the homologous pairs orient at the cell's center in preparation for separating, the chromosomes randomly sort. The resulting cells from this meiotic division will have a mixture of chromosomes from each parent. This increases the possibilities for variety among descendent cells.

Anaphase 1 (**4**) occurs next as the chromosomes move to separate ends of the cell. This phase differs from the anaphase of mitosis where one of each chromosome pair (rather than one chromatid) separates. In telophase 1 (**5**), the nuclear envelope may or may not form, depending on the type of organism. In either case, the cell then proceeds to meiosis 2.

The nuclear envelopes dissolve (if they have formed) during prophase 2 (**6**) and spindle fibers form again. All else proceeds as in mitosis, through metaphase 2 (**7**), anaphase 2 (**8**), and telophase 2 (**9**). Again, as in mitosis, each chromosome splits into two chromatids. The process ends with cytokinesis (**10**), forming four distinct gamete cells.

Biosynthesis

Biosynthesis is the process of producing chemical compounds by living things. Organisms need to produce membranes and organelles as well as proteins that regulate cellular activity and molecules that store energy. Biosynthesis takes reactant molecules and with added energy (and often the action of enzymes) produces the products that are needed for cell or organism function.

Protein synthesis, as described earlier, involves DNA, RNA, and the processes of transcription and translation. Protein synthesis is a biosynthetic process vital to all life functions.

Enzymes are protein molecules that act as catalysts for organic reactions. (A catalyst is a substance that lowers the activation energy of a reaction. A catalyst is not consumed in the reaction.) Enzymes do not make reactions possible that would not otherwise occur under the right energy conditions, but they lower the activation energy, which increases the rate of the reaction.

Fig. 3-15: Effect of Enzyme on a Reaction. Adding an enzyme lowers the activation energy for a reaction.

Enzymes are named ending with the letters -ase, and usually begin with a syllable describing the catalyzed reaction (i.e., hydrolase catalyzes hydrolysis reactions, lactase catalyzes the breakdown of the sugar lactose). Thousands of reactions occur within cells, each controlled by one or more enzymes. Enzymes are synthesized within the cell at the ribosomes, as all proteins are.

Enzymes are effective catalysts because of their unique shapes. Each enzyme has a uniquely shaped area, called its **active site**. For each enzyme, there is a particular substance known as its **substrate**, which fits within the active site (like a hand in a glove). When the substrate is seated in the active site, the combination of two molecules is called the **enzyme-substrate complex**. An enzyme can bind to two substrates and catalyze the formation of a new chemical bond, linking the two substrates. An enzyme may also bind to a single substrate and catalyze the breaking of a chemical bond, releasing two products. Once the reaction has taken place, the unchanged enzyme is released.

The operation of enzymes lowers the energy needed to initiate cellular reactions. However, the completion of the reaction may either require or release energy. Remember from Chapter 2 that reactions requiring energy are called endothermic reactions. Reactions that release energy are called exothermic reactions. Endothermic reactions can take place in a cell by being coupled to the breakdown of ATP or a similar molecule. Exothermic reactions are coupled to the production of ATP or another molecule with high-energy chemical bonds.

Fig. 3-16: Enzyme Reaction. 1 - enzyme; 2 - substrate; 3&4 - enzyme-substrate complex; 5 - products.

Some enzymatic reactions require a non-protein substance called a **cofactor**. The cofactor binds to the active site. This allows the substrate to fit into the active site. Some cofactors are inorganic. **Inorganic cofactors** include metal ions—for example, iron, copper, or zinc. Other cofactors are organic molecules. **Organic cofactors** are also called **coenzymes**. Some coenzymes are not made by cells but must be obtained in the diet. Most vitamins are coenzymes (or precursors of coenzymes). **Prosthetic groups** are similar to cofactors; they also facilitate the enzyme reaction. However, prosthetic groups are bound to the enzyme, rather than being separate atoms or molecules.

In some cases, other substances compete to attach to an enzyme's active site. If one of these substances, known as an **inhibitor**, attaches to the enzyme first, the cellular reaction will not take place. Environmental conditions within the cell, such as high temperature or acidity, may also inhibit an enzymatic reaction. These conditions may change the shape of the active site and render the enzyme ineffective.

Enzyme reactions may also be controlled by mechanisms within the cell. Enzyme control (or **regulation**) may occur when the product of the reaction is also an inhibitor to the reaction. This slows down the production rate as the concentration of the product increases. In other cases, a particular molecule serves as a regulator by changing the structure of the active site, making the enzyme more or less effective.

Chapter 4

Structure and Function of Plants and Animals; Genetics

PLANTS (BOTANY)

Most of us commonly recognize plants as organisms that produce their own food through the process of photosynthesis. (Some bacteria are also photosynthetic.) However, the plant kingdom is divided into several classifications according to physical characteristics.

Vascular plants (tracheophytes) have tissue organized in such a way as to conduct food and water throughout their structure. These plants include some that produce seeds (such as corn or roses) as well as those that do not produce any seeds (such as ferns). **Nonvascular** plants (bryophytes), such as mosses, lack special tissue for conducting water or food. They produce no seeds or flowers and are generally only a few centimeters in height.

Another method of classifying plants is according to their method of reproduction. **Angiosperms** are plants that produce flowers as reproductive organs. **Gymnosperms**, on the other hand, produce seeds without flowers. These include conifers (cone-bearers) and cycads.

Plants that survive only through a single growing season are known as **annuals**. Other plants are **biennial**; their life cycle spans two growing seasons. **Perennial** plants continue to grow year after year.

Plant Anatomy

Plants have structures with attributes that equip them to thrive in their environment. Angiosperms and Gymnosperms differ mostly in the structure of their stems and reproductive organs. Gymnosperms are mostly trees, with woody,

Fig. 4-1: A Typical Flowering Plant (angiosperm).
Note descriptions of numbered structures in text.

instead of herbaceous stems. Gymnosperms do not produce flowers; instead they produce seeds in cones or cone-like structures.

Angiosperms

The shoot system of angiosperms includes the stem, leaves, flowers, and fruit, as well as growth structures such as nodes and buds (see Fig. 4-1:1-7). The signature structure of an angiosperm is the **flower (1)**, the primary reproductive organ. Before the flower blooms, it is enclosed within the **sepals (1-a)**, small, green, leaf-like structures, which fold back to reveal the flower **petals (1-b)**. The petals usually are brightly colored; their main function is to attract insects and birds, which may be necessary to the process of pollination. The short branch of stem, which supports the flower, is called the **pedicel (1-c).**

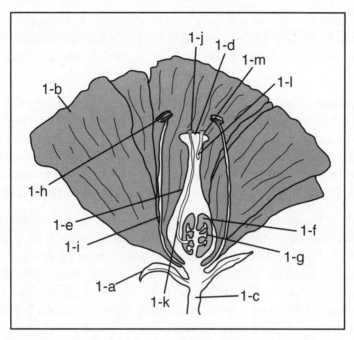

Fig. 4-2: Typical Flower. Note numbered explanations in text.

Usually (but depending on the species), a single flower will have both male and female reproductive organs. The **pistil** is the female structure, and includes the stigma, style, ovary, and ovules. The **stigma (1-d)** is a sticky surface at the top of the pistil, which traps pollen grains. The stigma sits above a slender vase-like structure, the **style (1-e)**, which encloses the ovary. The **ovary (1-f)** is the hollow, bulb-shaped structure in the lower interior of the pistil. (After seeds have formed, the ovary will ripen and become fruit.) Within the ovary are the **ovules (1-g)**, small round cases each containing one or more egg cells. (If the egg is fertilized, the ovule will become a seed.) In the process of meiosis in the ovule, an egg cell is produced, along with smaller bodies known as polar nuclei. The polar nuclei will develop into the endosperm of the seed when fertilized by sperm cells.

The male structure is the stamen, consisting of the **anther (1-h)** atop the long, hollow **filament (1-i)**. The anther has four lobes and contains cells (microspore mother cells) that become pollen. Some mature **pollen grains (1-j)** are conveyed (usually by wind, birds, or insects) to a flower of a compatible species, where they stick to the stigma. The stigma produces chemicals, which stimulate the pollen to burrow into the style, forming a hollow **pollen tube (1k)**. This tube is produced by the tube **nucleus (1-l)**, which has developed from a portion of the pollen grain. The pollen tube extends down toward the ovary. Behind the tube nucleus are two **sperm nuclei (1-m)**. When the sperm nuclei reach the ovule, one will join with an egg cell, fertilizing it to become a zygote (the beginning cell of the embryo). The other sperm nucleus merges with the polar bodies forming the endosperm, which will feed the growing embryo.

The **shoot apex (2)** is composed of **meristem** tissue (consisting of undifferentiated cells capable of quick growth and specialization), and is the region where elongation of the stem occurs. The **terminal bud** (the beginning of a new set of leaves) is also located at the shoot apex. Each year, as the plant continues to grow taller, a new terminal bud and shoot apex are produced. The spot where the previous year's terminal bud was located is then called a **terminal bud scar**.

Fruit (3) is a matured ovary, which contains the seeds (mature fertilized ovules). The fruit provides protection for the seeds, as well as a method to disburse them. For instance, when ripened fruit is eaten by animals the seeds are discarded or excreted in the animal's waste, transferring the seed to a new location for germination. Fruits that develop from a single ripened ovary are known as **simple fruits** (e.g., apple, corn, olive, acorn, cucumber). **Compound fruits** develop from many separate ovaries. They may be an **aggregate fruit,** in which many ovaries of a single flower fuse together (e.g., raspberry), or a **multiple fruit**, which forms from the fusing of several ovaries of separate flowers during ripening (e.g., strawberry or pineapple).

Each **seed** contains a tiny embryonic plant, stored food, and a seed coat for protection. When the seed is exposed to proper moisture, temperature, and oxygen, it germinates (begins to sprout and grow into a new plant). Stored food in a seed is found in the cotyledon. Angiosperms are also classified according to the structure of their cotyledons. Plants with two cotyledons in each seed are known as dicotyledons (**dicots**); those with only one are known as monocotyledons (**monocots**). The following chart outlines the major differences between monocots and dicots:

Dicots	Monocots
ex. oaks, flowers, vegetables	ex. grasses, lilies, palm trees
two cotyledons in seed	one cotyledon in seed
leaves have branched or networked veins	leaves have parallel veins
vascular bundles (collections of xylem and phloem tubes) are arranged in rings	stems have random arrangement of vascular bundles
taproot system with smaller secondary roots	fibrous roots
flowers with petals in multiples of four or five	flowers with petals in multiples of three

The **stem (4)** is the main support structure of the plant. The stem produces leaves and lateral (parallel with the ground) branches. **Nodes (5)** are the locations along the stem where new leaves sprout, and the space between nodes is the **internode**. New leaves begin as **lateral buds (6)**, which can be seen on growing plants.

The stem is also the main organ for transporting food and water to and from the leaves. In some cases the stem also stores food; for instance, a potato is a tuber (stem) that stores starch. The stem also contains meristem tissue.

Most of the stem tissue is made up of **vascular tissue**, including two varieties—**xylem** and **phloem**. Xylem tissue is composed of long tubular cells, which transport water up from the ground to the branches and leaves. Phloem tissue, made of stacked cells connected by sieve plates (which allow nutrients to pass from cell to cell), transports food made in the leaves (by photosynthesis) to the rest of the plant.

The **leaf (7)** is the primary site of photosynthesis in most plants. Most leaves are thin, flat, and joined to a branch or stem by a petiole (a small stem-like extension). The petiole houses vascular tissue, which connects the veins in the leaf with those in the stem.

The **cuticle**, which maintains the leaf's moisture balance, covers most leaf surfaces. Considering a cross-section of a leaf, the outermost layer is the **epidermis (7-a, e).** The epidermis is generally one cell thick. It secretes the waxy cuticle and protects the inner tissue of the leaf.

The mesophyll is composed of several layers of tissue between the upper and lower epidermis. The uppermost, the **palisade layer (7-b)**, contains vertically aligned cells with numerous chloroplasts. The arrangement of these cells maximizes the potential for exposure of the chloroplasts to needed sunlight. Most photosynthesis occurs in this layer.

The sugars produced by photosynthesis are transported throughout the plant via the **vascular bundles (7-c)** of xylem and phloem. The vascular bundles make up the veins in the leaf.

The next layer beneath the palisade cells is the **spongy layer (7-d)**, a layer of parenchyma cells separated by large air spaces. The air spaces allow for the exchange of gases (carbon dioxide and oxygen) for photosynthesis.

On the underside of the leaf there are openings ringed by guard cells (7-f). The openings are called stomata (7-g) (or stomates). The stomata serve to allow moisture and gases (carbon dioxide and oxygen) to pass in and out of the leaf, thus facilitating photosynthesis.

The root system of a typical angiosperm includes the **primary roots (8)**, which extend downward and the **lateral roots (9)**, which develop secondarily and extend horizontally, parallel with the ground surface. Roots function to provide water and

7-c
7-a
7-b
7-d
7-e
7-f
7-g

Fig. 4-3: Cross Section of a Leaf.

needed nutrients to the plant. Roots are structured to provide a large surface area for absorption. The network of the root system also anchors the plant.

Roots have four major structural regions, which run vertically from bottom to top. The **root cap** is composed of dead, thick-walled cells, and covers the tip of the root, protecting it as the root pushes through soil. The **meristematic region** is just above the root cap. It consists of undifferentiated cells, which carry on mitosis, producing cells that grow to form the **elongation region**. In the elongation region, cells differentiate, large vacuoles are formed, and cells grow. As the cells differentiate into various root tissues, they become part of the **maturation region**.

A cross-section of root tissue above the maturation region would reveal several types of **primary root tissue.** In the maturation region, the epidermis produces **root hairs (9-a)**, extensions of the cells, which reach between soil particles and retrieve water and minerals. The primary tissues include the outermost layer, the **epidermis (9-b)**. The epidermis is one cell layer thick and serves to protect the internal root tissue and absorb nutrients and water.

Inside the epidermis is a ring known as the **cortex (9-c)**, made up of large parenchyma cells. **Parenchyma** cells are present in many tissues of plants; they are thin-walled cells loosely packed to allow for flow of gases and uptake of minerals.

Inside the cortex is a ring of **endodermis (9-d)**, a single layer of cells, which are tightly connected so no substances can pass between cells. This feature allows the endodermis to act as a filter; all substances entering the vascular tissues from the root must pass through these cells. In the center of the root is the **vascular cylinder (9-e)**, including xylem and phloem tissue.

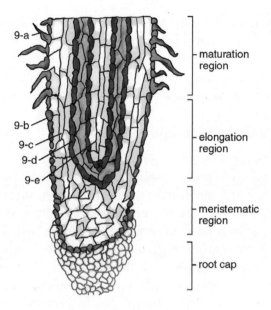

Fig. 4-4: Root Cross-section.

Plant Physiology

Water and Mineral Absorption and Transport

Although plants produce their own sugars and starches for food, they must obtain water, carbon dioxide, and minerals from their environment. Vascular plants have well-developed systems for absorption and transport of water and minerals.

Water is essential to all cells of all plants, so plants must have the ability to obtain water and transport water molecules throughout their structure. Most water is absorbed through the plant's root system, then makes its way in one of two pathways toward the xylem cells, which will transport water up the stem and to the leaves and flowers. The first pathway is for water to seep between the epidermal cells of the roots and between the parenchyma cells of the cortex. When water reaches the endodermal tissue, it enters the cells and is pushed through the vascular tissue toward the xylem.

A second pathway is for the water to pass through the cell wall and plasma membrane. Water travels along this intracellular route through channels in the cell membranes (plasmodesmata), until it reaches the xylem.

Once water reaches the xylem, hydrogen bonding between water molecules (known as **cohesion**) causes tension that pulls water through the water column up through the stem and on to the leaves (known as the **cohesion-tension process**). Some water that has traveled up through the plant to the leaves is evaporated, a process known as **transpiration**. As water is evaporated, it causes a siphoning effect (like sucking on a straw), which continues to pull water up from the root xylem, through the length of the plant and to the leaves.

Food Translocation and Storage

Food is manufactured by photosynthesis mostly in the leaves. The rest of the plant must have this food (carbohydrates) imported from the leaves. The leaves have source cells, which store the manufactured sugars. The food molecules are transferred from the source cells to phloem tissue through active transport (energy is expended to move molecules across the plasma membrane against the concentration gradient—from low concentration to high concentration). Once in the phloem, the sugars begin to build up causing osmosis to occur (water enters the phloem lowering the sugar concentration). The entrance of water into the phloem causes pressure, which pushes the water-sugar solution through **sieve plates** that join the cells. This pressure thrusts the water-sugar solution to all areas of the plant, making food available to all cells in the plant.

Plant Reproduction and Development

The reproductive cycle of plants occurs through the alternation of haploid (n) and diploid (2n) phases. Haploid cells have one complete set of chromosomes (n). Diploid cells have two sets of chromosomes (2n). Diploid and haploid stages are both capable of undergoing mitosis in plants. The diploid generation is known as a **sporophyte**. The reproductive organs of the sporophyte produce **gametophytes** through the process of meiosis. Gametophytes may be male or female and are haploid. The male gametophyte produces **sperm (male gamete)**; the female produces an **egg cell (female gamete)**. When a sperm cell **fertilizes** an egg cell (haploid cells join to form a diploid cell) they produce a **zygote**. The zygote will grow into an **embryo**, which resides within the growing seed.

We are accustomed to identifying particular plants according to their adult phase, which is only one phase of the life cycle. Various phyla of plants have their own identifiable life cycles, which include an **alternation of generations**.

Mosses and ferns alternate haploid and diploid phases, developing two distinct generations of the plant, each with its own recognizable form. One generation is haploid, the other diploid. The haploid phase is most prominent in mosses, while in ferns the diploid stage is most prominent.

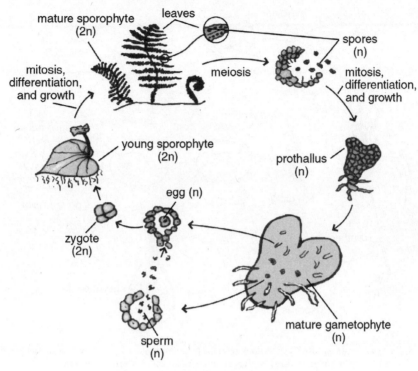

Fig. 4-5: Alternation of Generations in Ferns.

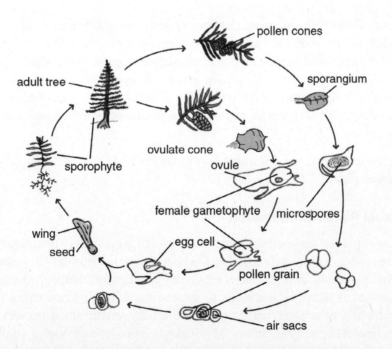

Fig. 4-6: Pine Life Cycle. The adult tree produces both male (pollen) and female (ovulate) cones that form the pollen and ovules that combine to produce a seed.

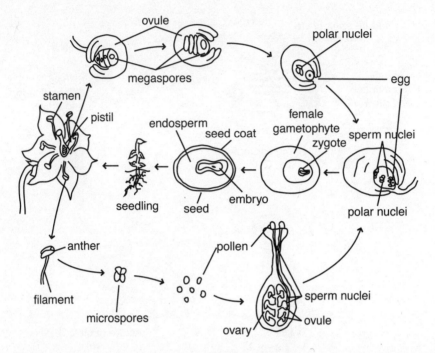

Fig. 4-7: Angiosperm Life Cycle. Pollen develops from the stamen; eggs develop from the pistil. The pollen ferilizes the egg, resulting in an embryo within the seed.

In conifers (such as pines), the sporophyte generation (diploid) is the familiar adult of the species. The process of meiosis produces the haploid gametophytes (male and female) from the male and female cone scales. The male gametophyte forms the male pollen grain and its attached air bladders, which assist it in being borne by the wind. The pollen contains sperm cells and tube cells, which will fertilize an egg cell of a female scale when they are brought into contact.

In angiosperms, the dominant adult generation is also the sporophyte—the flowering plant.

Asexual Plant Reproduction

Some plants may also reproduce through **vegetative propagation**—an asexual process. Asexual reproduction occurs through mitosis only (it does not involve gametes), and produces offspring genetically identical to the parent. While sexual reproduction leads to genetic variation and adaptation, asexual reproduction of a plant with a desirable set of genetic traits preserves these intact in successive generations. Many plants reproduce through a combination of sexual and asexual reproduction, reaping the advantages of each.

There are several types of plants that produce structures specifically designed to carry on vegetative propagation. These are described in the chart below:

Reproductive Structure	Description of Structure	Plants with these Structures
tubers	under-ground storage stems, develop new shoots after dormant season	potatoes
rhizomes	underground runners that develop into new plant	irises
stolens	above-ground runners that grow roots of their own then develop into new plant	strawberries
bulbs	underground storage units that grow into many new plants via division	amaryllis
corms	resemble bulbs but with enlarged, solid stem for food storage	gladiolus, crocus

Plant Growth and Development

Hormones are chemicals that regulate the growth, development, and function of an organism. Plant cells produce hormones that bring about physiological changes within plant tissues. Each type of hormone affects changes in particular cells known as target cells. The traits regulated by hormones are many and varied, but there are some particularly important ones in plants. Note the most common hormones and their functions in the following chart:

Hormone	Process Regulated or Influenced
giberellins (65 hormones)	cell division & cell elongation
cytokinins	cell division & fruit development
abscisic acid	opening and closing of stomata (controlling water lost through transpiration and formation of winter buds that put plant in dormant state)
ethylene	ripening of fruit (spoiling releases ethylene which stimulates ripening of surrounding fruit); metabolic activity (i.e., producing female flowers to increase fertilization
auxins	growth factors (i.e., tropisms)

A **tropism** is an involuntary response of an organism to an external stimulus such as light, water, gravity, or nutrients. For instance, plant stems are usually positively **phototropic** (they grow towards light), while plant roots are negatively phototropic (they grow away from light). Plant roots are positively **geotropic**; they grow toward the center of the earth, while stems are negatively geotropic, growing against gravity. Tropisms are thought to be caused by plant hormones, which react to the external stimulus causing some cells to grow quickly and others to grow slowly. Variations of auxin levels also influence the strength of petioles and stems, regulating when leaves or fruit drop.

There are other factors (besides hormones), which influence plant growth and development. For instance, plants respond to relative periods of light and darkness, a characteristic known as **photoperiodicity**. Light-sensitive chemicals in the leaves trigger a response in the plant, which encourages growth, flowering, or other reactions. It is this trait that causes flowering and growth of varying plants at different times of year.

ANIMALS (ZOOLOGY)

The animal kingdom includes a wide variety of phyla that have a range of body plans. This range includes certain invertebrates with relatively simple body plans as well as highly complex vertebrates (including humans). There are specific characteristics that differentiate animals from other living things. Organisms in the animal kingdom share the following traits:

1. Animal cells do not have cell walls or plastids.

2. Adult animals are multicellular with specialized tissues and organs.

3. Animals are heterotrophic (they do not produce their own food).

4. Animal species are capable of sexual reproduction, although some are also capable of asexual reproduction (ex. hydra).

5. Animals develop from embryonic stages.

In addition to the above traits, most adult animals have a symmetrical anatomy. Adult animals can have either radial symmetry (constituent parts are arranged radiating symmetrically about a center point) or bilateral symmetry (the body can be divided along a center plane into equal, mirror-image halves). There are a few exceptions to this rule, including the adult sponge whose body is not necessarily symmetrical. While there is wide variation in the physical structure of animals, the animal kingdom is usually divided into two broad categories—invertebrates and vertebrates. There are many more species of invertebrates than vertebrates.

Invertebrates are those species having no internal backbone structure; **vertebrates** have internal backbones. Invertebrates include sponges and worms, which have no skeletal structure at all, and arthropods, mollusks, crustaceans, etc., which have exoskeletons. In fact, there are many more phyla of invertebrates than vertebrates (about 950,000 phyla of invertebrates and only about 40,000 phyla of vertebrates).

Animal Anatomy

Tissues

Like all multicellular organisms, animal bodies contain several kinds of tissues, made up of different cell types. Differentiated cells may organize into specialized tissues performing particular functions. There are eight major types of animal tissue:

1) **Epithelial tissue** consists of thin layers of cells. Epithelial tissue makes up the layers of skin, lines ducts and the intestine, and covers the inside of the body cavity. Epithelial tissue forms the barrier between the environment and the interior of the body.

2) **Connective tissue** covers internal organs and composes ligaments and tendons. This tissue holds tissues and organs together, stabilizing the body structure.

3) **Muscle tissue** is divided into three types—smooth, skeletal, and cardiac. **Smooth** muscle makes up the walls of internal organs and functions in involuntary movement (breathing, etc.). **Skeletal** muscle attaches bones of the skeleton to each other and surrounding tissues. Skeletal muscle's function is to enable voluntary movement. **Cardiac** muscle is the tissue forming the walls of the heart. Its strength and electrical properties are vital to the heart's ability to pump blood.

4) **Bone tissue** is found in the skeleton and provides support, protection for internal organs, and ability to move as muscles pull against bones.

5) **Cartilage tissue** reduces friction between bones, and supports and connects them. For example, it is found at the ends of bones and in the ears and nose.

6) **Adipose tissue** is found beneath the skin and around organs providing cushioning, insulation, and fat storage.

7) **Nerve tissue** is found in the brain, spinal cord, nerves, and ganglion. It carries electrical and chemical impulses to and from organs and

limbs to the brain. Nerve tissue in the brain receives these impulses and sustains mental activity.

8) **Blood tissue** consists of several cell types in a fluid called plasma. It flows through the blood vessels and heart, and is essential for carrying oxygen to cells, fighting infection, and carrying nutrients and wastes to and from cells. Blood also has clotting capabilities, which preserve the body's functions in case of injury.

Tissues are organized into organs, and organs function together to form systems, which support the life of an organism. Studying these systems allows us to understand how organisms thrive within their ecosystem.

Systems

Many different body plans exist amongst animals, and each type of body plan includes systems necessary for the organism to live. Our discussion of systems here focuses on those found in most vertebrates. Vertebrates are highly complex organisms with several systems working together to perform the functions necessary to life. These include the digestive, gas exchange, skeletal, nervous, circulatory, excretory, and immune systems.

Digestive System

The **digestive system** (see Fig. 4-8) serves as a processing plant for ingested food. The digestive system in animals generally encompasses the processes of **ingestion** (food intake), **digestion** (breaking down of ingested particles into molecules that can be absorbed by the body), and **egestion** (the elimination of indigestible materials). In most vertebrates, the digestive organs are divided into two categories, the **alimentary canal,** and the **accessory organs**. The alimentary canal is also known as the **gastrointestinal** (or GI) **tract** and includes the mouth, pharynx, esophagus, stomach, small intestine, large intestine, rectum, and anus. The accessory organs include the teeth, tongue, salivary glands, liver, gallbladder, and pancreas.

The **mouth** (oral cavity, **1**) is the organ of ingestion and the first organ of digestion in the GI tract. The first step in digestion in many vertebrates occurs as food is chewed. Chewing is the initial step in breaking down food into particles of manageable size. Chewing also increases the surface area of the food and mixes it with saliva, which contains the starch-digesting enzyme amylase. Saliva is secreted by the **salivary glands** (**2**). Chewed food is then swallowed and moved toward the **stomach** (**3**) by peristalsis (muscle contraction) of the **esophagus** (**4**). The stomach is a muscular organ that stores incompletely digested food. The stomach continues the mechanical and chemical breakdown

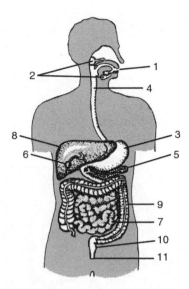

Fig. 4-8: Human Digestive System.

of food particles begun by the chewing process. The lining of the stomach secretes mucous to protect it from the strong digestive chemicals necessary in the digestive process. The stomach also secretes digestive enzymes and hydrochloric acid, which continue the digestive process to the point of producing a watery soup of nutrients, which then proceeds through the pyloric sphincter into the small intestine (the duodenum). The **pancreas (5)** and **gall bladder (6)** release more enzymes into the small intestine, the site where the final steps of digestion and most absorption occurs. The cells lining the **small intestine (7)** have protrusions out into the lumen of the intestine called **villi**. Villi provide a large surface area for absorption of nutrients. Nutrients move into the capillaries through or between the cells making up the villi. The enriched blood travels to the **liver (8)**, where some sugars are removed and stored. The indigestible food proceeds from the small intestine to the **large intestine (9)** where water is absorbed back into the body. The waste (**feces**) is then passed through the **rectum (10)** and excreted from the **anus (11)**.

There are, of course, variations in the digestive system among animals of various classifications. Some vertebrates such as cows and deer are **ruminants**; they consume large amounts of vegetation. These animals have several chambers in their stomachs. Chewed vegetation is regurgitated from the first two stomach chambers as **cud**, and is chewed again, allowing much of their food to be broken down mechanically. Bacteria in the digestive track then break down cellulose, the main constituent of a ruminant's diet.

Many invertebrates, such as insects and earthworms, have digestive systems resembling those of vertebrates, including a mouth, esophagus, stomach, and

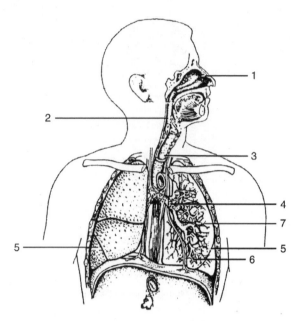

Fig. 4-9.: Human Respiratory System.

intestines. Many of these species also have a **crop**, an organ that stores food until it is processed for absorption. Other animals have only a sac-like digestive cavity that performs the necessary functions of digestion.

Respiratory or Gas Exchange System

Also known as the **respiratory system** (see Fig. 4-9), the **gas exchange system** is responsible for the intake and processing of gases required by an organism, and for expelling gases produced as waste products. In humans, air is taken in primarily through the **nose** (although gases may be inhaled through the mouth, the nose is better at filtering out pollutants in the air). The **nasal passages** (**1**) have a mucous lining to capture foreign particles. This lining is surrounded by epithelial tissue with embedded capillaries, which serve to warm the entering air. Air then passes through the **pharynx** (**2**) and into the **trachea** (**3**). The trachea includes the windpipe or **larynx** in its upper portion, and the **glottis**, an opening allowing gases to pass into the two branches known as the bronchi. The glottis is guarded by a flap of tissue, the **epiglottis**, which prevents food particles from entering the bronchial tubes. The **bronchi** (**4**) lead to the two **lungs** (**5**) where they branch out in all directions into smaller tubules known as **bronchioles** (**6**). The bronchioles end in **alveoli** (**7**), thin-walled air sacs, which are the site of gas exchange. The bronchioles are surrounded by capillaries, which bring blood with a high density of carbon dioxide and a low concentration of oxygen from the pulmonary arteries. At the alveoli, the carbon dioxide diffuses from the blood into the alveoli and oxygen diffuses from the alveoli into the blood. The oxygenated blood is carried away to tissues throughout the body.

All living organisms require the ability to exchange gases, and there are several variations to the means and organs utilized for this life process. Invertebrates such as the earthworm are able to absorb gases through their skin. Insects rely on the diffusion of gases through holes in the exoskeleton known as spiracles. In single-celled organisms such as the amoeba, diffusion of gases occurs directly through the plasma membrane.

Musculoskeletal System

The **musculoskeletal system** provides the body with structure, stability, and the ability to move. By definition, the musculoskeletal system is unique to vertebrates, although some invertebrates (such as mollusks and insects) have external support structures (exoskeletons) and muscle.

In humans, the musculoskeletal system is composed of joints, ligaments, cartilage, muscle groups, and 206 bones. The skeleton provides protection for the soft internal organs, as well as structure and stability allowing for an upright stature and movement. Bones also perform the important function of storing calcium and phosphates, and producing red blood cells within the bone marrow. The 206 bones forming the human skeleton are linked with movable joints, and joined by muscle systems controlling movement.

Skeletal muscles are voluntary—they are activated by command from the nervous system. **Smooth muscle** lines most internal organs, protecting their contents and function, and generally contracting without conscious intent. For instance, the involuntary (automatic) contraction of smooth muscle in the esophagus and lungs facilitates digestion and respiration. **Cardiac muscle** is unique to the heart. It is involuntary muscle (like smooth muscle), but cardiac muscle also has unique features, which cause it to "beat" rhythmically. Cardiac muscle cells have branched endings that interlock with each other, keeping the muscle fibers from ripping apart during their strong contractions. In addition, electrical impulses travel in waves from cell to cell in cardiac muscle, causing the muscle to contract in a coordinated way with a rhythmic pace.

Nervous System

The **nervous system** is a communication network that connects the entire body of an organism, and provides control over bodily functions and actions. Nerve tissue is composed of nerve cells known as **neurons**. Neurons carry impulses via electrochemical responses through their **cell body** and **axon** (long root-like appendage of the cell). Nerve cells exist in networks, with axons of neighbor neurons interacting across small spaces (**synapses**). Chemical

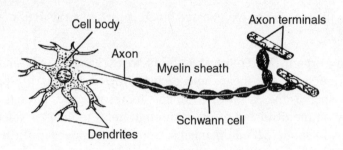

Fig. 4-10: A typical neuron.

neurotransmitters send messages along the nerve network causing responses specific to varying types of nerve tissue. The nervous system allows the body to sense stimuli and conditions in the environment and respond with necessary reactions. **Sensory organs**—skin, eyes, nose, ears, etc.—transmit signals in response to environmental stimuli to the **brain**, which then conveys messages via nerves to glands and muscles, which produce the necessary response.

The human nervous system (and that of many mammals) is anatomically divided into two systems, the central nervous system, and the peripheral nervous system. The following outline shows the components of each portion of the nervous system:

    I.   **Central Nervous System** (CNS)—two main components, the **brain** and the **spinal cord**. These organs control all other organs and systems of the body. The spinal cord is a continuation of the brain stem, and acts as a conduit of nerve messages.

    II.   **Peripheral Nervous System** (PNS)—a network of nerves throughout the body.

        A)   **Sensory Division**

            1.   **visceral sensory nerves**—carry impulses from body organs to the CNS

            2.   **somatic sensory nerves**—carry impulses from body surface to the CNS

        B)   **Motor Division**

            1.   **somatic motor nerves**—carries impulses to skeletal muscle from the CNS

            2.   **autonomic**

                a.)   **sympathetic** nervous system—carries impulses that stimulate organs

                b.)   **parasympathetic** nervous system—carries impulses back from organs

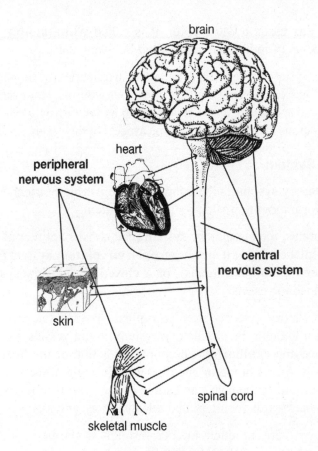

Fig. 4-11: Human Nervous System.

The brain of vertebrates has three major divisions, the forebrain, midbrain, and hindbrain. The **forebrain** is located most anterior, and contains the **olfactory lobes** (sense of smell), **cerebrum** (controls sensory and motor responses, memory, speech, and most factors of intelligence), as well as the **thalamus** (integrates senses), **hypothalamus** (involved in hunger, thirst, blood pressure, body temperature, hostility, pain, pleasure, etc.), and **pituitary gland** (releases various hormones). The **midbrain** is between the forebrain and hindbrain and contains the **optic lobes** (visual center connected to the eyes by the optic nerves). The **hindbrain** consists of the **cerebellum** (controls balance, equilibrium, and muscle coordination) and the **medulla oblongata** (controls involuntary response such as breathing and heartbeat).

Within the brain, nerve tissue is grayish in color and is called **gray matter**. The nerve cells, which exist in the spinal cord and throughout the body, have insulation covering their axons. This insulation (called the **myelin sheath)** speeds electrochemical conduction within the axon of the nerve cell. Since the myelin sheath gives this tissue a white color, it is called **white matter**. The myelin sheath is made up of individual cells called Schwann cells.

The nervous systems of vertebrates and some invertebrates are highly sophisticated, providing conscious response and unconscious controls. However, the nervous systems of some species of invertebrates (such as jellyfish) are relatively simple networks of neurons that control only some aspects of their body functions.

Circulatory System

The **circulatory system** is the conduit for delivering nutrients and gases to all cells and for removing waste products from them.

In invertebrates, the circulatory system may consist entirely of diffusion in the gastrovascular cavity, or it may be an **open circulatory system** (where blood directly bathes the internal organs), or a **closed circulatory system** (where blood is confined to vessels).

Closed circulatory systems are also typical of vertebrates. In vertebrates, **blood** flows throughout the circulatory system within **vessels**. Vessels include **arteries**, **veins**, and **capillaries**. The pumping action of the **heart** (a hollow, muscular organ) forces blood in one direction throughout the system. In large animals, valves within the heart, and some of the vessels in limbs, keep blood from flowing backwards (being pulled downward by gravity).

Blood carries many products to cells throughout the body, including minerals, infection-fighting white blood cells, nutrients, proteins, hormones, and

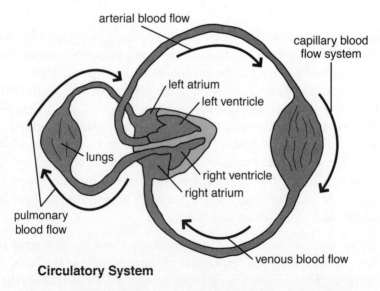

Circulatory System

Fig. 4-12: Human Circulatory System. Blood flows from the heart through arteries to the capillaries throughout the body and returns via the veins.

metabolites. Blood also carries dissolved gases (particularly oxygen) to cells and waste gases (mainly carbon dioxide) away from cells. The process of cellular metabolism is a fundamental process of life and cannot proceed without a continuous supply of oxygen to every living cell within the body.

Capillaries (tiny vessels) surround all tissues of the body and exchange carbon dioxide for oxygen. Oxygen is carried by **hemoglobin** (containing iron) in red blood cells. Oxygen enters the blood in the lungs and travels to the heart, then through **arteries** (larger vessels that carry blood away from the heart), then **arterioles** (small arteries), to capillaries. The blood picks up carbon dioxide waste from the cells and carries it through capillaries, then **venules** (small veins) and **veins** (vessels that carry blood toward the heart), back to the heart and on to the lungs. Thus, blood is continually cycled.

Excretory System

The **excretory system** is responsible for collecting waste materials and transporting them to organs that expel them from the body. There are many types of waste that must be expelled from the body, and there are many organs involved in this process.

The primary excretory organs of most vertebrates are the kidneys. The **kidneys** filter metabolic wastes from the blood and excrete them as **urine** into the urinary tract. The urinary tract carries the fluid that is eventually expelled from the body. Urine is typically 95% water, and may contain urea (formed from breakdown of proteins), uric acid (formed from breaking down nucleic acids), creatinine (a byproduct of muscle contraction), and various minerals and hormones.

The **liver** produces **bile** from broken-down pigments and chemicals (often from pollutants and medications) and secretes it into the small intestine, where it proceeds to the large intestine and is expelled in the feces. The liver also breaks down some nitrogenous molecules (including some proteins), excreting them as urea.

The **lungs** are the sites of excretion for carbon dioxide. The **skin** is an accessory excretory organ; salts, urea, and other wastes are secreted with water from sweat glands in the skin.

Immune System

The **immune system** functions to defend the body from infection by bacteria and viruses. The **lymphatic system** is the principal infection-fighting component of the immune system. The organs of the lymphatic system in humans and other higher invertebrates include the lymph, lymph nodes, spleen, thymus, and tonsils. **Lymph** is a collection of excess fluid that is absorbed from between cells into a special system of vessels, which circulates through the lymphatic system and finally dumps into the bloodstream. Lymph also collects plasma proteins that have leaked into interstitial fluids.

Lymph nodes are small masses of lymph tissue whose function is to filter lymph and produce lymphocytes. **Lymphocytes** and other cells are involved in the immune system. Lymphocytes begin in bone marrow as stem cells and are collected and distributed via the lymph nodes. There are two classes of lymphocytes: B cells, and T cells. **B cells** emerge from the bone marrow mature, and produce **antibodies**, which enter the bloodstream. These antibodies find and attach themselves to foreign **antigens** (i.e., toxins, bacteria, foreign cells, etc.). The attachment of an antibody to an antigen marks the pair for destruction.

The **spleen** contains some lymphatic tissue, and is located in the abdomen. It filters larger volumes of lymph than nodes can handle. The **tonsils** are a group of lymph cells connected together and located in the throat.

The **thymus** is another mass of lymph tissue, which is active only through the teen years, fighting infection and producing T cells. **T cells** mature in the thymus gland. Some T cells (like B cells) patrol the blood for antigens, but T cells are also equipped to destroy antigens themselves. T cells also regulate the body's immune responses.

Homeostatic Mechanisms

All living cells, tissues, organs, and organisms must maintain a tight range of physical and chemical conditions in order for them to live. Conditions such as temperature, pH, water balance, sugar levels, and so on, must be monitored and controlled in order to keep them within the accepted ranges that will not inhibit life. When the conditions of an organism are within acceptable ranges, it is said to be in **homeostasis**. Organisms have a special set of mechanisms that serve to keep them in homeostasis. Homeostasis is a state of dynamic equilibrium, which balances forces tending toward change with forces acceptable for life functions.

Homeostasis is achieved mostly by actions of the sympathetic and parasympathetic nervous systems by a process known as **feedback control**. For instance, when the body undergoes physical activity, muscle action causes a rise in temperature. If not checked, rising temperature could destroy cells. In this instance, the nervous system detects rising temperature and reacts with a response that causes sweat glands to produce sweat. The evaporation of sweat cools the body.

There are many instances of feedback control. These take effect when any situation arises that may drive levels out of the normal acceptable range. In other words, the homeostatic mechanism is a reaction to a stimulus. This reaction, called a **feedback response**, is the production of some counterforce that levels the system.

Hormonal Control in Homeostasis and Reproduction

Hormones are chemicals produced in the endocrine glands of an organism, which travel through the circulatory system and are taken up by specific targeted organs or tissues, where they modify metabolic activities.

Hormonal control occurs through one of two processes. The first is the **mobile receptor mechanism**. A hormone is manufactured in response to a particular **stimulus**. The hormone (for instance, a **steroid**) enters the bloodstream from one of the ductless endocrine glands that manufacture hormones. The steroid passes through the cell membrane of the targeted cell and enters the cytoplasm. The hormone combines with a particular protein known as a receptor, creating the **hormone-receptor complex**. This complex enters the nucleus and binds to a DNA molecule causing a gene to be transcribed. The mRNA molecule leaves the nucleus for the endoplasmic reticulum, where it encodes a particular protein. The protein migrates to the site of the stimulus and counteracts the source of the stimulus. The result is homeostasis, a balance of the counterproductive forces.

The second process targets receptors on a cell's membrane. A particular **receptor** exists on the membrane when the cell is in a particular condition (for instance, containing an excess of glucose). When the hormone binds with the receptor on the membrane, the receptor changes its form. This triggers a chain of events within the cytoplasm resulting in the production or destruction of proteins, thus moderating the conditions.

Hormones control many physiological functions, from digestion, to conscious responses and thinking, to reproduction. In humans, for instance, women of childbearing age have a continuous cycle of hormones. The hormone cycle causes the release of eggs at specific times. If the egg is fertilized, a different combination of hormones stimulates a chain of events that promotes the development of the embryo.

Animal Reproduction and Development

Reproduction in multicellular animals is a complex process that generally proceeds through the steps of **gametogenesis** (gamete formation) and then **fertilization**.

Gametes are the sex cells formed in the reproductive organs—sperm and eggs. When a sperm of one individual combines with the egg cell of another, the resulting cell is known as a **zygote**. A **zygote** then develops into a new individual. In the case of **spermatogenesis** (sperm formation), diploid **primary spermatocytes** are formed from special cells (**spermatogonia**) in the testes. The primary spermatocytes then undergo meiosis I, forming haploid **secondary spermatocytes** with a single chromosome set. (Please see the section on meiosis in Chapter 3.) The secondary spermatocytes go through meiosis II, forming **spermatids**, which are haploid. These spermatids then develop into the **sperm cells**.

In human female reproductive organs, egg cells are formed through a similar process known as **oogenesis**. **Primary oocytes** are typically present in great number in the female's ovaries at birth. Primary oocytes undergo meiosis I, forming one **secondary oocyte** and one smaller **polar body**. Both the secondary oocyte and the polar body undergo meiosis II; the polar body producing two polar bodies (not functional cells), and the oocyte producing one more polar body and one haploid **egg cell**. The egg cell is now ready for fertilization, and if there are sperm cells present, the egg may be fertilized, forming a diploid cell with a new combination of chromosomes, the zygote.

All multicellular organisms that reproduce sexually begin life as a zygote. The zygote then undergoes a series of cell divisions known as **cleavage**. After the first few divisions, the cluster of cells is called a morula. The **morula** then continues cell division, and the cluster begins to take shape as a thin layer of cells surrounding an internal cavity, the **blastula**. As cell division continues, the cells migrate and rearrange themselves, transforming the blastula into a two-layered cup shape, called the **gastrula** (a process known as **gastrulation**). As the gastrula develops, the cup shape reforms itself into a double-layered tube. The outer layer of the gastrula tube will become the **ectoderm**, which later will develop into the skin, some endocrine glands, and the nervous system. The inner layer of the tube will become the **endoderm**, the precursor of the gut lining and various accessory structures. With further development, a third layer, between the ectoderm and endoderm arises—the **mesoderm**. The mesoderm layer will eventually form muscles, and organs of the skeletal, circulatory, respiratory, reproductive, and excretory systems. The ectoderm, mesoderm, and endoderm collectively are called the **germ layers**. As the germ layers develop, the embryo becomes recognizable, and differentiation continues until the organ systems are fully developed.

In addition to forming the tissues and organ systems of vertebrates, the germ layers also develop into **extraembryonic membranes** (i.e., membranes not part of the embryos themselves, see Fig. 4-13). The first of these membranes is the **chorion** (**1**). In egg-laying vertebrates, the chorion lies in contact with the innermost surface of the shell, while in other vertebrates it is the outermost membrane surrounding the **embryo** (**2**) and in contact with the **uterus** (**3**). In both cases, the chorion functions in regulating the passage of gases and water

Fig. 4-13: Human Extraembryonic Membranes.

from the embryo to its surrounding environment. In embryos without shells, the chorion also controls passage of nutrients and wastes between the embryo and the mother.

Within the chorion is the **amnion** (**4**), a fluid-filled (**amniotic fluid**) sac enclosing the embryo. The amniotic fluid cushions the embryo and helps keep temperatures constant. The fluid also keeps the amnionic membrane from sticking to the developing embryo.

The third membrane is the **allantois** (**5**). It arises from the developing digestive tract. In humans and other vertebrates that bear live young, the allantois appears in the third week of development and becomes part of the **umbilical cord**. It contains blood vessels, which function to exchange gases and nutrients between the embryo and the mother. In egg-laying reptiles, the allantois is a reservoir for wastes. It fuses with the chorion, forming the **chorioallantoic membrane**, which regulates gas exchanges through the shell.

The **yolk sac membrane** (**6**), enclosing the **yolk sac** (**7**), also forms from the developing digestive tract and also becomes part of the umbilical cord. The yolk sac stores nutrients for use by the embryo. The yolk sac is larger and contains more material in egg-laying species, since there is no continuing contact with the mother. The yolk sac cells also give rise to gametes, which develop in reproductive organs of the embryo.

In mammals, the outer cells of the embryo and the inner cells of the uterus combine to form the **placenta**. The placenta is the connection between the mother and embryo; it is the site of transfer for nutrients, water, and wastes between them. The embryo synthesizes its own blood that is kept separate from the mother's blood. In the placenta, the vessels (that connect the circulatory system of the embryo through the umbilical cord to the placenta) pass right next to the mother's blood vessels. Nutrients, water, and oxygen diffuse from the mother's blood to the embryo's blood, while wastes and carbon dioxide diffuse into the mother's blood supply.

PRINCIPLES OF HEREDITY (GENETICS)

The process by which characteristics pass from one generation to another is known as **inheritance**. The study of the principles of heredity (now called genetics) advanced greatly through the experimental work of **Gregor Mendel** (c. 1865). Mendel studied the relationships between traits expressed in parents and offspring, and the hereditary factors that caused expression of traits.

Mendel systematically bred pea plants to determine how certain hereditary traits passed from generation to generation. First, he established true-breeding plants, which produce offspring with the same traits as the parents. For example, the seeds of pea plants with yellow seeds would grow into plants that produced yellow seeds. Green seeds grow into plants that produce green seeds. Mendel named this first generation of true-breeding plants the parent or P_1 **generation**; he then bred the plant with yellow seeds and the plant with green seeds. Mendel called the first generation of offspring the F_1 **generation**. The F_1 generation of Mendel's yellow seed/green seed crosses contained only yellow seed offspring.

Mendel continued his experiment by crossing two individuals of the F_1 generation to produce an F_2 **generation**. In this generation, he found that some of the plants (one out of four) produced green seeds. Mendel performed hundreds of such crosses, studying some 10,000 pea plants, and was able to establish the rules of inheritance from them. The following are Mendel's main discoveries:

- Parents transmit hereditary factors (now called **genes**) to offspring. Genes then produce a characteristic, such as seed-coat color.

- Each individual carries two copies of a gene, and the copies may differ.

- The two genes an individual carries act independently, and the effect of one may mask the effect of the other. Mendel coined the terms geneticists still use: "dominant" and "recessive."

Modern Genetics

We now know that **chromosomes** carry all the genetic information in most organisms. Most organisms have corresponding pairs of chromosomes that carry genes for the same traits. These pairs are known as **homologous chromosomes**. Genes that produce a given trait exist at the same position (or **locus**) on homologous chromosomes. Each gene may have different forms, known as **alleles.** For instance, yellow seeds and green seeds arise from different alleles of the same gene. A gene can have two or more alleles, which differ in their nucleotide sequence. That difference can translate into proteins that function differently, resulting in variations of the trait.

Sexual reproduction (meiosis) produces gamete cells with one-half the genetic information of the parents (paired chromosomes are separated and sorted independently). Therefore, each gamete may receive one of any number of combinations of each parent's chromosomes.

In addition, a trait may arise from one or more genes. (However, because one-gene traits are easiest to understand, we will use them for most of our examples.) If a trait is produced from a gene or genes with varying alleles, several possibilities for traits exist. The combination of alleles that make a particular trait is the **genotype**, while the trait expressed is the **phenotype**.

An allele is considered **dominant** if it masks the effect of its partner allele. The allele that does not produce its trait when present with a dominant allele is **recessive**. That is, when a dominant allele pairs with a recessive allele, the expressed trait is that of the dominant allele.

A **Punnett square** is a notation that allows us to easily predict the results of a genetic cross. In a Punnett square, a letter is assigned to each gene. Uppercase letters represent dominant traits, while lower case letters represent recessive traits (a convention begun by Mendel). The possible alleles from each parent are noted across the top and side of a box diagram; then the possible offspring are represented within the internal boxes. If we assign the allele that produces yellow seeds the letter **Y**, and the allele that produces green seeds **y**, we can represent Mendel's first cross between pea plants (**YY** × **yy**) by the following Punnett square:

	Y	Y
y	Yy	Yy
y	Yy	Yy

One parent pea plant had green seeds (green seeds is its phenotype), so it must not have had any of the dominant genes for yellow seeds (**Y**), therefore it must have the genotype **yy**. If the second parent had one allele for yellow and one for green, then some of the offspring would have inherited two genes for green. Since Mendel started with true-breeding plants, we may deduce that one parent had two genes for green seeds (**yy**) and the other two genes for yellow seeds (**YY**).

When both alleles for a given gene are the same in an individual (such as **YY** or **yy**), that individual is **homozygous** for that trait. Furthermore, the individual's genotype can be called homozygous. Both of the above parents (**P₁**) were homozygous. The children in the **F₁** generation all have one dominant gene (**Y**) and one recessive gene (**y**), their phenotype is yellow, and their genotype is **Yy**. When the two alleles for a given gene are different in an individual (**Yy**), that individual is said to be **heterozygous** for that trait; its genotype is heterozygous.

Breeding two **F₁** offspring from the example above produces the following Punnett square of a double heterozygous (both parents **Yy**) cross:

	Y	Y
Y	YY	Yy
y	Yy	yy

Through this Punnett square, we can determine that three-fourths of the offspring will produce yellow seeds. This is consistent with Mendel's findings. However, there are two different genotypes represented among the yellow seed offspring. One-half of the offspring were heterozygous yellow (**Yy**), while one-fourth were homozygous yellow (**YY**).

The example above shows a **monohybrid cross**—a cross between two individuals where only one trait is considered. Mendel also experimented with crossing two parents while considering two separate traits, a **dihybrid cross.**

The laws investigated by Mendel form the basis of modern genetics. However, Mendel's laws now incorporate modern terminology (i.e., "genes" rather than "hereditary factors," etc.).

The Law of Segregation

The first law of Mendelian genetics is the **law of segregation.** The law of segregation states that traits are expressed from a pair of genes in the individual (on homologous chromosomes). Each parent provides one chromosome of every pair of homologous chromosomes. Paired chromosomes (and thus corresponding genes) separate and randomly recombine during gamete formation.

The Law of Dominance

Mendel determined that one gene was usually dominant over the other. This is the **law of dominance**, Mendel's second law of inheritance. In Mendel's experiments, the first generation produced no plants with green seeds, leading him to recognize the existence of genetic dominance. The yellow-seed allele was clearly dominant.

The Law of Independent Assortment

Mendel also investigated whether genes for one trait always were linked to genes for another. In other words, Mendel experimented not only with pea seed-coat color, but also with pea-plant height (and a number of other traits in peas and other plants). He wanted to determine whether if the parent plant had green seeds and was tall, all plants with green seeds would be tall. These dihybrid cross experiments demonstrated that most traits were independent of one another. That is, a pea plant could be green and tall or green and short, yellow and tall or yellow and short. In most cases, genes for traits randomly sort into pairs (although some genes lie close to others on a chromosome and can therefore be inherited together). Since homologous chromosomes separate and independently sort in gamete formation, alleles are also separated and independently sorted, an assertion known as the **law of independent assortment**.

The following Punnett square demonstrates independent assortment. **Y** stands for the allele for yellow color, **y** for the allele for green, **T** for the allele tall, and **t** for short:

	TY	Ty	tY	ty
TY	TTYY	TTYy	TtYY	TtYy
Ty	TTYy	TTyy	TtYy	Ttyy
tY	TtYY	TtYy	ttYY	ttYy
ty	TtYy	Ttyy	ttYy	ttyy

Incomplete Dominance

Some traits have no genes that are dominant and instead produce offspring that are a mix of the two parents. For instance, in snapdragons a plant with red flowers crossed with a plant with white flowers produces offspring with pink flowers. This is known as **incomplete dominance**. Neither white nor red is dominant over the other. In incomplete dominance, the conventional way to symbolize the alleles is with a capital letter designating the trait (in this case **C** for color) and a superscript designating the allele choices (in this case ^{R} for red, ^{W} for white), making the possible alleles $\mathbf{C^R}$ and $\mathbf{C^W}$. The following Punnett square represents the incomplete dominance of the allele for red flowers $(\mathbf{C^R})$, the allele for white as $(\mathbf{C^W})$, and the combination resulting in pink as $(\mathbf{C^R C^W})$.

	$\mathbf{C^R}$	$\mathbf{C^R}$
$\mathbf{C^W}$	$\mathbf{C^R C^W}$	$\mathbf{C^R C^W}$
$\mathbf{C^W}$	$\mathbf{C^R C^W}$	$\mathbf{C^R C^W}$

In this case, two plants, one with white flowers, one with red, cross to form all pink flowers. If two of the heterozygous offspring of this cross are then bred, the outcome of this cross $(\mathbf{C^R C^W} \times \mathbf{C^R C^W})$ will be:

	$\mathbf{C^R}$	$\mathbf{C^W}$
$\mathbf{C^R}$	$\mathbf{C^R C^R}$	$\mathbf{C^R C^W}$
$\mathbf{C^W}$	$\mathbf{C^R C^W}$	$\mathbf{C^W C^W}$

One-fourth of the offspring will be red, one-half pink, and one-fourth white, a 1:2:1 ratio.

Multiple Alleles

In the instances above, two possible alleles exist in a species, so the genotype will be a combination of those two alleles. There are some instances where more than two choices of alleles are present. For instance, for human blood types there is a dominant allele for type A blood, another dominant allele for type B blood, as well as a recessive allele for neither A nor B, known as O blood. There are three different alleles and they may combine in any way. In multiple-allele crosses, it is conventional to denote the chromosome by a letter (in this case **I** for dominant, **i** for recessive), with a subscript letter representing the allele types (in this case **A**, **B**, or **O**). The alleles for A and B blood are co-dominant, while the allele for O blood is recessive. The possible genotypes and phenotypes then are as follows:

genotype	phenotype
$I^A I^A$	Type A blood
$I^B I^B$	Type B blood
$I^B i^O$	Type B blood
$I^A i^O$	Type A blood
$I^A I^B$	Type AB blood
$i^O i^O$	Type O blood

[Note: There is another gene responsible for the Rh factor that adds the + or − to the blood type.]

Linkage

While Mendel had established the law of independent assortment, later study of genetics by other scientists found that this law was not always true. In studying fruit flies, for instance, it was found that some traits are always inherited together; they were not independently sorted. Traits that are inherited together are said to be **linked**. Genes are portions of chromosomes, so most traits produced by genes on the same chromosome are inherited together. (The chromosomes are independently sorted, not the individual genes.)

However, an exception to this rule complicates the issue. During metaphase of meiosis I, when homologous chromosomes line up along the center of the dividing cell, some pieces of the chromosomes break off and move from one chromosome to another (change places). This random breaking and reforming of homologous chromosomes allows genes to change the chromosome they are linked to, thus changing the genome of that chromosome. This process, known as **crossing over**, adds even more possibility of variation of traits among species. It is more likely for crossing over to occur between genes that do not lie close together on a chromosome than between those that lie close together.

Gender is determined in an organism by a particular homologous pair of chromosomes. The symbols **X** and **Y** denote the sex chromosomes. In mammals and many insects, the male has an **X** and **Y** chromosome (**XY**), while the female has two **X**'s (**XX**). Genes that are located on the gender chromosome **Y** will only be seen in males. It would be considered a **sex-limited trait.** An example of a sex-limited trait is bar coloring in chickens that occurs only in males.

Some traits are **sex-linked**. In sex-linked traits, more males (**XY**) develop the trait because males have only one copy of the **X** chromosome. Females have a second **X** gene, which may carry a gene coding for a functional protein for the trait in question that may counteract a recessive trait. These traits (for example, hemophilia and colorblindness) occur much more often in males than females.

Still other traits may be **sex-influenced**. In this case, the trait is known as autosomal—it only requires one recessive gene to be expressed if there is no counteracting dominant gene. A male with one recessive allele will develop the trait, whereas a female would require two recessive genes to develop it. An example of a sex-influenced trait is male-pattern baldness.

Polygenic Inheritance

While the best-studied genetic traits arise from alleles of a single gene, most traits, such as height and skin color, are produced from the expression of more than one set of genes. Traits produced from interaction of multiple sets of genes are known as **polygenic traits.** Polygenic traits are difficult to map and difficult to predict because of the varied effects of the different genes for a specific trait.

Chapter 5

Ecology and Population Biology

ECOLOGY

Ecology is the study of how organisms interact with other organisms, and how they influence or are influenced by their physical **environment**. The word "ecology" is derived from the Greek term *oikos* (meaning "home" or "place to live") and *ology* (meaning "the study of"), so ecology is a study of organisms in their home. This study has revealed a number of patterns and principles that help us understand how organisms relate to their environment. First, however, it is important to grasp some basic vocabulary used in ecology.

The study of ecology centers on the ecosystem. An **ecosystem** is a group of populations found within a given locality, plus the inanimate environment around those populations. A **population** is the total number of a single species of organism found in a given ecosystem. Typically, there are many populations of different species within a particular ecosystem. The term **organism** refers to an individual of a particular species. Each species is a distinct group of individuals that are able to interbreed (mate), producing viable offspring. Although species are defined by their ability to reproduce, they are usually described by their morphology (their anatomical features).

Populations that interact with each other in a particular ecosystem are collectively termed a **community**. For instance, a temperate forest community includes pine trees, oaks, shrubs, lichen, mosses, ferns, squirrels, deer, insects, owls, bacteria, fungi, etc.

The part of the Earth that includes all living things is called the **biosphere**. The biosphere also includes the **atmosphere** (air), the **lithosphere** (ground), and the **hydrosphere** (water).

A **habitat** refers to the physical place where a species lives. A species' habitat must include all the factors that will support its life and reproduction. These factors may be **biotic** (i.e., living - food source, predators, etc.) and **abiotic** (i.e., nonliving - weather, temperature, soil features, etc.).

A species' **niche** is the role it plays within the ecosystem. It includes its physical requirements (such as light and water) and its biological activities (how it reproduces, how it acquires food, etc.). One important aspect of a species' niche is its place in the food chain.

Ecological Cycles

Every species within an ecosystem requires resources and energy in varying forms. The interaction of organisms and the environment can be described as cycles of energy and resources that allow the community to flourish. Although each ecosystem has its own energy and nutrient cycles, these cycles also interact with each other to form bioregional and planetary biological cycles.

The **energy cycle** supports life throughout the environment. There are also several **biogeochemical cycles** (the water cycle, the carbon cycle, the nitrogen cycle, the phosphorous cycle, the rock cycle, etc.), which are also important to the health of ecosystems. A biogeochemical cycle is the system whereby the substances needed for life are recycled and transported throughout the environment.

Carbon, hydrogen, oxygen, phosphorous, and nitrogen are called macronutrients; they are used in large quantities by living things. Micronutrients—those elements utilized in trace quantities in organisms—include iodine, iron, zinc, and copper.

Energy Cycle (Food Chain)

Since all life requires the input of energy, the **energy cycles** within the ecosystem are central to its well-being. On Earth, the Sun provides the energy that is the basis of life in most ecosystems. (An exception is the hydrothermal vent communities that derive their energy from the heat of the Earth's core.) Without the constant influx of solar energy into our planetary ecosystem, most life would cease to exist. Energy generally flows through the entire ecosystem in one direction—from producers to consumers and on to decomposers (consumers may also consume decomposers) through the **food chain.**

Photosynthetic organisms—such as plants, some protists, and some bacteria—are the first link in most food chains; they use the energy of sunlight to combine carbon dioxide and water into sugars, releasing oxygen gas (O_2). Photosynthetic organisms are called producers, since they synthesize sugar and starch molecules using the Sun's energy to link the carbons in carbon dioxide. Primary consumers (also known as herbivores) are species that eat photosynthetic organisms. Consumers utilize sugars and starches stored in cells or tissues for energy. Secondary consumers feed on primary consumers, and on the chain goes, through tertiary, quarternary (etc.) consumers. Finally, decomposers (bacteria, fungi, some animals) are species that recycle the organic material found in dead plants and animals back into the food chain.

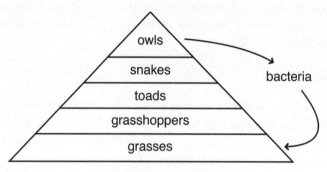

Fig. 5-1: A food chain pyramid.

Animals that feed only on other animals are called **carnivores** (meat-eaters), whereas those that consume both photosynthetic organisms and other animals are known as **omnivores**.

The energy cycle of the food chain is subject to the laws of thermodynamics. Energy can neither be created nor destroyed. However, every use of energy is less than 100% efficient; about 10% is lost as heat. When we call photosynthetic organisms producers, we mean that they produce food, using the Sun's energy to form chemical bonds in sugars and other biomolecules. Other organisms can use the energy stored in the bonds of these biomolecules.

The steps in the food chain are also known as **trophic levels**. Consider the pyramid diagram (Fig. 5-1) as one example of a food chain with many trophic levels. Grasses are on the bottom of the pyramid; they are the producers, the first trophic level. Producers are also known as **autotrophs**, as they produce their own food. Each trophic level is greater in **biomass** (total mass of organisms) than the level above it.

Grasshoppers represent the **second trophic level,** or primary consumers in this example of a food chain. Grasshoppers consume plants and are consumed (in this example) by toads, the secondary consumers, which represent the **third trophic level**. Snakes consume toads, and are in turn consumed by owls—making these the **fourth and fifth trophic levels**. In this example, bacteria are the decomposers that recycle some of the nutrients from dead owls (and other levels) to be reused by the first trophic level.

The pyramid illustrates a food chain; however, in nature it is never actually as simple as shown. Owls consume snakes, but they may also consume toads (a lower level in the pyramid) and fish (from an entirely different pyramid). Thus, within every ecosystem there may be numerous food chains interacting in varying ways to form a **food web**. Furthermore, all organisms produce waste products that feed decomposers. The food web represents the cycling and re-cycling of both energy and nutrients within the ecosystem. The productivity of the entire web is dependent upon the amount of photosynthesis carried out by photosynthesizers.

Water Cycle

The availability of water is crucial to the survival of all living things. Water vapor circulates through the biosphere in a process called the **hydrologic cycle**. Water is evaporated via solar radiation from the ocean and other bodies of water into clouds. Water is also released into the atmosphere from vegetation (leaves) by transpiration. Some water is also evaporated directly from soil, but most water in the ground flows into underground aquifers, which eventually empty into the oceans. Water above ground flows into waterways, which also eventually flow into the ocean (a process known as runoff). Water vapor is then redistributed over land (and back into oceans as well) via clouds, which release water as precipitation.

The water cycle also has a profound effect on Earth's climate. Clouds reflect the Sun's radiation away from the Earth, causing cool weather. Water vapor in the air also acts as a **greenhouse gas**, reflecting radiation from the Earth's surface back toward the Earth, and therefore trapping heat. The water cycle also intersects nearly all the other cycles of elements and nutrients.

Nitrogen Cycle

Nitrogen is another substance essential to life processes, since it is a key component of amino acids (components of proteins) and nucleic acids. The nitrogen cycle recycles nitrogen. Nitrogen is the most plentiful gas in the atmosphere, making up 78% of the air. However, neither photosynthetic organisms nor animals are able to use nitrogen gas (N_2), which does not readily react with other compounds, directly from the air. Instead, a process known as nitrogen fixing makes nitrogen available for absorption by the roots of plants. **Nitrogen fixing** is the process of combining nitrogen with either hydrogen or oxygen, mostly by **nitrogen-fixing bacteria**, or to a small degree by volcanoes and **lightning**.

Nitrogen-fixing bacteria live in the soil and perform the task of combining gaseous nitrogen from the atmosphere with hydrogen, forming ammonium (NH_4^+ ions). (Some cyanobacteria, also called blue-green bacteria, are also active in this process.) Ammonium ions are then absorbed and used by plants. Other types of nitrogen-fixing bacteria live in symbiosis on the nodules of the roots of legumes (beans, peas, clover, etc.), supplying the roots with a direct source of ammonia.

Some plants are unable to use ammonia, instead, they use **nitrates**. Some bacteria perform **nitrification**, a process, which further breaks down ammonia into nitrites (NO_2^-), and yet again another bacteria converts nitrites into nitrates (NO_3^-).

Nitrogen compounds (such as ammonia and nitrates) are also produced by natural, physical processes such as volcanic activity. Another source of usable nitrogen is lightning, which reacts with atmospheric nitrogen to form nitrates.

In addition, nitrogen passes along through the food chain, and is recycled through decomposition processes. When plants are consumed, the amino acids are recombined and used, a process that passes the nitrogen-containing molecules on through the food chain or web. Animal waste products, such as urine, release nitrogen compounds (primarily ammonia) back into the environment, yet another source of nitrogen. Finally, large amounts of nitrogen are returned to the Earth by bacteria and fungi, which decompose dead plant and animal matter into ammonia (and other substances), a process known as **ammonification.**

Various species of bacteria and fungi are also responsible for breaking down excess nitrates, a process known as **denitrification**, which releases nitrogen gas back into the air. The nitrogen cycle involves cycling nitrogen through both living and non-living entities.

Carbon Cycle

The carbon cycle is the route by which carbon is obtained, used, and recycled by living things. Carbon is an important element contained in the cells of all species. The study of organic chemistry is the study of carbon-based molecules.

Earth's atmosphere contains large amounts of carbon in the form of carbon dioxide (CO_2). Photosynthetic organisms require the intake of carbon dioxide for the process of photosynthesis, which is the foundation of the food chain. Most of the carbon within organisms is derived from the production of carbohydrates through photosynthesis. The process of photosynthesis also releases oxygen molecules (O_2), which are necessary to animal respiration. Animal respiration releases carbon dioxide back into the atmosphere in large quantities.

Since plant cells consist of molecules containing carbon, animals that consume photosynthetic organisms are consuming and using carbon from the photosynthetic organisms. Carbon is passed along the food chain as these animals are then consumed. When animals and photosynthetic organisms die, decomposers, including the detritus feeders, bacteria, and fungi, break down the organic matter. Detritus feeders include worms, mites, insects, and crustaceans, which feed on dead organic matter, returning carbon to the cycle through chemical breakdown and respiration.

Carbon dioxide (CO_2) is also dissolved directly into the oceans, where it is combined with calcium to form calcium carbonate, which is used by mollusks to form their shells. When mollusks die, the shells break down and often form limestone. Limestone is then dissolved by water over time and some carbon may be released back into the atmosphere as CO_2, or used by new ocean species.

Finally, organic matter that is left to decay, may, under conditions of heat and pressure be transformed into coal, oil, or natural gas (the **fossil fuels**). When fossil fuels are burned for energy, the combustion process releases carbon dioxide back into the atmosphere, where it is available to plants for photosynthesis.

Phosphorous Cycle

Phosphorous is another mineral required by living things. Unlike carbon and nitrogen, which cycle through the atmosphere in gaseous form, phosphorous is only found in solid form, within rocks and soil. Phosphorous is a key component in ATP, NADP (a molecule that, like ATP, stores energy in its chemical bonds), and many other molecular compounds essential to life.

Phosphorous is found within rocks and is released by the process of erosion. Water dissolves phosphorous from rocks, and carries it into rivers and streams. Here phosphorous and oxygen react to form phosphates, which end up in bodies of water. Phosphates are absorbed by photosynthetic organisms in and near the water and are used in the synthesis of organic molecules. As in the carbon and nitrogen cycles, phosphorous is then passed up the food chain and returned through animal wastes and organic decay.

New phosphorous enters the cycle as undersea sedimentary rocks. These rocks are thrust up during the shifting of the Earth's tectonic plates. New rock containing phosphorous is then exposed to erosion and enters the cycling process.

POPULATION GROWTH AND REGULATION

The population growth of a species is regulated by limiting factors that exist within the species' environment. Population growth maintains equilibrium in all species under normal conditions because of these limiting factors. A population's overall growth rate is affected by the birth rate (**natality**) and death rate (**mortality**) of the population. The rate of increase within a population is represented by the birth rate minus the death rate. When the birth rate within a population equals the death rate, the population remains at a constant level.

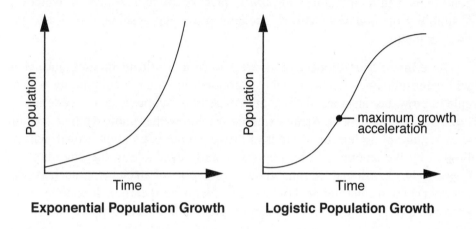

Exponential Population Growth   **Logistic Population Growth**

There are two models of population growth, the exponential curve (or J-curve) and the logistic curve (or the S-curve). The exponential curve represents populations in which there is no environmental or social limit on population size, so the rate of growth accelerates over time. Exponential population growth exists only during the initial population growth in a particular ecosystem, since as the population increases the limiting factors become more influential. In other words, a fish population introduced into a pond would experience exponential population growth until food and space supplies began to limit the population.

The logistic curve reflects the effects of limiting factors on population size, where growth accelerates to a point, then slows down. The logistic curve shows population growth over a longer period of time, and represents population growth under normal conditions.

Population growth is directly related to the life characteristics of the population such as the age at which an individual begins to reproduce, the age of death, the rate of growth, etc. For instance, species that grow quickly, mature sexually at an early age, and live a long life would have a population growth rate that exceeds that of species with a short life span and short reproductive span.

In general, most populations have an incredible ability to increase in numbers. A population without limiting factors could overpopulate the world in several generations. It is the limits existing within each ecosystem that keep this from happening.

Limiting Factors

Many factors affect the life of an ecosystem, which may be permanent or temporary. Populations within an ecosystem will be affected by changes in the environment from **abiotic factors** (physical, non-living factors such as fire, pollution, sunlight, soil, light, precipitation, availability of oxygen, water conditions, and temperature) and **biotic factors** (biological factors, including availability of food, competition, predator-prey relationships, symbiosis, and overpopulation).

These biotic and abiotic factors are known as **limiting factors** since they will determine how much a particular population within a community will be able to grow. For instance, the resource in shortest supply in an ecosystem may limit population growth. As an example, we know that photosynthetic organisms require phosphorous in order to thrive, so the population growth will be limited by the amount of phosphorous readily available in the environment. Conversely, growth may be limited by having more of an element (such as heat or water) than it can tolerate. For example, plants need carbon dioxide to grow; however, a large concentration of carbon dioxide in the atmosphere is toxic.

Ecologists now commonly combine these two ideas to provide a more comprehensive understanding of how conditions limit growth of populations. It may be stated that the establishment and survival of a particular organism in an area is dependent upon both 1) the availability of necessary elements in at least the minimum quantity, and 2) the controlled supply of those elements to keep it within the limits of tolerance.

Limiting factors interact with each other and generally produce a situation within the ecosystem that supports homeostasis (a steady-state condition). **Homeostasis** is a dynamic balance achieved within an ecosystem functioning at its optimum level. Homeostasis is the tendency of the ecological community to stay the same. However, the balance of the ecosystem can be disturbed by the removal, or decrease, of a single factor or by the addition, or increase, of a factor.

Populations are rarely governed by the effect of a single limiting factor; instead, many factors interact to control population size. Changes in limiting factors have a domino effect in an ecosystem, as the change in population size of one species will change the dynamics of the entire community. The number of individuals of a particular species living in a particular area is called the population **density** (number of organisms per area).

Both abiotic and biotic limiting factors exist in a single community; however, one may be dominant over the other. Abiotic limiting factors are also known as **density-independent factors**. That is, they are independent of population density. For instance, the populations around Mount St. Helens were greatly affected by its eruption in 1980, and this effect had nothing to do with the population levels of the area before the eruption. In this situation, the density-independent physical factors dominated the population changes that took place.

Pollution is a major density-independent factor in the health of ecosystems. Pollution is usually a byproduct of human endeavors and affects the air or water quality of an ecosystem with secondary effects. In addition to producing pollution, humans may deliberately utilize chemicals such as pesticides or herbicides to limit growth of particular species. Such chemicals can damage the homeostatic mechanisms within a community, causing a long term upset in the balance of an ecosystem.

In other situations, biotic factors, called **density-dependent factors** may be the dominant influence on population in a given area. Density-dependent factors include population growth issues and interactions between species within a community.

Within a given area, there is a maximum level the population may reach at which it will continue to thrive. This is known as the **carrying capacity** of the environment. When an organism has reached the carrying capacity of the ecosystem, the population growth rate will level off and show no net growth. Populations also occupy a particular geographic area with suitable conditions. This total area occupied by a species is known as the **range**. Typically, populations will have the greatest density in the center of their range, and lower density at the edges. The area outside the range is known as the area of intolerance for that species, since it is not able to survive there. Environmental changes will affect the size and location of the range, making it a dynamic characteristic.

Over time, species may move in or out of a particular area, a process known as **dispersion**. Dispersion occurs in one of three ways—through **emigration** (permanent one way movement out of the original range), **immigration** (permanent one way movement into a new range), and **migration** (temporary movement out of one range into another, and back). Migration is an important process to many species and communities, since it allows animals that might not survive year round in a particular ecosystem to temporarily relocate for a portion of the year. Therefore, migration gives the opportunity for greater diversity of species in an ecosystem.

Two or more species living within the same area and that overlap niches (their function in the food chain) are said to be in **competition** if the resource they both require is in limited supply. If the niche overlap is minimal (other sources of food are available), then both species may survive. In some cases, one of the species may be wiped out in an area due to competition, a situation called **competitive exclusion**. This is a rare but plausible occurrence.

A **predator** is simply an organism that eats another. The organism that is eaten is known as the **prey**. The **predator/prey** relationship is one of the most important features of an ecosystem. As seen in our study of the energy cycle, energy is passed from lower trophic levels to higher trophic levels, as one animal is consumed by another. This relationship not only provides transfer of energy up the food chain, it also is a population control factor for the prey species. In situations where natural predators are removed from a region, the overpopulation occurring amongst the prey species can cause problems in the population and community. For instance, the hunting and trapping of wolves in the United States has led to an overpopulation of deer (the prey of wolves), which in turn has caused a shortage of food for deer in some areas, causing these deer populations to starve.

When two species interact with each other within the same range it is known as **symbiosis**. **Amensalism** is one type of symbiosis where one species is neither helped nor harmed while it inhibits the growth of another species. **Mutualism** is another form of symbiosis where both species benefit. **Parasitism** is symbiosis in which one species benefits, but the other is harmed. (Parasites are not predators, since the parasitic action takes a long period of time and may not actually kill the host.)

When the entire population of a particular species is eliminated, it is known as **extinction**. Extinction may be a local phenomenon, the elimination of a population of one species from one area. However, species extinction is a worldwide phenomenon, where all members of all populations of a species die.

The extinction of a single species may also cause a chain reaction of secondary extinctions if other species depend on the extinct species. Conversely, the introduction of a new species into an area can also have a profound effect on other populations within that area. This new species may compete for the niche of native population or upset a predator/prey balance. For example, the brown tree snake (native to Australia) was introduced into islands in the Pacific years ago. (They probably migrated on ships.) The brown snake has caused the extinction of several species of birds on those Pacific islands. The bird populations could not withstand the introduction of this new predator.

Ultimately, the survival of a particular population is dependent on maintaining a **minimal viable population** size. When a population is significantly diminished in size, it becomes highly susceptible to breeding problems and environmental changes that may result in extinction.

Community Structure

Community structure refers to the characteristics of a specified community including the types of species that are dominant, major climatic trends of the region, and whether the community is open or closed. A **closed community** is one whose populations occupy essentially the same range with very similar distributions of density. These types of communities have sharp boundaries called **ecotones** (such as a pond aquatic ecosystem that ends at the shore). An **open community** has indefinite boundaries, and its populations have varying ranges and densities (such as a forest). In an open community, the species are more widely distributed and animals may actually travel in and out of the area.

An open community is often more able to respond to calamity and may be therefore more resilient. Since the boundaries are subtler, the populations of a forest, for instance, may be able to move as necessary to avoid a fire. If, however, a closed community is affected by a traumatic event (for example, a pond being polluted over a short period of time) it may be completely wiped out.

Communities do grow and change over time. Some communities are able to maintain their basic structure with only minor variations for very long periods of time. Others are much more dynamic, changing significantly over time from one type of ecosystem to another. When one community completely replaces another over time in a given area, it is called **succession**. Succession occurs both in terrestrial and aquatic biomes.

Succession may occur because of small changes over time in climate or conditions, the immigration of a new species, disease, or other slow-acting factors. It may also occur in direct response to cataclysmic events such as fire, flood, or human intervention (for example, clearing a forest for farmland). The first populations that move back into a disturbed ecosystem tend to be hardy species that can survive in bleak conditions. These are known as **pioneer communities.**

An example of terrestrial succession occurs when a fire wipes out a forest community. The first new colonization will come from quick growing species such as grasses, which will produce over time a grassland ecosystem. The decay of grasses will enrich the soil, providing fertile ground for germination of seeds for shrubs brought in by wind or animals. The shrubs will further prepare the soil for germination of larger species of trees, which over time will take over the shrub-land and produce a forest community once again.

When succession ends in a stable community, the community is known as the **climax community**. The climax community is the one best suited to the climate and soil conditions, and one that achieves a homeostasis. Generally, the climax community will remain in an area until a catastrophic event (fire, flood, etc.) destroys it.

BIOMES

A **biome** is an ecosystem that is generally defined by its climate characteristics. Each biome includes many types of community interacting within the climatic region. There are several major biomes that have been identified by ecologists. There are two basic types of biome—terrestrial and aquatic. **Terrestrial biomes** are those that exist on land, **aquatic biomes** are within large bodies of water. The following table gives the name of the major biomes with their major characteristics:

Biome	Temperature	Precipitation Level	Features
Tropical Rain Forest	warm	high	dense forest, heavy rainfall, abundant vegetation, relatively poor soil
Savanna	warm	moderate	grassland, light seasonal rains
Chaparral	hot summer, temperate winter	low in summer, high in winter	trees, shrubs, small animals, prolonged summer
Temperate Grassland	moderate and seasonal	low for most of year	large land tracts of grassland, shrubs and annuals, rodents, and some larger carnivores
Desert	extreme hot or cold	very low	sandy or rocky terrain, sparse vegetation, mainly succulents, small animals, rodents, reptiles
Tundra	extreme cold	low	modified grassland, permafrost, short growing season w/ some plants and animals
Taiga	cold	moderate	snow most of year, thick coniferous forests, wide variety of animal life
Temperate Deciduous Forest	moderate, seasonal	moderate	many trees (that lose leaves in cold season), mosses, grasses, shrubs, abundant animal life
Marine Aquatic	varied	not applicable	large amounts of dissolved minerals (particularly salts) in the water, huge array of aquatic animal and plant life
Freshwater Aquatic	varied	not applicable	still or running water with little dissolved minerals, large array of aquatic plant and animal life

Island Biogeography

Biogeography is the study of how photosynthetic organisms and animals are distributed in a particular location, plus the history of their distribution in the past. Island biogeography is a subdiscipline that investigates the distribution of species in an island habitat. The study of island biogeography is of particular interest to ecologists, since islands are closer to being a closed system (that is, they have less interaction with other ecosystems) than other environments.

Since islands are by nature separated from other land ecosystems, species of both photosynthetic organisms and animals found on a particular island usually have arrived there by natural **dispersal** processes (by air or sea). For instance, there are many plant species with adapted seeds, which will float in water or be carried long distances by air and remain viable. Birds are adapted for dispersion, as are many species of insect, and many sea animals (e.g., tortoises, snails, etc.). Dispersal to an island is dependent on geographic as well as historical factors. Distance from other land masses is an important geographic factor. Obviously, the closer the island is to other land, the easier dispersal of species to that island will be. Conversely, islands separated by long stretches of water will have less dispersion. Prevailing winds and ocean currents are also geographic factors that will affect species introduction. Historical factors such as climate shifts (for instance, the shift to an ice age), drought, volcanic action, plate shifting (where the continental plates of the Earth's crust move slowly), etc., will also affect which species are able to travel to a given island. In recent history, dispersion has also occurred through human intervention. Species that inhabit a given ecosystem because humans transported them there are known as **introduced** species.

In some cases, new species develop from parents that were dispersed to the island. These new species are **native** to that island. Arrival of a species on an island, however, does not insure that it will survive and thrive there. In order to become an established part of the island ecosystem, a species must find a suitable habitat and niche. Ultimately, the species must be able to reproduce for many generations in its new setting, or it will not remain a part of the ecosystem. If the island contains a habitat suitable for the newly arrived species, then that species has a chance of survival in its new environment. Islands may contain several habitats; consequently, islands that support numerous habitats will be more likely to have a wider diversity of species.

Islands may also develop new habitats over time as the climate and geology change, and depending on the size and age of the island. In general, the larger and older the island, the more species it will support. The one exception to this is an old island whose soil has eroded and lost its nutrients. In this case, its habitats may not be able to support life. Also, the harsher the climate (high or low temperature or water conditions) of the island, the fewer species it will have. The geology of the island (whether it is volcanic in origin, for instance) determines the characteristics of the soil, and thus has a direct effect on habitability as well.

PRINCIPLES OF BEHAVIOR

The study of **ethology** involves studying how animals act and react within their environments. Behavior simply is what an organism does and how it does it. Some behavioral characteristics are learned; others are instinctive (inherited).

Behavioral characteristics of animals may include how they acquire food, how they seek out and relate to a mate, how they respond to danger, or how they care for young. Behavior may be as simple as a reflex or may involve responses and interactions between the endocrine, nervous, and musculoskeletal systems.

Some behaviors are extremely simple in nature; they are a response to an environmental stimulus. These basic behaviors are innate; they exist from birth and are genetic in origin (they are inherited). **Innate behaviors** are the actions in animals we call **instincts**. Innate behaviors are highly stereotyped; all individuals of a species perform these behaviors in the same way. **Stereotyped behaviors** are of four basic varieties:

- **taxes** (plural of taxis) are directional responses either toward or away from a stimulus,

- **kineses** are changes in speed of movement in response to stimuli,

- **reflexes** are an automatic movement of a body part in response to a stimulus, and

- **fixed action patterns** (FAP) are complex but stereotyped behaviors in response to a stimulus.

The fixed action pattern is the most complex of stereotyped behaviors. It is a pre-programmed response to a particular stimulus known as a **releaser** or a **sign stimulus**. FAPs include courtship behaviors, circadian rhythms, and feeding of young. Organisms automatically perform FAPs without any prior experience (FAPs are not learned).

Some animal behaviors are learned. **Learned behaviors** may have some basis in genetics, but they also require learning. Generally, there are three types of learned behavior in animals: conditioning, habituation, and imprinting.

Conditioning involves learning to apply an old response to a new stimulus. The classic example of conditioning is that of Pavlov's dogs. Ivan Pavlov was a scientist who studied animal behavior. Dogs have an innate behavior to begin salivating when they see food. Pavlov was able to train dogs to salivate when they heard a bell ring. He trained, or conditioned, them by ringing the bell every time he fed the dogs. The dogs were conditioned to produce an instinctive behavior (salivating) in response to a new stimulus (bell).

B.F. Skinner was another scientist who studied conditioning. Skinner started with the thesis that learning happens through changes in overt behavior. Skinner believed that when a particular behavior is rewarded, the individual is being conditioned to repeat that behavior. Reinforcement of good behaviors results in repeating that behavior.

Habituation is a learned behavior where the organism produces less and less response as a stimulus is repeated, without a subsequent negative or positive action. For instance, a cat might innately respond to a dog's approach by hissing and raising its hair. However, if the dog regularly approaches, but never attacks, the cat eventually learns that the dog is not a threat and ceases to exhibit the fear behavior. Habituation safeguards species from wasting energy on irrelevant stimuli.

Imprinting is a learned behavior that develops in a critical or sensitive period of the animal's lifespan. Konrad Lorenz (a behavioral scientist) was able to show that baby geese responded to their mother's physical appearance shortly after birth. During the critical period after birth, the gosling learns to recognize his mother. However, if another object is exposed to the gosling during that critical period (immediately following hatching) the gosling would interpret the substituted object to be its mother. Imprinting generally involves learning a new releaser for an established FAP.

Social Behavior

Some animal species demonstrate **social behavior**—behavior patterns that take into account other individuals. One aspect of animal behavior regards the physical land area that an individual lives in. Animals will develop a **home range** (an area in which they spend most of their time). Animals may also develop an area of land as their **territory**, which lies within the home range, but is the area the individual will defend as his own. The establishment of a territory implies the recognition by one individual that other individuals exist, thus it is a simple social behavior.

Sexual and mating behaviors often rely on complex interactions of the endocrine, nervous, and musculoskeletal systems. In many cases, an individual will compete with another for a particular mate. There are often complex rituals, which are performed before the actual mating experience, involving many instinctive responses to stimuli and learned behaviors. The sexual and parenting behaviors of animals are social traits that are extremely diverse between species.

In some species, social interactions are highly complex; for instance, an entire population may function as a hierarchy (or society), where individuals have specified roles and status. Insects such as ants and bees, some species of birds, and many primates are among the groups that form societies.

A **society** is an organization of individuals in a population in which tasks are divided, in order for the group to work together. For instance, bees are social insects with a hierarchy (including a queen bee and worker bees). Some individuals are responsible for caring for the queen, others work within the nest, and others gather nectar from outside sources to be brought to the nest. Most of the population is female; the males are called drones and their only responsibility is mating. This division of labor allows the society to perform a higher function than if each individual acted on it own. Within a society, the individuals may be constantly growing, changing, and adapting, while the functions of the community remain the same over time.

While the social behavior of insects is more a question of division of labor, societies of primates are built around the idea of **dominance**. Older, more established individuals, compete for status within the community. A hierarchy is formed through actual competitions among individuals. The community member(s) at the top of the hierarchy enjoy privileges related to their selection of food and mates. This hierarchy is challenged as individuals mature, causing a succession of leaders.

Social behavior is highly dependent on communication within the population, and the ability of individuals to adapt behavior according to the needs of the society as a whole. Social animals exhibit a characteristic known as **altruism**, that is, having traits that tend to serve the needs of the society as a whole in addition to its own individual needs.

SOCIAL BIOLOGY

Human Population Growth

As with the study of population growth among other species, human population growth is a direct function of human birth and death rates (natality and mortality). People are able to reason around many of the limiting factors (for example, problems of food shortage or disease), making human population growth a much more complex situation. Furthermore, reproductive behaviors of humans are also subject to the reasoning process, unlike the instinctual mating behaviors of most animals.

The development of vaccines and antibiotics has greatly increased the lifespan of people in recent history, decreasing the mortality rate. Infant mortality rates have steeply declined in the last 150 years, as safer birthing processes and infant care have been developed. On the other hand, the development of contraceptives has reduced the natality rate in many countries.

Thomas Malthus is one of the most famous human population scientists. In the 1780s Malthus recognized the exponential properties of population growth and calculated that the Earth's food supply would eventually be exhausted by human overpopulation. However, Malthus's calculations did not take into account new technologies allowing for higher yield of food production. So, while the Earth's population has indeed increased exponentially (passing the six billion mark in 2000), and the doubling time (the amount of time it takes for a population to double in size) is decreasing significantly, the Earth has so far been able to support its population for the most part. (The Earth has an adequate food supply at present, yet people may currently starve because they are unable to produce food in their region and/or may be politically unable to import food.)

A theory known as **demographic transition** proposes that there are progressive demographic time periods of human population growth. In the first period, birth and death rates are approximately equal, allowing the population to be in equilibrium with the environment. Social evolution (i.e., ability to fight disease, mass produce food, etc.) causes the birth rate to overtake the death rate, in turn causing rapid population growth throughout another period. Agrarian lifestyles (where families have numerous children to "work the farm") become less common and children become a liability in urban society. However, **biomedical progress** of urban society causes a lowering of the infant mortality rate. Society then faces a period of dramatic population growth, most of it within cities. The final stage occurs as developed industrialized nations work to lower birth rates through contraceptive practices.

As the human population proceeds through demographic transition, the **age composition** (the relative numbers of individuals of specific ages within the population) changes. As birth rates increase, the population tends to shift toward youth, whereas medical advancements may increase the average age of the population. For instance, in 1900 approximately 40% of Americans were under 18, in 1960, 36% and in 1996, only 26% of Americans were under 18. Demographic transition also has an effect on the population growth rate.

Meanwhile, the introduction of **genetic engineering** in recent history has produced a complex array of implications. Genetic engineering is the intentional alteration of genetic material of a living organism. Genetic engineering of plant species has produced species able to resist drought, disease, or other threats—providing for more abundant food production. Genetic engineering is also responsible for disease-fighting breakthroughs such as the production of human insulin to fight diabetes. (Insulin is produced industrially using genetically engineered bacteria that produce human insulin.) The future of genetic engineering, however, is uncertain as we confront the ethical questions regarding the possibility of choosing characteristics of children, or cloning humans.

The growth of human population has also had a profound effect on the biosphere. **Environmental pollution** (the addition of contaminants to the air and water by human intervention and industry) has profoundly affected the ecosystems of the Earth. Most pollution has occurred in recent decades as industrialization has increased.

Progress has been made in the **management of resources** in the recent past. In our discussion of energy and biochemical cycles (early in this chapter), we noted that our biosphere has natural mechanisms that allow for the recycling of energy and nutrients. Careful resource management, including the active human intervention of recycling energy, water, nutrients, and chemicals, will encourage the natural cyclic processes within the biosphere to maintain a viable balance.

PART II
Physical Science

Chapter 6

Atomic Chemistry

STRUCTURE OF THE ATOM

The study of matter is known as **chemistry**. All matter is made up of **atoms**. The properties of matter are a result of the structure of atoms and their interaction with each other. An **element** is a substance that cannot be broken down into any other substances. The simplest unit of an element that retains the element's characteristics is known as an *atom*. Each atom of a given element has a nucleus containing a unique number of **protons** and usually a similar number of **neutrons**. The nucleus is surrounded by **electrons**.

Elements are listed by atomic number on the **periodic table of the elements**. The **atomic number** is the number of protons found in the nucleus of an atom of that element. In an uncharged atom, the number of protons is equal to the number of electrons.

The mass of an atom consists of the cumulative mass of all the particles in the atom, which includes protons, neutrons, and electrons. The mass of the electrons is insignificant relative to the mass of protons or neutrons. Therefore, the **atomic mass** is calculated by adding up the masses of the protons and neutrons. For example, a helium atom consists of two protons and two electrons. It would have an atomic mass of 4 amu (atomic mass units—the mass of one proton or neutron).

Atoms with the same number of protons but different numbers of neutrons are called **isotopes** of one another. For example, carbon-12 and carbon-14 are the same element (carbon), which is defined as having 6 protons. The difference in the **mass numbers** indicates that carbon-12 has 6 neutrons, while carbon-14 has 8 neutrons. In nature, elements naturally occur as a combination of more than one isotope. The average mass number takes into account the relative frequencies of the different isotopes. The average mass number is also called the **atomic weight**. This number is also the **molar mass** of the element, or the

THE PERIODIC TABLE

METALS

NONMETALS

KEY

Atomic Number → Group Classification
Atomic Weight → Symbol

( ) indicates most stable or best known isotope

	4 IVA IVB
22 Ti	47.88

TRANSITIONAL METALS

Alkali Metals

Alkaline Earth Metals

Halogens

Noble Gases

LANTHANIDE SERIES

ACTINIDE SERIES

Fig. 6-1: The Periodic Table of the Elements. Elements are listed by atomic number.

mass in grams of one mole of atoms. (6.02×10^{23} atoms constitute one mole of atoms.) For example:

Naturally occurring lead (Pb) exists as a combination of four isotopes, Pb-204, Pb-206, Pb-207, and Pb-208. Given the natural abundance of each isotope described in the following chart, calculate the average mass number of lead.

Pb-204	0.42%
Pb-206	24.10%
Pb-207	22.10%
Pb-208	52.40%

Solution: Multiply the frequency, expressed as a fraction, by the mass of each isotope. Then add the contributions of each isotope together to get the total average mass. [0.8568 + 49.65 + 45.75 + 1090 = 205.0.]

Electrons have a charge of –1, while protons have a charge of +1. Neutrons have no charge. The number of protons in the nucleus of an atom carries a positive charge equal to this number; that is, if an atom's nucleus contains 4 protons, the charge is + 4. Since positive and negative charges attract, the positive charges of the nucleus attract an equal number of negatively charged electrons.

Electrons travel freely in a three-dimensional space that may be called an **electron cloud**, an **electron shell**, or an **orbital**. Current models of the atom follow the principles of **quantum mechanics**, which predict the probabilities of an electron being in a certain area at a certain time. Although the term "orbital" is used, electrons do not orbit the nucleus like a planet orbiting a sun. The orbital (or electron cloud or electron shell) represents a probability of finding an electron at a particular location.

Each shell has a particular amount of energy related to it, and is therefore also referred to as an **energy level**. Energy levels are named utilizing a *quantum number* and a *letter designation* (i.e., 1s, 2s, 2p, etc.). The quantum number of the energy level closest to the nucleus is 1, and progresses as the levels get farther from the nucleus (2, 3, etc.). The letter designation indicates the shape of that particular energy level. The energy level closest to the nucleus has the least energy related to it; the farthest has the most. Each energy level has a limited capacity for holding electrons and each energy level requires a different number of electrons to fill it. Lower energy levels (closer to the nucleus) have less capacity for electrons than those farther from the nucleus.

Since electrons are attracted to the nucleus, electrons fill the electron shells closest to the nucleus (lowest energy levels) first. Once a given level is full, electrons start filling the next level out. The outermost occupied energy level of an element is called the **valence shell**. The number of electrons in the valence shell will determine the combinations that this atom will be likely to make with other atoms. Atoms are more stable when every electron is paired and are most stable when their valence shell is full. The tendency for an atom toward stability means that elements having unpaired or partially-filled valence shells will easily gain or lose electrons in order to obtain the most stable configuration.

Electrons give off energy in the form of **electromagnetic radiation** when they move from a higher level, or an excited state, to a lower level. The energy represented by light, using Planck's equation, represents the difference between the two energy levels of the electron. Atoms contain electromagnetic energy that is found in discrete bundles, expressed by the equation below:

Energy and Electromagnetic Radiation

$$\mathbf{E} = h\,v \text{ or, since } c = v\,\lambda, \text{ then } \mathbf{E} = \frac{hc}{\lambda}$$

where: E = Energy of the photon, J

h = Planck's constant, 6.63×10^{-34} J • sec

v = frequency of light, sec^{-1}

λ = wavelength of light, m

c = speed of light, 3.00×10^{8} m/sec

PERIODIC TRENDS

Atomic Radii: Moving from left to right across a period, the atomic radius decreases. Moving down a group from top to bottom, the atomic radius increases. *Cations* (positive ions) have smaller radii than their corresponding neutral atoms. *Anions* (negative ions) have larger radii than their corresponding neutral atoms.

Ionization Energy: Moving from left to right across a period, ionization energy increases. Moving down a group from top to bottom, ionization energy decreases. More energy is needed for each successive ionization. Significantly more energy is needed to break a full shell of electrons. Elements with low ionization energies are more easily oxidized.

Electron Affinity: Moving from left to right across a period, electron affinity increases. Moving down a group from top to bottom, electron affinity generally decreases.

Electronegativity: Moving from left to right across a period, electronegativity increases. Moving down a group from top to bottom, electronegativity decreases.

NUCLEAR REACTIONS AND EQUATIONS

Alpha Decay occurs when the nucleus of an atom emits a package of two protons and two neutrons, called an *alpha particle* (α), which is equivalent to the nucleus of a helium atom. This usually occurs with elements that have a mass number greater than 60. Alpha decay causes the atom's atomic mass to decrease by four units and the atomic number by two units. For example:

$$^{238}_{92}U \rightarrow \alpha \, \text{particle} \, (^4_2He) + ^{234}_{90}Th$$

Beta Decay occurs when the nucleus emits a *beta particle* (β-) that degrades into an electron as it passes out of the atom. This usually occurs with elements that have a mass number greater than their atomic weight. Beta decay causes the mass number to remain the same but increases the atomic number by one. Beta decay converts a neutron into a proton. For example:

$$^{234}_{90}Th \rightarrow \beta^- \, \text{particle} \, (^{\,0}_{-1}e) + ^{234}_{91}Pa$$

Positron Decay occurs when the nucleus emits a particle that degrades into a *positron* as it passes out of the atom. This usually occurs with elements that have a mass number smaller than their atomic weight. Positron decay causes the mass number to remain the same but decreases the atomic number by one. Positron decay converts a proton into a neutron and a positron. For example:

$$^{13}_{7}N \rightarrow ^{\,0}_{+1}e + ^{13}_{6}C$$

Gamma Radiation consists of *gamma rays* (γ), which are high-frequency, high-energy, electromagnetic radiation that are usually given off in combination with alpha and beta decay. Gamma decay can occur when a nucleus undergoes a transformation from a higher-energy state to a lower-energy state. The resulting atom may or may not be radioactive. Gamma rays are photons, which have neither mass nor charge.

RATE OF DECAY; HALF-LIFE

Half-life is the time it takes for 50 percent of an isotope to decay. Nuclear decay represents a "first-order" reaction in that it depends on the amount of material and the rate constant. For example:

Strontium-85 has a half-life of 65.2 days. How long will it take for 20 grams of strontium-85 to decay into five grams of strontium-85?

Solution:

It takes two half-lives to decrease the amount of strontium-85 from 20 grams to 5 grams.

$$2 \times 65.2 \text{ days} = 130.4 \text{ days.}$$

Chapter 7

Chemistry of Reactions

COMMON ELEMENTS

There are numerous elements on the *Periodic Table of Elements* that are more commonly found on Earth, and more likely to interact with other elements. Properties of each element, such as mass, electronegativity, valence electrons, etc., make a particular element fit for interaction with other elements in a variety of ways. The most common elements encountered in chemical reactions are found on the following table:

Atomic Number	Symbol	Common Name
1	H	Hydrogen
2	He	Helium
6	C	Carbon
7	N	Nitrogen
8	O	Oxygen
11	Na	Sodium
12	Mg	Magnesium
14	Si	Silicon
15	P	Phosphorus
16	S	Sulphur
17	Cl	Chlorine
19	K	Potassium
20	Ca	Calcium
24	Cr	Chromium
26	Fe	Iron
29	Cu	Copper
30	Zn	Zinc
47	Ag	Silver
53	I	Iodine
79	Au	Gold
80	Hg	Mercury
82	Pb	Lead
88	Ra	Radium

Chemical Bonds

Valence properties of atoms provide opportunities for them to bond with other atoms. A **covalent bond** between atoms is formed when atoms *share* electrons. For instance, hydrogen has only one electron, which is unpaired, leaving the 1s valence shell one electron short of full. Oxygen has 6 electrons in the valence shell; it needs 2 more electrons in the valence shell for that shell to be full. It is easy for 2 hydrogen atoms to share their electrons with the oxygen, making the effective valence shells of each full.

A **molecule** is two or more atoms held together by shared electrons (covalent bonds). A **compound** is formed when two or more different atoms bond together chemically to form a unique substance (i.e., H_2O, CH_4).

Charged atoms are called **ions**. An atom that loses one or more electrons becomes a positively charged particle, or a positive ion. We call this positively charged ion a **cation**. An atom that gains one or more electrons becomes a negative ion, or an **anion**. Positive and negative ions are attracted to each other in a bond called an **ionic bond**. An ionic bond is the strongest bond and is stronger than a covalent bond. Na+Cl- (sodium chloride or table salt) is an example of a substance held together by ionic bonds.

Some molecules have a weak, partial negative charge at one region of the molecule and a partial positive charge in another region. Molecules that have regions of partial charge are called **polar molecules**. For instance, water molecules (which have a net charge of 0) have a partial negative charge near the oxygen atom and a partial positive charge near each of the hydrogen atoms. Thus, when water molecules are close together, their positive regions are attracted to the negatively charged regions of nearby molecules; the negative regions are attracted to the positively charged regions of nearby molecules. The force of attraction between water molecules is called a **hydrogen bond**. A hydrogen bond is a weak chemical bond between molecules.

Attractions between Molecules

Van der Waals forces are momentary forces of attraction that exist between molecules and are much weaker than the forces of chemical bonding. These forces are created by the chance movement of electrons in a system of atoms bonded together. The strength of attraction is proportional to the number of electrons in the molecule. These forces are weak relative to polar intermolecular forces, and they become apparent only if there are many electrons, or if the molecules come very close together.

A **polar intermolecular attraction** can exist between two polar molecules. The slightly positive end of one molecule forms an electrostatic attraction to the slightly negative end of another molecule. A **hydrogen bond** occurs when a hydrogen atom is involved with a polar intermolecular attraction to a more electronegative atom. Polar intermolecular attractions are much stronger than van der Waals forces.

Structure and Physical Properties

Physical properties of substances are related to the forces between atoms and molecules. Hardness, melting point, and boiling point are all measures of the strength of interatomic or intermolecular attraction holding the molecule together. Stronger attraction results in lower vapor pressures.

Network covalent crystals have the strongest attraction holding atoms together. They have the highest melting points and are the hardest of all crystals. **Ionic crystals** have strong electrostatic forces holding atoms together. They tend to have high melting and boiling points, and are poor conductors in the solid phase (because the electrons are in fixed positions). However, when ionic crystals are in an aqueous solution (dissolved in water), they are good conductors because the charge is mobile.

Nonpolar molecules, held together predominantly with van der Waals forces, are soft crystals, are easily deformed, and vaporize easily. They have much lower melting and boiling points than polar compounds of similar molar mass. Nonpolar molecules are poor conductors and tend to be more volatile because of their high vapor pressure.

Polar molecules have intermolecular attractions that are weaker than ionic forces but are much stronger than nonpolar dispersion forces. The melting and boiling points of polar compounds depend on the strength of the dipole moment (difference in charge between the poles) of the two compounds. The stronger the cumulative dipole moment, the greater the intermolecular attraction and the higher the melting and boiling points.

Hydrogen bonds have the strongest polar intermolecular attraction because the hydrogen atom has only one electron. When that electron leaves, the exposed proton of the hydrogen nucleus is strongly attracted to the slightly negative charge of the other molecule. Consequently, polar molecules with hydrogen bonds have higher melting and boiling points than polar molecules of similar molar mass that do not have hydrogen bonds.

Summary of strength of attraction:

Ionic > covalent > metallic > polar intermolecular > nonpolar intermolecular

---

Thus, if an ionic attraction needs to be broken to melt a solid, it will take more energy than if a covalent attraction needs to be broken, which will take more energy than a metallic attraction, and so on.

Chemical Reactions

Chemical reactions occur when molecules interact with each other to form one or more molecules of another type. Chemical reactions that occur within cells provide energy, nutrients, and other products that allow the organism to function.

There are several categories of chemical reactions. Chemical reactions are symbolized by an equation where the reacting molecules (**reactants**) are shown on one side and the newly formed molecules (**products**) on the other, with an arrow between indicating the direction of the reaction. Some chemical reactions are simple, such as the breakdown of a compound into its components (a **decomposition** reaction):

$$AB \rightarrow A + B$$

A simple **combination** reaction is the reverse of decomposition:

$$A + B \rightarrow AB$$

When one compound breaks apart and forms a new compound with a free reactant, it is called a **replacement** reaction:

$$AB + C \rightarrow AC + B$$

Chemical reactions may require an input of energy or they may release energy. Reactions that require energy are called **endothermic** reactions. Reactions that release energy are termed **exothermic**.

All chemical reactions are subject to the **laws of thermodynamics**. The first law of thermodynamics (also known as the law of conservation of matter and energy) states that matter and energy can neither be created nor destroyed. In other words, the sum of matter and energy of the reactants must equal that of the products. The second law of thermodynamics, or the law of increasing disorder (or **entropy**), asserts that all reactions spread energy, which tends to diminish its availability. So, although we know from the first law that the energy must be equal on both sides of a reaction equation, reaction processes also tend to degrade the potential energy into a form that cannot perform any useful work.

Properties of Water

Water exhibits unique characteristics that affect the processes of life. Water is able to dissolve many types of organic and inorganic substances. This property promotes several biological processes such as muscle contraction, nerve stimulation, and transport across membranes (permeability).

Because water molecules are polar, certain types of chemicals dissociate in water. Some chemicals yield protons and others accept protons when dissolved in water. An **acid** is a chemical that donates protons (H+ ions) when dissolved in water. Acidity, then, is a measure of the concentration of H+ ions in a solution. A chemical that accepts protons (H+ ions) when dissolved in water is a **base**. The **pH** (standing for potential of hydrogen) scale is a measurement of H+ ions in solution. The pH of a substance can range from 0-14. A pH of 7 is neutral (as is pure water). A pH below 7 is acidic and a pH above 7 is basic (or alkaline). Acids and bases neutralize each other when dissolved together in water. The neutralization of an acidic solution with a basic solution produces a salt (an ionic compound) and water. Acids, bases, and salts are important chemicals to many life processes.

The transparent quality of water keeps it from disturbing processes within cells that require light (such as in photosynthetic and light-sensing cells).

Water also exhibits unique responses to temperature change. Most substances contract upon becoming a solid; however, water expands as it solidifies (a process we call freezing), forming a loose lattice structure (crystal). This crystalline form also makes frozen water (ice) less dense than liquid water. This accounts for lakes and other bodies of water freezing on the top first (insulating the water and organisms below from harsh temperature changes).

Water has a high specific heat; it resists changes in temperature. The presence of water in an environment will tend to moderate the effect of harsh temperature changes.

Hydrogen bonds between water molecules also give water a high surface tension, allowing small particles, and even some organisms (such as the water strider) to rest on the surface. This surface tension also causes liquid water in air to form drops (rain).

Chemical Structure of Organic Compounds

Organic compounds are the building blocks of all living things. The special properties exhibited by the various types of organic molecules allow for the specialized functions within the cells and tissue of living things. Organic compounds are defined as those that contain carbon. Organic molecules may also include hydrogen, oxygen, nitrogen, sulfur, phosphorous, and some metal ions. It is important to have a basic understanding of the properties and chemical structure of carbohydrates, proteins, and other organic compounds. Organic substances include many types of molecules active in biological processes (or biomolecules), such as carbohydrates, lipids, proteins, and nucleic acids.

Carbohydrates

Carbohydrates are made up of varying combinations of only carbon, hydrogen, and oxygen. The ratio of hydrogen to oxygen in carbohydrates is always 2:1, just as in water (H_2O)—thus the name *carbo* (carbon) *hydrate* (plus water).

Fig. 7-1: Structural formula of Cyclic Glucose (a common hexose).

Sugars and **starches** are both forms of carbohydrates. The basic sugar unit is a **monosaccharide**, which usually contains 3 to 7 carbon atoms plus attached oxygen and hydrogen atoms. The most common monosaccharides are called hexoses (six carbon sugars); they are usually in a ring-shaped (or cyclic) structure.

Two monosaccharide molecules may join together, producing a **disaccharide** and liberating a molecule of water. Table sugar is a disaccharide of glucose and fructose (the most common monosaccharides). When three monosaccharides join together, the chain is then called a **trisaccharide**. When more than three monosaccharides merge, the resultant molecule is known as a **polysaccharide**.

Plants store energy by synthesizing polysaccharides known as **starches**. Starches are stored within the plant's cells until energy is needed. Plants also synthesize starches that provide structure to their cells; the most common is a plant fiber known as **cellulose** (a long chain of water-insoluble polysaccharides). **Glycogen** is a polysaccharide composed of many joined glucose units. Many animals use glycogen as a short-term storage molecule for energy. In mammals, glycogen is found in muscle and liver tissue.

Lipids

Lipids are organic compounds composed of carbon, hydrogen, and oxygen. The ratio of hydrogen to oxygen in lipids is always greater than 2:1. Lipids are hydrophobic (from the Greek for "water fearing") and will not dissolve in water. Lipids include waxes, steroids, phospholipids, and fats. These various types of substances perform many functions within cells. Some form structural components of cell membranes (phospholipids), some provide moisture barriers (waxes), and others are primarily used to store energy (fats). Other lipids serve as vitamins or hormones.

Fats are highly efficient lipid molecules used for long-term energy storage. When an organism takes in more carbohydrates than are necessary for its current energy use, the excess energy is stored in fat molecules. The energy is stored in chemical bonds between the atoms of lipid molecules. When these bonds are broken, energy is released. In addition to storing energy, fats also function in organisms to provide a protective layer that insulates internal organs and maintains heat within the body.

Proteins

Proteins are present in every living cell. Proteins are large un-branched chains of **amino acids**. Amino acids are single links (**monomers**) that join together to form linear chains with many links (**polymers**). Amino acids contain carbon, hydrogen, oxygen, nitrogen, and sometimes sulfur. There are twenty common amino acids that can combine in various sequences to form thousands of different proteins. Amino acids are connected into chains by a water-releasing (dehydration) reaction that forms peptide bonds. For this reason, proteins may also be called **polypeptides**.

Proteins found in living things may have dozens or hundreds of amino acids. The long linear strings of amino acids form unique shapes by folding up in various ways. The shape of different protein molecules is the characteristic that allows them to perform specific functions within cells.

Enzymes are special proteins that act as **catalysts** for reactions. A catalyst is a substance that changes the speed of a reaction without being affected itself. Enzyme names have the suffix -ase (such as polymerase, lactase).

Nucleic Acids

There are two groups of nucleic acids, deoxyribonucleic acid (**DNA**) and ribonucleic acid (**RNA**). Each type is composed of chains of nucleotides.

Nucleotides are the monomers that form nucleic acids, which are polymers. Each nucleotide has a sugar (from the pentose group) attached to a phosphate group and a nitrogenous base. The sugar and phosphate groups alternate in long chains forming the backbone of the DNA or RNA molecule. In DNA, the sugar molecule is deoxyribose; in RNA, it is ribose. RNA chains are generally single strands, but DNA strands pair up to form a shape like a twisted ladder. This **double-helix** structure of DNA was discovered and modeled by two scientists, James Watson and Francis Crick, in the 1950s. DNA and RNA structure is therefore known as the **Watson-Crick** model.

The nitrogen bases in DNA include adenine, cytosine, guanine, and thymine (A, C, G, and T). In RNA, thymine is replaced by the base uracil (U). The nucleic acid bases form complementary pairs, that is, cytosine (C) and guanine (G) pair together forming hydrogen bonds, while thymine (T - or uracil in RNA - U) pairs with adenine (A). [A sequence of GATTACA would then pair with the sequence CTAATGT, or with the RNA sequence CUAAUGU.] This pairing allows DNA and RNA strands to accurately duplicate themselves and to encode the order of amino acids in proteins.

Fig. 7-2: A DNA Molecule. Each molecule of DNA consists of a chain of nucleo-tides (each containing a phosphate group, a sugar, and a nitrogenous base). Two chains bond together with hydrogen bonds, forming a double-helix structure.

Chapter 8

Physics

HEAT

Heat is energy that flows from an object that is warm to an object that is cooler. It is important to understand the difference between heat and temperature. **Temperature** is the measure of the **average kinetic energy** of a substance. The atoms and molecules of all substances are constantly in motion. The energy of the motion of the atoms and molecules in a substance is called its kinetic energy. Temperature is a measure of that energy. The faster the particles in a substance move (more energy), the higher the temperature will be. The slower the particles move (less energy), the lower the temperature.

The theoretical temperature at which particle motion stops is called *absolute zero* (or 0 Kelvin). This temperature has never been reached by any known substance.

When substances come in contact, the hotter (greater energy) substance transfers kinetic energy to the cooler (lower energy) one—heat has been expended. Heat is measured in calories or joules.

Energy (including heat) may be transferred from one object to another by three processes—radiation, conduction, and convection. **Radiation** is the transfer of energy via waves. Radiation can occur through matter, or without any matter present. Radiation from the Sun passes through space (very low density of matter) to reach Earth. **Convection** involves the movement of energy by the movement of matter, usually through currents. For instance, convection moves warm air up, while cool air sinks. In a fluid, the heat will move with the fluid. **Conduction** is movement of energy by transfer from particle to particle. Conduction can only occur when objects are touching. A pan on a stove heats water by conduction. An oven cooks by convection—warming food by movement of hot air. A microwave cooks by radiation—waves travel into food, adding kinetic energy.

Specific Heat

Different substances have different capacities for storing energy. For example, it may take twenty minutes to heat water to 75°C. The same mass of aluminum might require five minutes and the same amount of copper may take only two minutes to reach the same temperature. However, water will retain the kinetic energy (stay hot) longer than the aluminum or copper. The measure of a substance's ability to retain energy is called **specific heat**. Specific heat is measured as the amount of heat needed to raise the temperature of one gram of a substance by one degree Celsius.

THE LAWS OF THERMODYNAMICS

The Laws of Thermodynamics explain the interaction between heat and work (energy) in the universe. The First Law says that matter and energy can neither be created nor destroyed. This law is also known as the **Law of Conservation of Matter and Energy**. The Second Law is also known as the **Law of Entropy** and states that whenever energy is exchanged, some energy becomes unavailable for use (entropy increases). The Third Law or the **Law of Absolute Zero** says that absolute zero cannot be attained in any system (that is, energy of motion of particles cannot be stopped). The *Zeroth Law of Thermodynamics* is so named because it was accepted by scientists after the first three laws were named, but it underlies them all—thus the name "zeroth." The Zeroth Law says that when two bodies are in contact that they will move toward a state of thermodynamic equilibrium—where both bodies eventually reach the same temperature.

STATES OF MATTER

All matter has physical properties that can be observed. These properties affect the way substances react with each other under various conditions. Physical properties include color, odor, taste, strength, hardness, density and state.

Solids, Liquids, Gases, Plasma

Matter exists in one of four states—solid, liquid, gas, or plasma. Under most conditions elements will be in the solid, liquid, or gas phase. Plasma only exists in the case of extreme heat and ionization—in this state ions and electrons move about freely, giving plasma properties different from the other three states. The center of the Sun and stars are thought to be plasma.

A solid has molecules in fixed positions giving the substance definite shape. Solids have a definite volume. In a solid the molecules are packed and bonded together. The strength of the bonds determines the strength of the solid and its melting point. When heat energy is applied to the bonds they break apart, the molecules can move about and the substance becomes a liquid.

A liquid has definite volume but not definite shape since the molecules are loosely attracted. The loose attractions between molecules allow for the shape of the substance to mold to its surroundings. When a liquid is cooled the molecules become bonded and the substance becomes a solid. Heat energy is lost since the molecules are moving less. When heat energy is added to a liquid, the weak attractions holding the molecules together break apart causing the molecules to move about randomly and the liquid becomes a gas.

A gas is a substance with relatively (relative to solids and liquids) large distances and little attraction between molecules. The molecules are free to move about randomly. Gases have no definite shape or volume since temperature and pressure can impact the density.

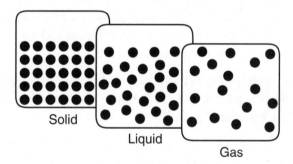

Fig. 8-1: Solids, liquids, and gases differ in the arrangement and density of molecules.

Different substances have different conditions under which they exist in a solid, liquid, or gas. The state that a substance exists in at room temperature depends on how the molecules are bonded together.

The following are some terms that are important to know related to substances and their states:

— **melting point**—temperature at which a substance changes from solid to liquid form

— **heat of fusion**—heat required to melt 1kg of a solid at its melting point (also known as enthalpy of fusion)

— **freezing point**—temperature at which a substance changes from liquid to solid

- **boiling point**—temperature at which a substance changes from liquid to gas

- **heat of vaporization**—amount of energy required to change 1kg of liquid of a substance to a gas (also known as enthalpy of vaporization)

- **evaporation**—escape of individual particles of a substance into gaseous form

- **condensation**—change of a gaseous substance to liquid form

- **diffusion**—mixing of particles in a gas or liquid

Density

Density is the measure of how much matter exists in a given volume. The density of a substance is determined by measuring the mass of a substance and dividing it by the volume (**D=m/v**). Substances that are less dense will float when placed in a denser substance. Denser substances will sink in a less dense liquid. It is important to understand that density is a function of mass (amount of matter), not weight (attraction of gravity on mass). Density has to do with how tightly packed the atoms in a substance are.

Consider this: Which weighs more, a pound of lead or a pound of feathers? Neither. A pound is a pound; but the volume of a pound of feathers will be much greater than a pound of lead.

Pressure is a measure of the amount of force applied per unit of area. Pressure exerted on a gas may affect its density, by compressing its volume. Liquids and solids are much less responsive to pressure. **Pascal's principle** states that the pressure exerted on any point of a confined fluid is transmitted unchanged throughout the fluid. Therefore, if you exert pressure on a liquid, it will exert that same pressure on its surroundings. **Archimedes's principle** states that when an object is placed in a fluid, the object will have a buoyant force equal to the weight of the displaced fluid. Archimedes's principle results in **buoyancy,** a decrease in the measured apparent weight of an object in a fluid due to the net upward force caused by the displaced fluid. This apparent decrease in weight of the object is a result of the force of the displaced fluid acting in an upward direction opposing the object.

Gravity

The **mass** of an object refers to *the amount of matter* that is contained by the object; however, the **weight** of an object is *the force of gravity acting upon that* *object.* *Mass* is related to how much stuff is there while *weight* refers to the pull of the Earth (or any other planet or object) upon that stuff.

The mass of an object (measured in kg) will be the same no matter where in the universe the object is located. Mass is never altered by location, the pull of gravity, speed or even the existence of other forces. A 51kg object will have a mass of 51 kg whether it is located on Earth, the Moon, or anywhere else. The amount of mass and the gravitational field of the Earth (or the Moon, etc.) imparts weight to an object. The weight of an object, however, will vary according to where in the universe the object is. Weight depends upon the mass of the celestial body that is exerting the gravitational field and the distance from the center of the gravitational field of the body upon the mass experiencing the field.

Gravity is a property of all matter; all matter exerts a gravitational force on all other matter. Gravity acts at a distance and attracts bodies of matter toward each other. The gravity of the Moon affects the water in the Earth's oceans, causing the tides. In the study of atomic particles, there is even a weak force of gravity between all particles.

The gravity on the Earth is greater than the gravity on the Moon, since the Earth has much more matter or mass than the Moon. The force of gravity on an object caused by the mass of the Earth equals the mass of the object (m) times the acceleration caused by gravity (g). The equation is:

$$F = mg$$

This acceleration caused by gravity on Earth, *g* (more commonly called the acceleration of gravity) equals 9.8 m/s^2 in the metric system and 32 ft/s^2 in the English system.

The weight of an object is the measurement of the force of gravity on that object. When you weigh something on a scale, the weight is actually the force of gravity on that object:

$$Weight = mg$$

The mass of the Moon is less than the mass of the Earth, so the acceleration of gravity (*g*) is less on the Moon than the Earth. If you put an object on the Moon and weighed it, its weight would be 1/6 the weight on Earth. In other words, a 180-pound man would only weigh 30 pounds on the Moon.

The fundamental units of measure used in the metric system are the meter, kilogram, and second, or *mks* system. To get the weight of an object in the metric system, you multiply the mass in kilograms by the acceleration of gravity (9.8 m/s^2), resulting in the units of kg-m/s^2 or *Newtons*.

The universal gravitational law, first described by Sir Isaac Newton, states that *the force of gravity between two objects is proportional to the product of the masses of the objects and inversely proportional to the square of the distance between them*—in simple English—as objects get further apart, the effect of gravity drops dramatically. The equation below shows this relationship . . . the mass of one body is designated as M, the mass of a second as m, and the distance between them is r; the force of attraction between the two bodies is F.

$$F = G\frac{Mm}{r^2}$$

where G is the universal gravitational constant $G = 6.67 \times 10^{-11}$ N(m²/kg²) (Newton-meter squared per kilogram squared).

If you drop an object relatively near the Earth, it will speed up according to the acceleration of gravity (g). When you let go of the object, its velocity is zero. Since $g = 32$ ft/s² $= 9.8$ m/s², the velocity will be 32 ft/s (9.8 m/s) after one second. Because the object is accelerating, the velocity after 2 seconds will be 2 s $\times$ 32 ft/s/s = 64 ft/s (19.6 m/s). After 10 seconds, the velocity will be 10 s $\times$ 32 ft/s/s = 320 ft/s or 98 m/s.

Although a falling object will continue to accelerate until it is made to stop (when it hits the ground), air resistance will slow down that acceleration. Air resistance is approximately proportional to the square of the velocity, so as the object falls faster, the air resistance increases until it equals the force of gravity. The point at which these forces are equal is called its *terminal velocity*. For instance, a falling baseball reaches 94 miles per hour or 42 meters/second; it would remain at that velocity and no longer accelerate. A penny dropped from a high building will accelerate until it reaches around 230 mph.

The acceleration of the force of gravity on falling bodies is *independent of the mass* of the falling object. Therefore, a 15-pound weight would fall at the same rate as a 2-pound weight and would hit the ground at the same time if dropped from the same height. In addition, gravity of the mass of an object is also *independent of the velocity* of the object parallel to the ground. For example, two bullets are positioned at the same initial height. One is shot from a gun horizontal to the surface. The other bullet is dropped at the exact same time as the bullet is fired from the gun. Both bullets will hit the ground at the exact same time, if no incidental air resistance or friction exists.

$$F = ma$$

Since *force = mass times acceleration*, the universal gravity equation implies that as objects are attracted and get closer together, the force increases and the acceleration between them also increases.

CLASSICAL MECHANICS

Mechanics is the study of things in motion. **Classical mechanics** involves particles bigger than atoms and slower than light. **Newton's Laws of Motion** form the basis of most of our understanding of things in motion. These three laws are:

#1 Law of Inertia: A particle at rest will stay at rest and a particle in motion will stay in motion until acted upon by an outside force,

#2 Law of Force versus Mass: The rate of change of a particle is directly proportional to its mass and the force that is exerted on it, or

$$F = m \times a \text{ or } \mathbf{F = ma}$$

(where F is force, m is mass, and a is acceleration),

#3 Law of Action and Reaction: Mutual interactions between bodies produce two forces that are equal in magnitude and opposite in direction; one body exerts a force on the second and the second body exerts an equal force on the first.

The study of classical mechanics is predominately involved with evaluating relationships of motion using equations. When studying relationships in classical mechanics, we usually identify quantities in terms of both their magnitude and direction. These mathematical quantities are called **vectors**. A vector recognizes both the size and direction of the dimension being considered. For example, velocity involves both a *speed* and a *direction* of the object. The formula for momentum (p) would then be written as $\mathbf{p} = m\mathbf{v}$, where **p** and **v** are both vector quantities, that is, they represent both a quantity of magnitude (or size) and a direction in which the object is moving. Vectors are identified with either bold letters or an arrow over the letter that indicates direction. It is important to understand how to do vector multiplication in standard physics courses. However, it will not be necessary to practice with vectors in a basic physics course, except to know that this is a standard procedure that may be described in some physics problems you may encounter as you study the material.

The following definitions and equations are those central to the general study of classical mechanics:

— **Work** is the movement of a mass over a distance:

$$\text{Work} = \text{Force} \times \text{Distance}$$

$$W = F \times d \text{ or } W = Fd$$

— **Speed** is the rate of change of an object's distance traveled.

$$s = \frac{d}{t}$$

— **Displacement** measures the change in position of an object, using the starting point and ending point and noting the direction. Consider that displacement may be in some cases the same as distance, but in other cases very different. For instance, if a biker traveled from point A to B to C to D in the following diagram, the distance would equal A+B+C+D. However, the displacement would be 0 since the biker started and ended at the same location (ending with no displacement).

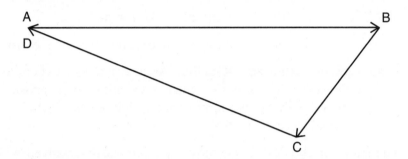

— **Velocity** is the rate of change of displacement; it includes both speed and direction.

$$v = \frac{d}{t}$$

(where v is velocity and has a directional component of plus or minus; d is displacement, t is time)

— **Friction** is the rubbing force that acts against motion between two touching surfaces. Friction between any two objects depends upon the surface attractions or the roughness or smoothness of the two surfaces. The measurement of the amount of friction between any two given objects can be determined experimentally and is designated by the Greek symbol mu, μ, called the *coefficient of friction*. There are tables that give standard coefficients of friction for some objects that have already been determined experimentally. If μ approaches zero, then there is very little friction. As the value for μ increases, it indicates that there is increasing friction between the objects. For example, tires with worn tread on an icy road would have a low coefficient of friction (μ), and therefore a car with such tires would likely skid. Tires with heavy tread would have a higher coefficient of friction (the addition of sand on the road or chains on the tires would increase this even further) and greatly decrease the likelihood of the car skidding on an icy road.

— **Acceleration** is the *rate of change of velocity*; it can act in the direction of motion, at an angle, or opposite to the direction of motion.

$$a = \frac{v_2 - v_1}{t_2 - t_1}$$

— **Momentum** is the product of mass and velocity; the quantity of motion for an object.

$$p = mv$$

(where p = momentum)

— **Force** is the push or pull exerted on an object.

$$F = ma$$

$$F = \frac{W}{d}$$

It is also important to note measurements related to mechanics. In science, all measurements are recorded and reported in **metric** units, known as the Système Internationale (International System) or **SI** units:

Mass—measure in kilograms

Length—measured in meters

Time—measured in seconds

Volume—measured in liters

THEORY OF RELATIVITY

Classical mechanics and its resultant laws and equations hold true for systems where we can recognize certain *frames of reference*. For instance, when a person is traveling on a train going east and walking toward the rear of the train (to the west) while tossing a ball in the air, each of the movements can be described within their own frame of reference whether that be in reference to a point on the ground such as a GPS point (the ball is moving east at x velocity), a spot on the train (the ball is moving west at x velocity), or the person (the ball is moving upward at x velocity).

In 1905, Albert Einstein expanded on the work of Faraday, Lorentz, and Maxwell to propose his "**Special Theory of Relativity**." He stated it in the following two postulates again in 1954:

1. ". . . the same laws of electrodynamics and optics will be valid for all frames of reference for which the equations of mechanics hold good. . . . A co-ordinate system that is moved uniformly and in a straight line relative to an inertial system is likewise an inertial system. By the 'special principle of relativity' is meant the generalization of this definition to include any natural event whatever: thus, every universal law of nature which is valid in relation to a co-ordinate system C must also be valid, as it stands, in relation to a co-ordinate system C' which is in uniform translatory motion relative to C."

2. "The second principle, on which the special theory of relativity rests, is the 'principle of constant velocity of light in vacuo.' This principle asserts that light in vacuo always has a definite velocity of propagation (independent of the state of motion of the observer or of the source of the light). The confidence which physicists place in this principle springs from the successes achieved by the electrodynamics of Maxwell and Lorentz."

Albert Einstein (1954). Ideas and Opinions. Crown Trade Paperbacks.

In basic terms, Einstein's Special Relativity states that

- **the speed of light is a constant,**

- **the laws of physics are the same in all inertial (non-accelerating) reference frames**.

The famous equation that resulted from this theory is

$$E = mc^2$$

where E is energy, m is the mass of an object and c is the speed of light.

What these two postulates logically say is that if you measure the velocity of light c to have a particular value, then no matter which inertial (non-accelerated) reference frame you are moving in, you will always measure it to have the same value; this is an experimental fact. It follows that the velocity of light will be the same regardless of the motion of the object against which it is being measured.

Classical mechanics "works" because for objects at speeds not approaching the speed of light and at masses much greater than atomic particles, the equations are appropriate. However, Einstein postulated that the speed of light was the only true constant, and that time and distance would always be made relative in order to maintain the speed of light as a constant. In other words, if a plane is traveling toward a given point at 500 miles per hour and shoots a missile forward at 100 mph you would presume the missile to be traveling 600 mph at takeoff. The light that is leaving from the plane's warning beacons is presumably also traveling at 500 miles per hour plus the speed of light when it leaves the plane. However, according to Einstein's special theory of relativity, since the speed of light is always constant, the light is actually traveling at the constant speed for light, not that plus 500 mph.

Einstein proposed several experiments to test his special theory of relativity which required equipment and technology unavailable during his time, but which have now been carried out and verified. The experiments have served to confirm Einstein's proposed theories. The theory of special relativity poses questions as to how distance and time might be distorted by travel at the speed of light or by travel in high gravitational fields which may mimic the effect of speed of light travel. In addition, the special theory of relativity has also added understanding to the field of *quantum mechanics*—the world of very small objects, namely subatomic particles. Scientists have long known through experimentation that subatomic particles did not follow the laws of classical mechanics, but rather have their own rules for motion. Quantum mechanics explains these classical discrepancies adequately to allow us to work at the subatomic level.

Chapter 9

Energy

ELECTRICITY AND MAGNETISM

Electrical charges consist of **electrons** (with their negative charge) gathered on the surface of an object. When the electrical charges are not moving, it is called *static electricity*. When a positively charged ion attracts the electron, a spark may occur, which is a transfer or discharge of the electrical charge.

Electrical charges may also move from atom to atom within substances that are called **conductors**. A flow of electrons through a conductor is an **electrical current**. Some elements are good conductors (such as metals); others are poor conductors (called **insulators**). Plastic, rubber, glass, and wood are insulators.

An electrical **circuit** is the path that an electric current follows. Every electric circuit has four parts —

    (1)   a *source* of *voltage* [a battery, generator, or AC source],

    (2)   a set of *conductors* [wires],

    (3)   a *load* [light, meter, appliance, etc.], and

    (4)   a *switch*.

A **closed circuit** is one that has a continuous path for electron flow (no interruptions). An **open circuit** has no flow of electrons because the pathway is interrupted (by a switch, disconnection, etc.).

Voltage refers to the *electromotive force* that pushes electrons through the circuit. **Amperage** is the measure of the amount of electron flow or current. **Resistance** is a hindrance to current due to objects that deter the current by their size, shape or type of conductor.

Series & Parallel Circuits

In a series circuit, there is only one path along which the electrons may flow, moving around the circuit along this single pathway from the positive to the negative pole of the battery (source). The current flows through each component in succession. Linking this group of electric cells in a series means that the voltage of the circuit will be equal to the sum total of the voltages in each cell added together.

In a parallel circuit, the electrical devices are connected to provide two or more paths through which the current may flow. Linking electrical cells in parallel will increase the amperage of the circuit (the current of the circuit will equal the sum of the currents in each cell).

Fig. 9-1. Series and Parallel Circuits

Magnetism

Magnetism is defined as the ability of a substance to produce a magnetic field. The magnetic field acts like point charges (in electricity) producing north (N) and south (S) poles. When magnets are placed in close proximity to each other, the similar poles repel, while opposite poles attract. Magnets can be either permanent or temporary. Permanent magnets are ones that contain natural magnetic ore, such as iron, cobalt or nickel, the three natural elements with magnetic properties. Temporary magnets are ones that can be induced to carry a magnetic field, but will not hold the magnetic field permanently. Electromagnets are electrically induced magnets usually created by wrapping coils of wire around an iron core.

WAVES: SOUND AND LIGHT

The study of waves is very important in science. Many things in nature travel in waves, including sound, light, and water. A wave has no mass of its own; it is simply movement within a medium, a disturbance that does not cause the medium itself to move significantly.

There are different types of waves with different types of movement. Light and ocean waves travel in transverse waves. A **transverse wave** causes particles to move up and down while the wave moves forward (perpendicular to the wave motion). Sound and some earthquake waves travel as longitudinal (compression) waves. In a **longitudinal wave** the particles move back and forth but in the same direction as (parallel with) the wave motion.

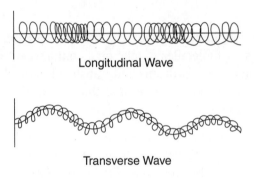

Longitudinal Wave

Transverse Wave

Fig. 9-2. Longitudinal and Transverse Waves

Properties of waves are described with the following terms. The **wavelength** of a wave is defined as the distance from one crest (or top) of a wave to the next crest on the same side. The **frequency** of a wave is the number of wavelengths that pass a point in a second.

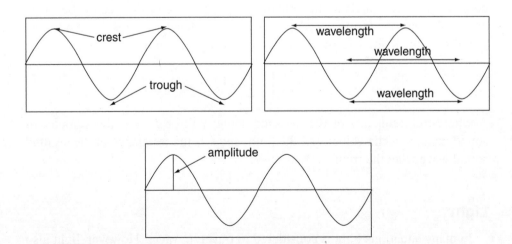

Fig. 9-3. Properties of Waves

Waves also interact with each other in various ways. Wave **interference** can occur between waves. Interference can increase wave amplitude if the crests and troughs of the waves coincide. If the crest and trough of two waves coincide, they can cancel each other or reduce the amplitude. Waves can also be **reflected** when they hit a surface.

The speed of a wave can be described by the equation: $v = f\lambda$; where $v =$ the speed of the wave, $f =$ frequency of the wave, $\lambda =$ wavelength of the wave.

Sound

Sound travels in longitudinal waves. Sound waves are made when an object vibrates and causes air molecules to take on a compression wave motion. This motion is picked up by our eardrums and translated in our brains into sounds. Changes in wavelength account for volume changes, while changes in frequency result in pitch changes.

Anyone who has stood beside a train track and heard the sound of the train whistle or horn has noticed that it sounds the same as the train approaches. But, as soon as the train passes by, the pitch of the horn begins to drop at a regularly reducing pattern as the train passes and moves away from the listener. This phenomenon is known as the "Doppler effect." What is happening here?

As the train approaches, the sound coming to the ear is being pushed by compression waves so that it arrives at the speed of sound, which is the sum of the speed of sound in air plus the speed of the train. Since the sound wave hits the ear drum at the speed of sound or greater, it maintains its regular pitch. However, as the train passes the ear, the speed of the sound wave will begin to decrease proportionately to the ratio of the speed of sound, divided by the speed of sound minus the train's speed away from the listener. This results in a lowering of the horn's pitch according to the following equation:

$$f_0 = \left(\frac{v}{v - v_s} \right) f_s$$

where the frequency of the detected sound will be f_o, v is the velocity of sound in air, v_s is the velocity of the train, and f_s is the frequency of the emitted sound wave from the train.

Light

In many situations light is considered to travel in waves. However, light also has characteristics indicative of a particle, rather than simply a wave. To understand how light affects how things are seen, it is important to understand the ways that light moves by reviewing the following terms:

Diffraction—the bending of a light wave around an obstacle

Reflection—the bouncing of a wave of light off an object

Refraction—the change of direction of a wave as it passes from one medium to another

The Light Spectrum—A spectrum is used to identify the arrangement of the components of a light wave according to wavelength. The visible spectrum of light is the arrangement of the visible wavelengths in a beam of light in the order red, orange, yellow, green, blue, indigo, violet. (Indigo has been recently removed from the official visible light spectrum. So that you may remember, use this mnemonic, "Roy G. Biv, where did Indi go?" Get it? "Where did Indi go?" Because indigo isn't there any longer. Funny, huh?)

Different kinds of light have different spectra. Fluorescent light has sharper bands than incandescent light (light bulb). Sunlight has more blue and violet in its spectrum.

Light travels in straight lines until it hits an object. In order to see an object your eye must intercept a ray of light traveling straight from it. You can determine a path of light by sighting along two points (like two pins stuck into a sheet of paper). When you turn your eye so that you see only one pinhead (the other is behind the first), your eye and the two pinheads are all in the same straight-line path of light.

Chapter 10

The Universe

ASTRONOMY

Galaxies

Beginning with Tycho Brahe, Johannes Kepler and Isaac Newton, scientists began to make significant progress in understanding the ways that the stars and planets move in the celestial sphere. Scientists began to work out sophisticated mathematical relationships in a discipline known as **celestial mechanics** to clarify the movement of objects in the Milky Way. However, it was not until the early twentieth century that astronomers started to understand the bigger picture of the mechanics of the expanding universe.

Edwin Hubble (the famous space telescope is named for his work) identified a **redshift** in the light spectrum of velocities of galaxies that indicated that galaxies are moving away from one another. At the same time, Albert Einstein was still attempting to understand issues related to his theory of general relativity. With the distortion of space-time caused by the effects of gravity tending to pull the universe together, Einstein was concerned how it was kept from completely collapsing when described by his gravitational constant. The expanding universe seemed to be contradicting Einstein's observations. However, recent scientific speculations of "dark energy" are giving additional credibility to Einstein's gravitational constant.

The Big Bang

The expansion of the universe recognized by Hubble gives further support to the evidence of a *Big Bang* to explain the origin of the universe, speculated to have occurred nearly 13 billion years ago. The series of events from that initial moment to the present involved the cooling of elementary particles starting with very light things (electrons) expanding into stellar clouds, then converting to matter and energy to form galaxies and clusters of galaxies. Photons in the early universe combined to form the *cosmic microwave background* (CMB) that resulted in radio wavelengths that we observe today. Through further cooling, coalescence, and expansion, stars and galaxies formed under gravitational forces. Speculation and theory combine to attempt to explain this through complex physics. There is significant room for further learning as we send probes into space in search of more answers.

Stars

The core of our Sun, along with most stars, begins with hydrogen. With the core temperature of stars being over 10 million Kelvin, and the tremendous pressures they contain, protons can fuse together to produce helium, gamma ray energy, positrons and neutrinos. These neutrinos are nearly massless and chargeless. They do not interact with other matter very much and flow almost unimpeded throughout the universe. It is speculated that neutrinos produced in the center of the Sun sweep through the average human's body here on Earth at a rate of billions per second.

Stars are huge masses of plasma with colossal amounts of energy and gravity. Many stars are held in by magnetic fields, but particles slip through occasional holes in the fields. The atoms are so hot, the protons, neutrons, and electrons move rapidly and react with each other, thus releasing energy. This energy moves out from stars in electromagnetic waves producing heat and light. We are too far from most stars to notice their heat, but their light still reaches us.

The stars consist of incredible amounts of matter. Since we know all matter has gravity, stars have very large gravitational forces. Many stars have their own systems, like our solar system with planets, asteroids, and Moons orbiting them.

The stars are arrayed in the sky in patterns that ancient people named for various creatures and objects (scales, scorpions, archers, etc.). We call these the zodiac. Travelers have used the zodiac for navigation since biblical times. In addition, Polaris, the North Star, sits directly over our North Pole so it can be used to determine directions on the Earth.

The Sun is our own star that the Earth and the rest of the planets in our solar system orbit.

Sun

The Sun is the source of light energy for plants to produce food for themselves and all living things on Earth. The Sun is also our source of warmth and power. Our Sun is actually a star. It is the nearest and most important star to us. The Sun is about 740 times greater in mass than all the rest of our solar system combined. It is hard to comprehend how massive the Sun is since we see it from a vast distance. The amount of matter contained in the Sun is so great that the gravity from it keeps all the planets in their orbits. Using scientific notation, we calculate the size of the Sun as 1.989×10^{30} kilograms. This works out to be about 2 octillion metric tons. An octillion is a billion-billion-billion.

The Sun releases incredible amounts of energy as protons interact with each other (*nuclear fusion*). The energy is in the form of heat and light radiation, providing heat and light for life on Earth and can be so intense that it is danger-ous. The Earth's atmosphere protects us from much of the harmful effects of radiation from the Sun.

Solar System

In 1919, the International Astronomical Union (IAU) was designated with the job of defining and naming planets and Moons in our solar system. Our solar system consists of all of the common celestial bodies such as planets, Moons, asteroids, and various types of space debris, which orbit our star, the Sun. In 2006 and 2008, the IAU General Assembly introduced two new plan-etary categories to include *dwarf planets* and *plutoids* respectively.

The Sun is incredibly huge in relation to all the other objects in the solar sys-tem. With a diameter of 1.4 million kilometers (~110 times Earth's diameter), its enormous mass results in the gravitational forces that hold our eight planets and three dwarf planets, their Moons, various asteroids, comets, plutoids, and other smaller space particles in its orbit (see Fig. 10-1).

The characteristics of the planets vary greatly because of their size, composi-tion, and distance from the Sun. It is easy to remember the nine planets in order, starting with the closest to the Sun, by learning the following sentence: My Very Educated Mother Just Served Us Nine Pickles. The beginning letter of each word in this sentence is the beginning letter of a planet (Mercury, Venus, Earth, Mars, Jupiter, Saturn, Uranus, Neptune, and Pluto). However, recent modifications to the names of the planets and dwarf planets are redefining old standards. The new scheme reclassifies Pluto as a "plutoid" along with Eris, Pluto's twin dwarf, and adds Ceres as a third unique dwarf planet in the Solar System, just inside the Asteroid Belt. It is expected that new plutoids will be identified in the near future as further discoveries are made and classified. To learn about these new modifica-tions, visit *www.nasa.gov* to regularly check for changes.

The IAU illustrates the nature of science as a continuous adjustment in terms as new information becomes available. Take the current definition of a planet, for example. The latest description of a planet is "a celestial body that (a) is in

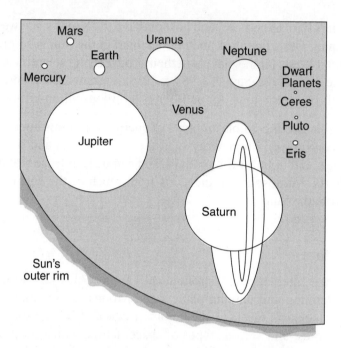

Approximate Relative Sizes of Sun and Planets

Fig. 10-1: Approximate relative sizes of planets in relation to the Sun.

orbit around the Sun, (b) has sufficient mass for its self-gravity to overcome rigid body forces so that it assumes a hydrostatic equilibrium (nearly round) shape and (c) has cleared the neighborhood around its orbit."

The new definition of a "dwarf planet" (introduced in 2006) is "a celestial body that (a) is in orbit around the Sun, (b) has sufficient mass for its self-gravity to overcome rigid body forces so that it assumes a hydrostatic equilibrium (nearly round) shape, (c) has not cleared the neighborhood around its orbit, and (d) is not a satellite."

The IAU promised to come up with a new name for the trans-neptunian dwarf planets that are similar to Pluto. They did not disappoint, proposing the name "plutoids" to describe these new discoveries. The IAU Committee on Small Body Nomenclature (CSBN) made the proposal to the Board of Division III, which was accepted by the IAU Working Group for Planetary System Nomenclature (WGPSN) and approved by the IAU Executive Committee in 2008 in Oslo, Norway.

These "plutoids" are now identified as small celestial bodies that "orbit the Sun at a semi-major axis greater than Neptune's which possess a sufficient mass for their self-gravity to overcome rigid body forces so that they assume a hydrostatic equilibrium (near-spherical) shape, and that have not cleared the

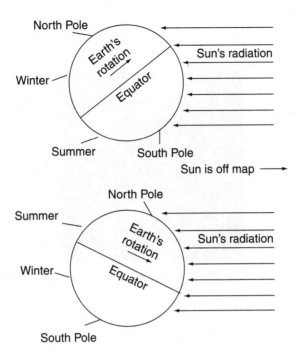

Fig. 10-2: Tilt of the Earth and seasons.

neighborhood around their orbit." Thus, Pluto and Eris are identified as plutoids, along with a third one identified in July of 2008 as MakeMake. More
plutoids are destined to be named as they are discovered. This will undoubtedly
occur with the improvements being made to the Hubble Space Telescope and
the launching of other exploratory vehicles anticipated in the coming years.

Our calendar year is a measure of the time the Earth takes in orbiting the Sun.
Each year Earth completes one trip around the Sun in 365.2422 days, or about
365¼ days. The seasons we experience on Earth are a result of the inclination
of the Earth on its axis. That is, if you drew a line through the Earth's poles, this
line is not perpendicular with its orbit around the Sun (see Fig. 10-2).

The Earth's axis tilts at an angle of twenty-three and one-half degrees with
its orbit. The tilt means that the Northern Hemisphere will be tilted toward the
Sun for half the orbit, and the Southern Hemisphere will be tilted for the other
half (half-a-year). The hemisphere tilted toward the Sun absorbs more of the
solar radiation during that half of the year and experiences summer. The hemisphere tilted away from the Sun experiences winter.

The orbit of the Moon around the Earth occurs approximately every twenty-
nine days. This is the origin of our months. A day is the time the Earth takes to
rotate one time on its axis. An hour is simply a division of the rotation of the

Earth (one day) obtained by taking the globe and dividing it into twenty-four time zones.

Fig 10-3: Image of the Moon taken by NASA's Galileo spacecraft in 1992.

Moon

Our view of the Moon is constantly changing as the Moon orbits Earth and as Earth rotates on its axis. Our daily view of the Moon changes as it moves around Earth along its regular orbital path. The changes we see in the shape and location of the Moon are regular in their occurrence because of the regular nature of the rotation and orbit. The Moon orbits around the Earth once approximately every twenty-nine days (one lunar month). The Moon's rotation on its axis is synchronous with its orbit, so we always see the same side of the Moon reflecting the sunlight.

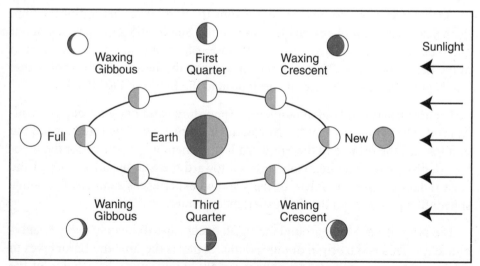

Fig. 10-4: The phases of the Moon.

The Moon does not emit any of its own light, but reflects the light from the Sun. Our daily view of the Moon changes during its orbit of the Earth. The phases that we see are a result of the angle between the Earth, Moon, and Sun as viewed by us from Earth.

A *new moon* occurs when the Moon is directly between the Earth and the Sun. At this point, the Moon will rise at about 6:00 am and set at about 6:00 pm (on standard, not daylight saving, time). The lighted side of the Moon is toward the Sun, so our view is of the dark side only (we don't see it at all).

Following the new moon, the Moon (continuing its orbit) moves so that we see an increasing portion of the lit side each night. We call this the *waxing crescent moon*.

In about a week, the angle between the Earth, Sun, and Moon is 90°, allowing us to see half its lighted surface, the *first quarter*. This 90° angle means the Moon rises halfway through the day at about noon, and sets at about midnight.

For the following week, we see more of the Moon's surface each night (*waxing gibbous*) until the full moon, which marks the middle of the lunar orbit (and the lunar month).

During the *full moon*, the Earth/Moon/Sun angle is 180° meaning the Earth is between the Sun and the Moon so we see the entire bright half of its surface. The full moon rises near Sundown and sets near Sunrise, opposite the Sun (see Fig. 10-5).

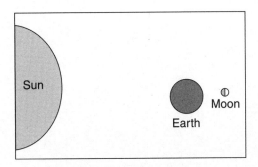

Fig. 10-5: Positioning of full Moon.

During the remaining two weeks of the lunar month, the Moon wanes through another gibbous moon to the *third quarter* (the other half of the Moon's lit surface is visible rising around noon and setting at midnight). It wanes through another *crescent moon* and on until it returns to the beginning of the orbital—the new moon.

We view the Moon "rising" in the east and "setting" in the west as the Earth rotates on its axis. The Moon's orbit is nearly in the same plane as the orbits of the planets around the Sun, so we view the Moon near that plane in the sky called the *ecliptic*.

The tilt of the Earth on its axis means the ecliptic is visible (to those in the northern hemisphere of the Earth) in the southern sky at varying heights through the seasons.

Chapter 11

Earth

The blue-green planet Earth is home to over 6.5 billion people. It is an ob-late spheroid with a surface area of over 5.1×10^8 square kilometers (nearly 200 million square miles). Revolving around the Sun at an average distance of 1.49×10^8 kilometers (9.3 million miles), it leans at an angle of 23.5 degrees to provide most of the inhabitants with four changing seasons. Its mass is ap-proximately $6.0. \times 10^{24}$ kilograms and a volume of 1.08 billion cubic kilome-ters (260 billion cubic miles). Studies in geosciences and biosciences have led to numerous discoveries of the Earth's surface and interior to aid in the ability to understand the wonders of our world. Understanding the interior and it struc-tures (geology), the oceans, seas and rivers (hydrology), and the skies above (meterology) is the focus of this chapter.

ATMOSPHERE

The atmosphere is comprised of several layers of gases immediately sur-rounding the Earth. Earth's atmosphere is an essential feature that allows our planet to sustain life. It extends approximately 560 km (350 miles) from the surface of the Earth, though the actual thickness varies from place to place. Our atmosphere makes Earth a habitable planet for people, plants, and animals, by absorbing the Sun's energy, recycling and preserving water and chemicals needed for life, and by moderating our weather patterns. The atmosphere is at-tracted and maintained by the force of gravity of the Earth.

Without the protection of our atmosphere, Earth would be subjected to the extreme freezing temperatures found in the vacuum of space. The Earth would also be bombarded by dangerous amounts of radiant energy from the Sun. Our atmosphere is specifically formulated to provide us with an environment suited to our needs.

Earth's atmosphere (Fig. 11-1) is made up of about 78% nitrogen, 21% oxy-gen, slightly less than 1% argon, and the remaining fraction of 1% contains small amounts of other gases (including carbon dioxide, helium, hydrogen, krypton, methane, neon, nitrogen dioxide, nitrous oxide, ozone, sulfur dioxide, water vapor, and xenon).

Composition of Atmosphere

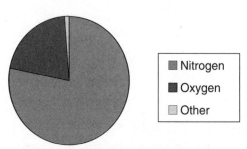

Fig. 11-1: Atmospheric composition.

We identify five distinct layers (called *strata*) of atmosphere: the troposphere, stratosphere, mesosphere, thermosphere, and exosphere. Each layer differs from the others by its temperature, density, and chemical composition. Four transition zones separate the four atmospheric layers: the tropopause, stratopause, mesopause, and thermopause.

The troposphere is the atmospheric layer closest to the Earth's surface. It extends to an altitude of approximately 8 to 15 kilometers (5 to 9 miles). The force of gravity is strongest nearest the surface of the Earth, thus the number of gas molecules per area (density) is greatest at the lowest altitudes. In addition, the density of gas molecules decreases as altitude increases. Therefore, the troposphere is the densest atmospheric layer, accounting for most of the mass of the atmosphere.

The troposphere contains 99% of the water vapor found in the atmosphere. Water vapor in the air absorbs solar energy and absorbs heat that radiates back from the Earth's surface. The water vapor concentration within the troposphere is greatest near the equator and lowest at the poles.

Nearly all weather phenomena experienced on Earth are caused by the interactions of gases (including water vapor) within the troposphere. The temperature of the troposphere decreases as altitude increases from about 16°C (60°F) nearest Earth's surface to –65°C (–85°F) at the tropopause. (Temperatures are averages of all the temperatures over the surface of the Earth and across all seasons.) For every kilometer in altitude above the Earth, the temperature drops approximately 6°C within the troposphere.

The troposphere is separated from the next layer (the stratosphere) by the tropopause.

The stratosphere is above the troposphere. The stratosphere extends from the tropopause (found approximately 14 km or 9 miles above the Earth's surface) to approximately 48 km (30 miles) above the Earth's surface. The stratosphere contains much less water vapor than the troposphere. The gases of the stratosphere are much less dense than in the troposphere as well.

The temperature within the lower stratosphere (up to about 25km altitude) is mostly constant. In the upper stratosphere, the temperature rises gradually with increased altitude to a temperature of approximately 3°C. The rising temperatures are caused by the absorption of ultraviolet radiation from the Sun by ozone molecules.

Ozone (O_3) molecules form the ozone layer at the upper ranges of the stratosphere. Ozone molecules absorb solar ultraviolet radiation, which is converted to kinetic energy (heat). This process accounts for the increased temperature levels as altitude increases within the stratosphere. The ozone layer also performs the crucial function of protecting organisms from the harmful effects of too much ultraviolet radiation.

The stratosphere is separated from the next atmospheric layer (the mesosphere) by the stratopause.

The **mesosphere** is the atmospheric layer found at approximately 50–80km altitude. The mesosphere is characterized by temperatures decreasing with increased altitude from about 3°C at the stratopause to –110 °C at 80km. The mesosphere has a low density of molecules with very little ozone or water vapor. The atmospheric gases of the upper mesosphere separate into layers of gases according to molecular mass. This phenomenon is caused by the weakened effects of gravity on the gas molecules (because of distance from Earth). Lighter (low molecular mass) gases are found at the higher altitudes.

The **mesopause** separates the stratosphere from the next layer, the thermosphere.

The **thermosphere** is found at altitudes of approximately 80 to 480 kilometers. Gas molecules of the thermosphere are widely separated, resulting in very low gas density. The absorption of solar radiation by oxygen molecules in the thermosphere causes the temperature to rise to approximately 1980°C at the upper levels of the thermosphere.

The final layer, the **exosphere** extends from the **thermopause** at approximately 480km to an altitude of 960 to 1000 kilometers. The exosphere, however, is difficult to define and is more of a transitional area between Earth and space than a distinct layer. The low gravitational forces at this altitude hold only the lightest molecules, mostly hydrogen and helium. Even these are at very low densities.

In addition to the names of the five atmospheric layers, some other terms describe various levels of the atmosphere. The troposphere and tropopause together are sometimes referred to as the "lower atmosphere." The stratosphere and mesosphere are sometimes called the "middle atmosphere," while the thermosphere and exosphere are together known as the "upper atmosphere." Still other scientists call the troposphere, mesosphere, and stratosphere together as the "homosphere," and the thermosphere and exosphere as the "heterosphere."

The **ionosphere** includes portions of the mesosphere and thermosphere. The term ionosphere refers to the portion of the atmosphere where ultraviolet radiation causes excitation of atoms resulting in extreme temperatures. Under extreme temperature conditions, electrons are actually separated from the atoms. The highly excited atoms are left with a positive charge. Charged atoms (ions) form layers within the thermosphere. The charged layers are referred to as the ionosphere. The charged particles within the ionosphere deflect some radio signals. While some radio frequencies are not affected by the ionosphere, others are. This reflection of some radio signals causes some radio frequencies (particularly AM transmissions) to be received far from their origination point.

Solar flares create magnetic storms in the thermosphere near Earth's poles. These storms temporarily strip electrons from atoms. When the electrons rejoin the atoms, brilliant light (in green and red) is emitted as they return to their normal state. These lights are called **auroras**, or the Northern and Southern lights.

The total weight of the atmosphere exerts force on the Earth. This force is known as **atmospheric pressure** and can be measured with a **barometer**.

EARTH'S LAYERS

The **geosphere** is the solid or mineral part of the Earth. It consists of layers, from the outer crust down to the inner core separated according to density and temperature. There are two ways to classify the composition of the geosphere:

1) chemically, into crust, mantle, and core, or

2) functionally, into lithosphere and asthenosphere.

Crust, Mantle and Core

The density of the Earth averages three times that of water. This density varies depending upon the layer of the Earth being considered.

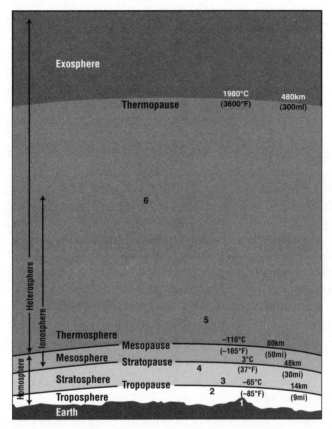

Fig 11-2: Layers of the atmosphere. 1: Mt. Everest; 2: Commercial Jet; 3: Fighter Jet; 4: Ozone Layer; 5: Auroras; 6: Space Shuttle.

The **crust** is the outermost layer of the geosphere, what we think of as "the Earth." It includes the mountains, valleys, continents, ocean beds, etc. The crust is rich in oxygen, silicon, and aluminum, with lesser amounts of other elements like iron, nickel, etc. It has low density (2.5 to 3.5 gm/cm^3), that allows it to float on the denser mantle. It is brittle and breaks relatively easily. It is made up mostly of sedimentary rocks resting on a base of igneous rocks. Several separate tectonic plates float beneath it on the surface of the mantle.

It is estimated that the entire surface of the Earth can re-form in about 500 million years through erosion and subsequent re-creation through tectonic activity.

The **mantle** is the complex middle layer of the geosphere. It is a broad layer of dense rock and metal oxides that lies between the molten core and the crust and extends to a depth of between 40 to 2,900 kilometers. It accounts for around 82% of the Earth's volume and is thought to be made up mostly of iron, magnesium, silicon, and oxygen. Analysis of seismic waves show that the material that makes up the mantle behaves as a plastic—a substance with the properties of a solid but flows under pressure. More precisely, the mantle consists of rigid and plastic zones.

The **core** is the innermost layer of the geosphere, composed of mostly iron and nickel. It extends from a depth of about 2,900 kilometers to nearly 6,400 kilometers (1,800 to 3,900 miles). It is extremely hot, even after thousands (to millions) of years of cooling. The core has two layers, the liquid **outer core**, and the solid iron **inner core** at the Earth's center. Even with the high temperatures at the center (up to 7,500K, hotter than the Sun's surface), this layer is solid due to the immense pressure of the overlying layers.

The material that makes up the Earth's interior is similar to that of liquid steel, but it maintains a fluidic consistency. This results in the migration of Earth's material toward the equator due to angular momentum caused by the spinning of the Earth. The effect is that the equatorial radius is about 21 kilometers larger than the polar radius, which results in its oblate spheroid shape.

Another way to classify the layers is into the lithosphere and asthenosphere. The rigid outermost layer of the geosphere (from the Greek, *lithos*—stone) is called the **lithosphere**. The upper layer of the lithosphere is the crust. Beneath the crust is a layer of rigid mantle. The **asthenosphere** is the molten plastic outer mantle of hot silicate rock beneath the lithosphere (from the Greek, *asthenos*—devoid of force).

The Discontinuities

The **Mohorovicic** discontinuity or **Moho** is the sharp boundary between the crust and mantle. The **Gutenberg** discontinuity separates the mantle from the core.

The Hydrosphere

The Earth is unique among planets in the solar system because of the large quantities of water that cover its surface. This water is responsible for much of its formation and dynamics. The interconnections between climate and geophysical processes due to hydrology are complex. Two-thirds of the planet's surface are covered by water at an average ocean depth of 3.9 kilometers (12,795 feet). The water area is 3.6×10^8 square kilometers (nearly 140 million square miles).

The Magnetosphere

The magnetic field that surrounds the Earth extends thousands of miles into outer space. It mimics a bar magnet with the poles being approximately located at the north and south poles and a neutral area at the equator. The poles shift slightly over time. The power of the Earth's magnet is not very strong, being approximately .5 Gauss at the surface of the Earth.

The location of the North Magnetic Pole was determined in 1996 by a Canadian expedition and certified by magnetometer and theodolite at 78°35.7′N 104°11.9′W. In 2005, the location was at 82.7°N 114.4°W, slightly west of Ellesmere Island in Northern Canada. It is clear that the magnetic field moves over time.

The Geologic Column

The estimated age of Earth is determined by radiometric dating and geological estimates to be about 4.6 billion years. The geologic column represents the layers of the Earth near the surface that contain fossils and various types of sediment. The geologic column is currently used as a tool of evolutionary uniformitarian scientists to display a "progression" of life from simple species in the deepest (oldest) layers to more complex species in the layers closer to the surface (younger). The layers are categorized into Eras, Periods, and Epochs. Fig. 11-3 represents the general arrangement of the geological column.

Geologic Time Scale

Eon	Era	Period	Epoch	Age (my)
Phanerozoic *(Visible Life)*	Cenozoic *(Recent Life)* *(Age of Mammals)*	Quaternary	Holocene	0.01
			Pleistocene	1.6
		Tertiary	Pliocene	5.3
			Miocene	23.7
			Oligocene	36.6
			Eocene	57.8
			Paleocene	66.4
	Mesozoic *(Middle Life)* *(Age of Reptiles)*	Cretaceous		144
		Jurassic		208
		Triassiac		245
	Paleozoic *(Ancient Life)*	Permian		286
		Pennsylvanian		320
		Mississippian		360
		Devonian		408
		Silurian		438
		Ordovician		505
		Cambrian		570
Proterozoic *(Early Life)*		Oldest Known Life		2500
Archean		Oldest Known Rocks		3900
Hadean		Age of Earth		4600

Fig. 11-3: Geologic Column.

Practice Tests

CLEP Natural Sciences

Practice Test 1

CLEP Natural Sciences

This test is also on CD-ROM in our special interactive
CLEP Natural Sciences TestWare®

(Answer sheets appear in the back of this book.)

TIME: 90 Minutes
120 Questions

DIRECTIONS: Each of the following group of questions consists of five lettered terms followed by a list of numbered phrases or sentences. For each numbered phrase or sentence, select the one choice that is most clearly related to it. Each choice may be used once, more than once, or not at all.

Questions 1–5 _____

(A) Mammalia

(D) Aves

(B) Amphibia

(E) Chondrichthyes

(C) Reptilia

_____ 1. Cold-blooded animals with bony skeletons, webbed feet, and separate sexes

_____ 2. Cold-blooded animals with horny scales and a bony skeleton that lay eggs

_____ 3. Cartilaginous fish

_____ 4. Warm-blooded animals, mostly with wings, that lay eggs

_____ 5. Animals with a hairy body and highly developed brain that have live births (in most cases) and produce milk

Questions 6–10 _____

    (A) Secretory vesicle

    (B) Smooth endoplasmic reticulum

    (C) Microvilli

    (D) Nucleolus

    (E) Nuclear pore

_____   6. Communication channel between the cytoplasm and nucleoplasm

_____   7. Extensions that provide extra surface area for absorption

_____   8. Contain digestive enzymes

_____   9. Packets that carry substances (hormones, fats, etc.) synthesized within the cell

_____   10. Network of membranes that deliver lipids and proteins throughout the cytoplasm

Questions 11–13 _____

    (A) KCl   (D) SiC

    (B) NaF   (E) $HC_2H_3O_2$

    (C) Cu

_____   11. Atoms are held together with network covalent attraction.

_____   12. Atoms are held together with covalent attraction.

_____   13. Atoms are held together with metallic attraction.

Questions 14–18 _____

(A) Nodes

(B) Nonvascular plants

(C) Angiosperms

(D) Gymnosperms

(E) Lateral buds

_____ 14. Bryophytes

_____ 15. Flowering plants

_____ 16. Shoots and roots

_____ 17. Produce seeds without flowers

_____ 18. Conifers and cycads

Questions 19–21 _____

(A) Radiation

(B) Convection

(C) Irradiation

(D) Conduction

(E) Diffusion

_____ 19. An athlete with a sore shoulder places a warm compress on it to transfer energy to soothe the muscle.

_____ 20. On a cold February morning, a blower system in a car warms up after several minutes and blows air through vents in the floor, dashboard, and windshield. Eventually, the driver is able to unbutton his coat and stay warm when the outside temperature is still 23°F.

_____ 21. Getting ready for a fall cruise inspires a young lady to spend a couple of weeks going to a local spa and reclining under a tanning lamp. However, such practices might result in dangerous overexposure to ultraviolet rays that can lead to cancer or premature aging of the skin.

Questions 22–24 _____

    (A) H_2 (D) KCl

    (B) $KMnO_4$ (E) Fe_2O_3

    (C) MgO

_____ 22. This substance is a very strong oxidizing agent.

_____ 23. The metal in this substance has an oxidation number of +2.

_____ 24. The oxidation potential of this substance is zero.

Questions 25–29 _____

    (A) Natality

    (B) J-curve

    (C) Population rate of growth

    (D) Mortality

    (E) S-curve

_____ 25. Exponential population growth curve; population growth accelerates

_____ 26. Birth rate minus death rate

_____ 27. Death rate

_____ 28. Birth rate

_____ 29. Logistic population growth curve; population growth accelerates and then slows down because of limits

---

DIRECTIONS: Each of the questions or incomplete statements below is followed by five possible answers or completions. Select the best choice in each case and fill in the corresponding oval on the answer sheet.

---

30. The evolution of plant species is considered to have begun with

    (A) autotrophic prokaryotic cells

    (B) heterotrophic eukaryotic cells

    (C) aerobic eukaryotic cells

    (D) pre-nucleic eukaryotic cells

    (E) aerobic prokaryotic cells

31. What type of a wave is a sound wave?

    (A) Compression   (D) Converse

    (B) Transverses   (E) Convex

    (C) Inverse

32. Salinity is a measure of dissolved solids in water. On average, 1,000 g of typical sea water contains 35 g of salt. The level of salinity is below average in areas where large amounts of fresh water enter the ocean and above average in hot, arid climates. The Mediterranean and the Red seas are adjacent to deserts. The water in these two seas would be expected to have

    (A) above-average salinity

    (B) below-average salinity

    (C) average salinity

    (D) no salt content

    (E) cold temperatures

33. The discoveries of Galileo Galilei (1564–1642) and Isaac Newton (1642–1727) precipitated the scientific revolution of the seventeenth century. Stressing the use of detailed measurements during experimentation enabled them to frame several universal laws of nature and to overthrow many of Aristotle's (384–322 B.C.E.) erroneous ideas about motion, which were based on sheer reasoning alone. One of these universal laws is now known as the law of inertia or Newton's first law of motion. According to this law, objects in motion tend to stay in motion and objects at rest tend to stay at rest unless acted upon by an external force. The more mass (inertia) an object has, the more resistance it offers to changes in its state of motion. According to the law of inertia, which of the following would offer the greatest resistance to a change in its motion?

    (A) A pellet of lead shot

    (B) A golf ball

    (C) A large watermelon

    (D) A feather

    (E) A sheet of notebook paper

34. The site of transfer for nutrients, water, and waste between a mammalian mother and embryo is the

    (A) yolk sac membrane   (D) umbilical membrane

    (B) uterus   (E) ovary

    (C) placenta

35. The process of genetic inheritance was first investigated and explained by

    (A) Robert Hooke   (D) Matthias Schleiden

    (B) Dmitri Mendeleev   (E) Gregor Mendel

    (C) Theodor Schwann

36. The first cells to evolve on Earth were most likely NOT

    (A) anaerobic   (D) aquatic

    (B) specialized   (E) small

    (C) prokaryotic

37. Which of the following best represents the sequence of human evolution?

    (A) *Australopithecus afarensis*, Cro-Magnon, *Homo erectus*, *Homo sapiens*, Modern man

    (B) Cro-Magnon, *Australopithecus afarensis*, *Homo erectus*, *Homo sapiens*

    (C) *Homo sapiens*, *Australopithecus afarensis*, *Homo erectus*, Cro-Magnon

    (D) *Australopithecus afarensis*, *Homo erectus*, Cro-Magnon, Modern man

    (E) Cro-Magnon, *Homo erectus*, *Australopithecus afarensis*, Modern man

38. Which of the following demonstrates pi bonding?

    (A) OH⁻

    (D) H_2S

    (B) H⁺

    (E) KCl

    (C) C_2H_2

39. The Sun crosses the celestial equator going north on March 21. This is known as the

    (A) solstice

    (D) spring equinox

    (B) lunar eclipse

    (E) autumnal equinox

    (C) solar eclipse

40. Cells of eukaryotes have all of the following EXCEPT

    (A) membraned organelles

    (B) DNA organized into chromosomes

    (C) a nucleus

    (D) DNA floating free in the cytoplasm

    (E) ribosomes

41. A small non-protein molecule such as iron that works with enzymes to promote catalysis is known as

(A) a protein

(D) a hormone

(B) an inorganic cofactor

(E) a carbohydrate

(C) a coenzyme

42. Which of the following will NOT inhibit enzymatic reactions?

(A) Temperature

(B) pH level

(C) Particular chemical agents

(D) Lack of substrate

(E) Large amount of enzyme

For questions 43–46, identify the answer that corresponds with the correct functional group.

(A)
$$\begin{array}{c} H \\ | \\ R-C-OH \\ | \\ H \end{array}$$

(D)
$$\begin{array}{c} R-C-R \\ || \\ O \end{array}$$

(B)
$$\begin{array}{c} R-C-H \\ || \\ O \end{array}$$

(E)
$$\begin{array}{c} R-C-OH \\ || \\ O \end{array}$$

(C)
$$\begin{array}{c} \quad\quad\quad H \\ \quad\quad\quad | \\ R-C-O-C-R \\ || \quad\quad | \\ O \quad\quad H \end{array}$$

_____ 43. Ketone

_____ 44. Alcohol

_____ 45. Ester

_____ 46. Aldehyde

47.   The conversion of light energy into chemical energy is accomplished by

    (A) catabolism

    (B) oxidative phosphorylation

    (C) metabolism

    (D) protein synthesis

    (E) photosynthesis

48.   Which of the following terms is defined as the increase in the statistical disorder of a physical system?

    (A) Enthalpy   (D) Euprophy

    (B) Entropy   (E) Empathy

    (C) Epathy

49.   Which of the following evolutionary developments is out of sequence?

    (A) Formation of coacervates occurred in primordial seas.

    (B) Development of eukaryotic cells took place.

    (C) The process of photosynthesis was developed within single cells.

    (D) Amphibians diversified into birds, then mammals.

    (E) A branch of mammals developed into primates, the direct ancestors of man.

50.   Energy flows through the food chain from

    (A) producers to consumers to decomposers

    (B) producers to secondary consumers to primary consumers

    (C) decomposers to consumers to producers

    (D) secondary consumers to producers

    (E) consumers to producers

51. If the Moon completely covers the sun as seen by an earthbound observer, there is a

    (A) total lunar eclipse   (D) partial solar eclipse

    (B) total solar eclipse   (E) parallax

    (C) partial lunar eclipse

52. The projection of the Earth's axis on the sky is the

    (A) celestial equator   (D) ecliptic

    (B) zenith   (E) zodiac

    (C) celestial poles

53. The process that releases energy for use by the cell is known as

    (A) photosynthesis   (D) cellular respiration

    (B) aerobic metabolism   (E) dark reaction

    (C) anaerobic metabolism

54. Which of the following is NOT a step in the translation portion of protein synthesis?

    (A) tRNA anticodons line up with corresponding mRNA codons

    (B) **a** ribosome attaches to the start codon on mRNA; ribosome adds tRNA whose anticodons complement the next codon on the mRNA string; and the process repeats to locate sequential amino acids

    (C) Ribosomal enzymes also link the sequential amino acids into a protein chain

    (D) As the protein chain is forming, rRNA moves along the sequence adding amino acids designated by codons on the mRNA

    (E) Terminating codon stops the synthesis process and releases the newly formed protein

55. Which of the following most closely represents the sequence leading to human evolution?

   (A) Coacervates, eukaryotes, plants, fish, amphibians, mammals, primates, man

   (B) Eukaryotes, plants, amphibians, fish, mammals, primates, man

   (C) Eukaryotes, coacervates, plants, fish, amphibians, mammals, primates, man

   (D) Coacervates, eukaryotes, plants, fish, amphibians, primates, mammals, man

   (E) Plants, eukaryotes, coacervates, fish, amphibians, mammals, primates, man

56. Water molecules are attracted to each other due to which of the following?

   (A) Polarity; partial positive charge near hydrogen atoms; partial negative charge near oxygen atoms

   (B) Inert properties of hydrogen and oxygen

   (C) Ionic bonds between hydrogen and oxygen

   (D) The crystal structure of ice

   (E) Brownian motion of hydrogen and oxygen atoms

57. The voltage across the terminal of a circuit containing a resistor is 12 V, and it contains a resistor connected to the circuit which reads 8 ohms. What is the amperage of the service?

   (A) 1.5 A

   (B) 48 A

   (C) 0.67 A

   (D) 15 A

   (E) 96 A

58. The percentage of Earth's surface that is water is

   (A) 10 percent   (D) 70 percent

   (B) 30 percent   (E) 90 percent

   (C) 50 percent

59. Traits that are produced by the expression of more than one set of genes are known as

    (A) polygenic traits   (D) monohybrid traits

    (B) autosomal traits   (E) dihybrid crosses

    (C) sex-limited traits

60. The major driving force of the evolution of species is known as

    (A) the Oparin Theory

    (B) natural selection

    (C) environmental determinism

    (D) Hardy-Weinberg Equilibrium

    (E) genetic drift

61. Which of the following items found on a bicycle is NOT a simple machine?

    (A) tire

    (B) pedal mechanism

    (C) rear wheel gear mechanism

    (D) horn

    (E) kickstand

62. Which of the following sets of quantum numbers (listed in order of n, l, ml, ms) describe the highest energy valence electron of nitrogen in its ground state?

    (A) 2, 0, 0, $+\frac{1}{2}$ (D) 2, 1, -1, $-\frac{1}{2}$

    (B) 2, 1, 1, $-\frac{1}{2}$ (E) 2, 1, -1, $+\frac{1}{2}$

    (C) 2, 1, 1, $+\frac{1}{2}$

63. The change of state from liquid to solid or solid to liquid involves a phase where the temperature remains constant. This phase is known as the

    (A) transition phase   (D) specific heat

    (B) heat of fusion   (E) equilibrium

    (C) heat of fission

64. Which of the following solid crystals has, on average, one atom per cubic unit cell?

    (A) Face-centered

    (B) Body-centered

    (C) Rhombic

    (D) All cubic crystals

    (E) Simple cubic crystals only

65. Which of the following is part of the alimentary canal?

    (A) Artery   (D) Bronchus

    (B) Sinus   (E) Esophagus

    (C) Vagus nerve

66. Which of the following experimental evidence was NOT considered supportive of the Oparin Hypothesis?

    (A) Amino acids can be produced in the laboratory by exposing simple inorganic molecules to electrical charge.

    (B) Guanine can be formed in the laboratory by thermal polymerization of amino acids.

    (C) Ultraviolet light induces the formation of dipeptides from amino acids in laboratory experiments.

    (D) In the laboratory, proteins are not useful as catalysts, indicating that early proteins were stable.

    (E) Phosphoric acid increases the yield of polymers in the laboratory, simulating the role of ATP in protein synthesis.

Questions 67–71

In snapdragons, a red flower crossed with a white flower produces a pink flower. In this illustration, R stands for red and W represents white. The Punnett square for a cross between a white snapdragon and a red snapdragon is shown here:

	R	R
W	RW	RW
W	RW	RW

67. The cross illustrated in this Punnett square is an example of

(A) a sex-linked trait   (D) a dihybrid cross

(B) multiple alleles   (E) complete dominance

(C) incomplete dominance

68. The symbol RW represents which of the following?

(A) The allele for red   (D) The allele for white

(B) The genotype for pink   (E) The genotype for white

(C) The phenotype for pink

69. In this cross, both parents have genotypes that are

(A) heterozygous for color   (D) dominant for pink

(B) homozygous for color   (E) dominant for white

(C) recessive for pink

70. Which of the following statements about this cross must be true?

(A) Both parents of the red snapdragon must have had the genotype RR.

(B) One of the parents of the red snapdragon must have had the genotype RR.

(C) Both parents of the red snapdragon must have been pink.

(D) Neither parent of the red snapdragon could be white.

(E) One parent of the red snapdragon could have been white.

71. If two of the heterozygous offspring (RW) of this cross are bred, what will be the ratio of phenotypes of the offspring?

(A) 0 red: 4 pink: 0 white   (D) 2 red: 0 pink: 2 white

(B) 2 red: 2 pink: 0 white   (E) 1 red: 2 pink: 1 white

(C) 1 red: 1 pink: 1 white

72. The physical place where a particular organism lives is called a

(A) niche   (D) habitat

(B) biosphere   (E) ecosystem

(C) lithosphere

73. What is the most likely explanation for the fact that a sample of solid nickel is attracted into a magnetic field, but a sample of solid zinc chloride is not?

(A) There are unpaired outer electrons in nickel.

(B) There is some iron mixed in with the nickel.

(C) There are unpaired outer electrons in zinc.

(D) The presence of chlorine keeps zinc from being attracted to the magnet.

(E) Nickel does not produce a magnetic field to oppose the one that is attracting it.

74. The specific heat of water is 4.2 J/g °C. What mass of water will be heated by 10°C by 840 J?

(A) 0.5 g   (D) 4.2 g

(B) 10 g   (E) 840 g

(C) 20 g

75. A light-year represents the

   (A) total amount of light energy that travels past a point on Earth in one year

   (B) total distance that an object travels in space at the speed of light in one year

   (C) total amount of time that a photon of light travels in order to reach a star, planet, or other extraterrestrial object

   (D) speed at which light travels in a year

   (E) speed of a photon in a vacuum when it collides with an x-ray

76. The half-life of C 14 is 5,730 years. A piece of cypress is measured to have ¾ of the carbon to be C 12 and ¼ C 14. How many years old is this piece of wood likely to be?

   (A) 5,730

   (B) 2,865

   (C) 4,297

   (D) 11,460

   (E) 1,435

77. Igneous rock forms are commonly called

   (A) marble   (D) granite

   (B) limestone   (E) sandstone

   (C) cement

78. Which of the following statements is true?

   (A) Despite the contraction of space, galaxies appear to be static relative to each other when observed.

   (B) The expansion of space makes galaxies appear to be moving apart, causing the color of their spectral lines to shift when observed.

   (C) Galaxies themselves are moving apart from each other.

   (D) Hubble's law states that the redshift in light coming from a distant galaxy is inversely proportional to its distance from Earth.

   (E) The actual motion of galaxies is questionable due to variations in Hubble's constant.

79. All of the following are major structural regions of roots EXCEPT the

   (A) meristematic region

   (B) elongation region

   (C) root cap

   (D) epistematic region

   (E) maturation region

80. When a yellow pea plant is crossed with a green pea plant, all the offspring are yellow. The law that best explains this is the law of

   (A) intolerance

   (B) dominance

   (C) interference

   (D) relative genes

   (E) codominance

81. Which of the following statements is true about electrons?

   (A) Electrons have a positive charge.

   (B) Electrons have less mass than protons and neutrons.

   (C) Electrons are found within the nucleus of atoms.

   (D) The number of electrons is equal to the number of protons in an ion.

   (E) An atom's valence number is the number of electrons in its lowest energy level.

82. What is the energy-generating mechanism of the stars, including the Sun?

   (A) Fission

   (B) Fusion

   (C) Spontaneous generation

   (D) Combustion

   (E) Stellar explosion

83. When measuring the flow of heat in a system, a natural process that starts at one equilibrium state and flows to another will go in what direction for an irreversible process which is impacted by the entropy of the system plus the environment?

   (A) Increase

   (B) Decrease

   (C) Remain static

   (D) Fluctuate between increases and decreases in a constant pattern

   (E) Increase steadily and then drop off, similar to the conservation of momentum in a closed system

84. What is the resistance of an electric can opener if it takes a current of 10 A when plugged into a 120 V service?

(A) 1,200 ohms   (D) 12 ohms

(B) 0.083 ohms   (E) 1.2 ohms

(C) 130 ohms

85. Photosynthesis would NOT proceed without which of the following that allow moisture and gases to pass in and out of the leaf?

(A) Surface hairs   (D) Epidermal cells

(B) Stomata   (E) Cilia

(C) Cuticles

86. In ferns, the individual we generally recognize as an adult fern is really which structure?

(A) A mature gametophyte   (D) A young sporophyte

(B) A prothallus   (E) A young gametophyte

(C) A mature sporophyte

87. Which of the following is the least polar molecule?

(A) H_2 (D) C_2H_2

(B) H_2O (E) NaH

(C) H_2S

88. Which state of matter does NOT have a definite shape or a definite volume?

(A) Solid   (D) Plasma

(B) Liquid   (E) Both (C) and (D)

(C) Gas

89. A person who has been exercising vigorously begins to sweat and breathe quickly. These reactions are involuntary responses known as

(A) fight or flight responses

(B) homeostatic mechanisms

(C) equilibrium responses

(D) stimulus receptors

(E) hormone reactions

90. The nervous system is an integrated circuit with many functions. Which of the following parts of the nervous system are matched with the wrong function?

(A) Forebrain—controls olfactory lobes (smell)

(B) Cerebrum—controls the function of involuntary muscles

(C) Hypothalamus—controls hunger and thirst

(D) Cerebellum—controls balance and muscle coordination

(E) Midbrain—contains optic lobes and controls sight

91. Fog is

(A) the same as smog

(B) caused when cold air moves over warm air

(C) a collection of minute water droplets

(D) associated with a tornado

(E) Both (C) and (D)

92. Land and sea (or lake) breezes form because of

(A) uneven heating of coastal environments

(B) the pressure gradient force

(C) the difference in temperature between land and water surfaces

(D) solar radiation

(E) a variety of factors involving temperature, pressure, and geographical components

93. An electric shock can restart a heart that has stopped beating. Which of the following statements is a valid reason for this fact?

(A) Electric shock stimulates the nervous system.

(B) Smooth muscle is affected by electric shock.

(C) The electric shock pushes blood through the stopped heart.

(D) Cardiac muscle of the heart responds to the electric shock.

(E) Electric shock causes air to enter the lungs.

94. When a hamburger is consumed by an individual, it passes through all of the following organs EXCEPT the

   (A) mouth   (D) stomach

   (B) esophagus   (E) small intestine

   (C) salivary glands

95. Each ecosystem can support a certain number of organisms—a number usually designated by the letter K and known as

   (A) ecodensity   (D) a community

   (B) population   (E) the biosphere

   (C) carrying capacity

96. Which of the following parts of an atom is NOT a subatomic particle?

   (A) A quark   (D) An electron

   (B) A boson   (E) A positron

   (C) A neutrino

97. The function of the gall bladder and pancreas is to aid digestion by producing digestive enzymes and secreting them into the

   (A) small intestine   (D) esophagus

   (B) large intestine   (E) mouth

   (C) stomach

98. Many insects have special respiratory organs known as

   (A) spiracles   (D) lungs

   (B) alveoli   (E) gills

   (C) cephalothorax

99. Most of Earth's photosynthesis takes place in which one of the following biomes?

   (A) Oceans   (D) Deserts

   (B) Tundra   (E) Tropical rainforests

   (C) Deciduous forests

100. Which of the following chemical equations represents a replacement reaction?

    (A) A + C ⊠ AC + B

    (B) A + B ⊠ AB

    (C) AB + C ⊠ AC + B

    (D) AB ⊠ A + B

    (E) AB + CD ⊠ A + B + C + D

101. The study of the interaction of organisms with their living space is known as

    (A) environmentalism   (D) ecology

    (B) habitology   (E) paleontology

    (C) zoology

102. What is the name of a distinct group of individuals that are able to mate and produce viable offspring?

    (A) A class   (D) A family

    (B) A community   (E) A species

    (C) A phylum

103. Which of the following is true concerning Einstein's theory of relativity?

    (A) As energy increases, the speed of light increases and mass is constant.

    (B) As energy increases, mass increases and the speed of light is constant.

    (C) As energy increases, the speed of light decreases and mass is constant.

    (D) As energy increases, mass decreases and the speed of light is constant.

    (E) As energy increases, the speed of light and mass will increase.

104. Which of the following is an autotroph?

   (A) *E. coli* bacteria

   (B) A Portuguese man-of-war

   (C) A portobello mushroom

   (D) An asparagus fern

   (E) A perch

105. The Michelson-Morley experiment in 1887 proved that the speed of light

   (A) is the same in all directions

   (B) can slow down in a vacuum

   (C) is slower in air than in liquid

   (D) is different on the Moon

   (E) continuously speeds up in a vacuum

106. Which of the following is NOT a fundamental geological principle?

   (A) The principle of original horizontality

   (B) The principle of supererogation

   (C) The principle of lateral continuity

   (D) The principle of fossil succession

   (E) The principle of uniformitarianism

107. Astronomers observing the redshift of light from a faraway star means that the star is

   (A) moving away from us   (D) a dwarf star

   (B) moving toward us   (E) a giant nova

   (C) ready to explode

108. The three most recent geological eras are

   (A) Paleozoic, Proterozoic, Archean

   (B) Mesozoic, Paleozoic, Cenozoic

   (C) Cenozoic, Mesozoic, Paleozoic

(D) Cenozoic, Archean, Paleozoic

(E) Recent, Tertiary, Quaternary

109. A form of symbiosis in which one species is benefited while the other is harmed is called

(A) parasitism

(D) altruism

(B) mutualism

(E) commensalism

(C) amensalism

110. An axis is

(A) a connecting line at the equator

(B) a connecting line between the poles

(C) a connecting line between orbits

(D) a pole

(E) a connecting line at the tropical zones

111. In order of magnitude, how many galaxies are there in the universe?

(A) Hundreds

(D) Billions

(B) Thousands

(E) Trillions

(C) Millions

112. An astronaut is traveling in a spacecraft that is slowing down. To the astronaut inside the spacecraft, the apparent force inside the craft is directed

(A) backward

(B) forward

(C) sideways

(D) vertically only

(E) nowhere because there is no force

113. The cells of which of the following organisms are most likely to be prokaryotic?

    (A) Mold
    (B) Seaweed
    (C) Blue-green algae
    (D) Fern
    (E) Hydra

114. The name for the imaginary object that centers on and surrounds Earth by which background stars are projected is called a(an)

    (A) geodesic dome
    (B) celestial sphere
    (C) stellar ball
    (D) Cartesian coordinate system
    (E) equatorial coordinate system

115. Why is stratospheric ozone depletion (destruction of the ozone layer) a serious concern?

    (A) It is a major cause of the "greenhouse effect."
    (B) It will increase the amount of ultraviolet radiation reaching the ground.
    (C) It causes acid rain.
    (D) It is really nothing to worry about.
    (E) It leads to global warming as more radiation enters through the hole in the atmosphere.

116. Mountain and valley breezes form because of

    (A) gravity and the pressure gradient force
    (B) the pressure gradient force and heating
    (C) gravity and heating
    (D) the pressure gradient force and the Coriolis force
    (E) high pressure forming near the top of the mountain due to warm air expansion forcing air up the mountain from the valley below

117. As you go down the periodic table and to the left, which of the following traits increases?

    (A) Atomic radius   (D) Ionization energy

    (B) Electronegativity   (E) Acidity of the oxides

    (C) Electron affinity

118. According to Newton's laws of motion, the greater the mass of an object, the greater the force necessary to change its

    (A) position   (D) shape

    (B) force   (E) density

    (C) state of motion

119. The top or peak of a sine wave is called the

    (A) crest   (D) period

    (B) trough   (E) frequency

    (C) amplitude

120. A wave does not carry along the medium through which it travels. Thus, it follows that

    (A) molecules of water in the ocean are pushed to shore by waves

    (B) the ocean's water molecules are thoroughly mixed each day by waves

    (C) debris in the ocean is washed ashore by waves

    (D) individual water molecules do not travel toward shore, but wave peaks do

    (E) waves move water, not swimmers

Practice Test 1

CLEP Natural Sciences

Answer Key

1. (B)	25. (B)	49. (C)	73. (A)	97. (A)
2. (C)	26. (C)	50. (A)	74. (C)	98. (A)
3. (E)	27. (D)	51. (B)	75. (B)	99. (A)
4. (D)	28. (A)	52. (C)	76. (D)	100. (C)
5. (A)	29. (E)	53. (D)	77. (D)	101. (D)
6. (E)	30. (E)	54. (A)	78. (B)	102. (E)
7. (C)	31. (A)	55. (A)	79. (D)	103. (B)
8. (C)	32. (A)	56. (A)	80. (B)	104. (D)
9. (A)	33. (C)	57. (A)	81. (B)	105. (A)
10. (B)	34. (C)	58. (D)	82. (B)	106. (B)
11. (D)	35. (E)	59. (A)	83. (A)	107. (A)
12. (E)	36. (B)	60. (B)	84. (D)	108. (C)
13. (C)	37. (D)	61. (D)	85. (B)	109. (A)
14. (B)	38. (C)	62. (C)	86. (C)	110. (B)
15. (C)	39. (D)	63. (B)	87. (A)	111. (D)
16. (C)	40. (D)	64. (E)	88. (E)	112. (B)
17. (D)	41. (B)	65. (E)	89. (B)	113. (C)
18. (D)	42. (E)	66. (D)	90. (B)	114. (B)
19. (D)	43. (D)	67. (C)	91. (C)	115. (B)
20. (B)	44. (A)	68. (B)	92. (E)	116. (C)
21. (A)	45. (C)	69. (B)	93. (D)	117. (A)
22. (B)	46. (B)	70. (D)	94. (C)	118. (C)
23. (C)	47. (E)	71. (E)	95. (C)	119. (A)
24. (A)	48. (B)	72. (D)	96. (D)	120. (D)

Detailed Explanations of Answers

Practice Test 1

1.   **(B)**   Amphibia include cold-blooded (ecothermic) animals with a bony skeleton that usually have four limbs with webbed feet and four toes, a large mouth and small teeth, a three-chambered heart, separate sexes, and fertilize eggs internally or externally (salamanders, frogs, etc.).

2.   **(C)**   Reptilia have horny epidermal scales, usually with paired limbs that have five toes. They have a bony skeleton and lungs (no gills). Most have a three-chambered heart. They are cold-blooded (ecothermic), have separate sexes, fertilize internally, and lay eggs (snakes, lizards, alligators).

3.   **(E)**   Chondrichthyes are fish with a cartilaginous endoskeleton, a two-chambered heart, between five and seven gill pairs, no swim bladder or lung, and internal fertilization (sharks, rays, etc).

4.   **(D)**   Aves includes warm-blooded (endothermic) birds having a spindle-shaped body (with head, neck, trunk, and tail), a long neck, paired limbs, wings for flying, a four-toed foot, feathers, leg scales, a bony skeleton, bones with air cavities, a beak, no teeth, and a well-developed nervous system. Aves also have a four-chambered heart, lungs with thin air sacs, separate sexes, and lay eggs with a hard calcified shell (birds—ducks, sparrows, etc.).

5.   **(A)**   Mammalia includes warm-blooded animals with hairy bodies, glands (sweat, scent, sebaceous, mammary), teeth, eyelids, four limbs (usually), external fleshy ears, a four-chambered heart, lungs, a larynx and a highly developed brain. They fertilize internally, give birth to live young (except monotremes), and produce milk (cows, humans, platypus, apes, etc.).

6.   **(E)**   Nuclear pores are holes in the nuclear membrane where the double nuclear membrane fuses together, forming a break or hole, allowing the selective intake and excretion of molecules to or from the nucleus. Thus, nuclear pores are the channel of communication between the cytoplasm and the nucleoplasm.

7. **(C)** Microvilli are filaments that extend from the cell membrane, particularly in cells that are involved in absorption (such as in the intestine). These filaments increase the surface area of the cell membrane, thus increasing the area available to absorb nutrients.

8. **(C)** Microvilli also contain enzymes that are involved in digesting certain types of nutrients.

9. **(A)** Secretory vesicles are packets of material packaged by either the Golgi apparatus or the endoplasmic reticulum. The secretory vesicle carries the substance produced within the cell to the cell membrane. The vesicle membrane fuses with the cell membrane, allowing the substance to escape the cell.

10. **(B)** Smooth endoplasmic reticulum is a network of continuous membranous channels that connect the cell membrane with the nuclear membrane and is responsible for the delivery of lipids and proteins to certain areas within the cytoplasm. Smooth endoplasmic reticulum lacks attached ribosomes.

11. **(D)** Silicon carbide (SiC) is held together with network covalent bonds, which creates a crystal entirely from covalent bonds and confers unusual strength (and a high melting point) upon the crystal.

12. **(E)** Acetic acid is a molecular compound that is held together with covalent bonds, in which electrons are shared between atoms, so that both atoms in the bond end up having a full octet of electrons.

13. **(C)** As a metal, copper is held together by metallic bonds, which involve delocalized d-orbital electrons.

14. **(B)** Nonvascular plants are known as bryophytes (mosses). They lack tissue that will conduct water or food.

15. **(C)** Angiosperms are those plants that produce flowers as reproductive organs.

16. **(C)** Angiosperms (flowering plants) have two main systems—the shoot system, which is mainly above ground, and the root system below ground.

17. **(D)** Gymnosperms produce seeds without flowers.

18. **(D)** Gymnosperms produce seeds without flowers, which include conifers (cone-bearers) and cycads.

19. **(D)** Conduction is the transfer of molecules by collisions, passing heat through one material into another.

20. **(B)** Convection is caused by the flow of heated liquid or gas through a volumetric medium.

21. **(A)** Radiation is waves traveling through space to transfer heat away from the energy source.

22. **(B)** The manganese ion in potassium permanganate has a +5 oxidation state, and is therefore readily reduced. When it is reduced, it forces another species to be oxidized. Therefore, the permanganate ion is a very strong oxidizing agent.

23. **(C)** The magnesium atom that is combined with oxygen has a +2 oxidation state. Oxygen carries a –2 oxidation state, and the sum of the oxidation states of oxygen and magnesium must total the charge on the compound, which is 0.

24. **(A)** Hydrogen gas by definition, since it is a standard, has an oxidation potential of 0.

25. **(B)** One of the modes of population growth is represented by the exponential curve (or J-curve). The rate of growth accelerates over time since there are no limiters of growth.

26. **(C)** The rate of increase within a population is represented by the birth rate minus the death rate.

27. **(D)** Mortality is the death rate within a population.

28. **(A)** Natality is the birth rate within a population.

29. **(E)** Another mode of population growth is represented by the logistic curve (or S-curve) for populations that encounter limiting factors in which acceleration occurs up to a point and then slows down.

30. **(E)** The evolution of plant species is considered to have begun with E-aerobic prokaryotic cells.

31. **(A)** A sound wave is a compression or longitudinal wave, which means that it compresses and rarefies as it moves through a medium. Transverse waves

oscillate up and down as they move through a medium. The other three terms are not commonly used to label sound waves.

32. **(A)** The desert areas increase evaporation of the water that is present, causing a concentration of salts.

33. **(C)** The property of an object that determines the object's resistance to motion is its mass. A large watermelon has a far greater mass than the pellet of lead shot, the golf ball, the feather, or the sheet of notebook paper. The mass of an object never changes. Its mass is equal to the object's weight divided by the acceleration due to gravity (g) at its current position in space.

34. **(C)** The placenta is the connection between the mother and embryo; it is the site of transfer for nutrients, water, and waste between them.

35. **(E)** Gregor Mendel studied the relationships between traits expressed in parents and offspring, and the genes that caused the traits to be expressed.

36. **(B)** The first cells to evolve were most likely unspecialized. Since the Earth's atmosphere was most likely lacking in oxygen, it is presumed that pre-plant cells were also anaerobic. Early cells were also small, aquatic, and pro-karyotic.

37. **(D)** A branch of bipedal primates gave rise to the first true hominids about 4.5 million years ago. The earliest known hominid fossils were found in Africa in the 1970s. The well-known "Lucy" skeleton was named *Australo-pithecus afarensis*. It was determined from the skeleton of *Australopithecus* that it was a biped that walked upright. It had a human-like jaw and teeth, but a skull that resembled that of a small ape. The arms were proportionately longer than humans', indicating the ability to still be motile in trees. The fossilized skull of *Homo erectus*, the oldest known fossil of the human ge-nus, is thought to be about 1.8 million years old. The skull of *Homo erectus* was much larger than *Australopithecus*, about the size of a modern human brain. *Homo erectus* was thought to walk upright and had facial features more closely resembling men than apes. A third fossil, the oldest to be designated *Homo sapiens,* is also called Cro-Magnon man, with a brain size and facial features comparable to modern men. Cro-Magnon *Homo sapiens* are thought to have evolved in Africa and migrated to Europe and Asia approximately 100,000 years ago.

38. **(C)** Acetylene shows a triple bond between the two carbons, which contains two pi bonds. In multiple bonds, the first bond is a sigma bond, in which electrons are shared along the internuclear axis. Any additional bonding

is created by the sideways overlap of unhybridized p-orbitals above and below the internuclear axis. None of the other options for answers contain multiple covalent bonds between any two atoms.

39. **(D)** Equinoxes are described as the two points on the celestial sphere where the ecliptic crosses the celestial equator. Since the crossing occurs on March 21 in this question, it is the spring equinox. Solstices occur in the summer and winter, and correspond to the ecliptic being farthest from the celestial equator. In general, when this crossing occurs on March 21, the Moon is not necessarily aligned with the Earth and the Sun, so the odds of an eclipse occurring are very low. The autumnal equinox occurs at the other end of the celestial sphere on September 22.

40. **(D)** The DNA of eukaryotes is organized into chromosomes within the nucleus.

41. **(B)** Inorganic cofactors are small non-protein molecules that promote proper enzyme catalysis. These molecules may bind to the active site or to the substrate itself. The most common inorganic cofactors are metallic atoms such as iron, copper, and zinc.

42. **(E)** Environmental conditions such as heat or acidity inhibit enzymatic reactions by changing the shape of the active site and rendering the enzyme ineffective. Certain chemicals inhibit enzymatic reactions by changing the shape of the enzyme's active site. If there is a lack of substrate, the enzyme will have no substance to affect. Thus, a large amount of enzyme is the only factor that will not inhibit enzymatic reactions.

43. **(D)** A ketone group has a double bond between oxygen and a carbon atom that is imbedded within a carbon chain.

44. **(A)** An alcohol group has a hydroxide group (OH) with the second bond from oxygen going to a carbon atom.

45. **(C)** An ester group is an ether with an additional double bond to an oxygen from an adjacent carbon.

46. **(B)** An aldehyde group has a double bond between an oxygen atom and a carbon that is one end of a carbon chain, or not otherwise bonded to any other carbons.

47. **(E)** The process of photosynthesis is the crucial reaction that converts the light energy of the Sun into chemical energy that is usable by living things.

48. **(B)** Entropy is defined as the new state variable that describes the increase of disorder in a system. Stated positively, it describes the amount of increase in the statistical disorder of a physical system.

49. **(C)** The development of photosynthetic cells took place before the development of eukaryotes. The first photosynthetic cells were prokaryotic.

50. **(A)** Energy flows through the entire ecosystem in one direction—from producers to consumers and on to decomposers through the food chain.

51. **(B)** The eclipse must be a solar eclipse because the Moon is between the Earth and the Sun. The solar eclipse is total because the Moon's disk covers the Sun from our view completely. Parallax has to do with the apparent displacement of a celestial object.

52. **(C)** The celestial poles are extensions of Earth's north and south geographic poles up into the sky. The celestial equator identifies the projection of Earth's equator. The zenith is the point directly overhead above an observer. The ecliptic is the line that describes the Sun's orbit across the celestial sphere. The zodiac is the name for the annual cycle of twelve stations along the ecliptic that the sun and planets travel along the celestial sphere.

53. **(D)** Cellular respiration is the process that releases energy for use by the cell. There are several steps involved in cellular respiration, some require oxygen (aerobic) and some do not (anaerobic).

54. **(A)** When tRNA anticodons line up with corresponding mRNA codons, it is the last step in the transcription process before translation begins. Translation begins as a ribosome attaches to the mRNA strand at a particular codon known as the start codon. This codon is only recognized by a particular initiator tRNA. The ribosome continues to add tRNA whose anticodons complement the next codon on the mRNA string. A third type of RNA is utilized at this point, ribosomal RNA or rRNA. Ribosomal RNA exists in concert with enzymes as a ribosome. In order for the tRNA and mRNA to link up, enzymes connected to rRNA at the ribosome must be utilized. Ribosomal enzymes also are responsible for linking the sequential amino acids into a protein chain. As the protein chain is forming, the rRNA moves along the sequence, adding the amino acids that are designated by the codons on the mRNA. At the end of the translation process, a terminating codon stops the synthesis process, and the protein is released.

55. **(A)** The most likely sequence leading to human evolution begins with coacervates, then eukaryotes, plants, fish, amphibians, mammals, primates, and, finally, man.

56. **(A)** The hydrogen atoms in water molecules have a partial positive charge, while the oxygen atoms in water have a partial negative charge, causing polarity. This polarity allows the oxygen of one water molecule to attract the hydrogen of another. The partial charges attract other opposite partial charges of other water molecules allowing for weak (hydrogen) bonds between the molecules. Inert means non-reactive; it does not explain the attraction between H and O. There are no ionic bonds within water molecules, only covalent bonds. A crystal structure forms in ice because of the attraction of hydrogen bonds; the crystal structure does not cause the attraction. Brownian motion is the random movement of atoms or particles caused by collisions between them; it does not explain attraction between atoms or molecules.

57. **(A)** Using Ohm's law, $V = IR$, we solve for $I = V / R$ with $V = 12$ V and $R = 8$ ohms. $I = 12.0$ V $/ 8.0$ ohms $= 1.5$ V $/$ ohm $= 1.5$ A. The other answers are results of erroneous calculations or misapplications of Ohm's law.

58. **(D)** Earth is approximately 70 percent water. Most of the water is in the oceans. Land makes up the remaining 30 percent.

59. **(A)** Traits, such as height and skin color, are produced from the expression of more than one set of genes and are known as polygenic traits.

60. **(B)** Evolution is driven by the process of natural selection, a feature of population genetics first popularized by Charles Darwin in his book *The Origin of Species* (published in 1859).

61. **(D)** The horn is not a simple machine. Simple machines are mechanical devices that alter the magnitude and direction of a force. They are represented by the following six objects: 1) lever, 2) wheel and axle, 3) pulley, 4) inclined plane, 5) pulley, and 6) screw. On a bike, the tire is a type of wheel. The pedal mechanism is a wheel and axle as well as a gear mechanism (two simple machines). The rear wheel gear mechanism is obviously one of the simple machines. The kickstand is a lever.

62. **(C)** Since nitrogen is in the second row, its highest energy electron is at $n = 2$, which is the first number. The second number signifies that its outer electron is in a p-orbital. The third number indicates the third p-orbital to receive an electron, since nitrogen is the third element in the p-block in the periodic table. The last number is the magnetic spin quantum number and signifies that the highest energy electron is the only electron in the orbital.

63. **(B)** Although there is a transition from one state of matter to another, there is no term "transition phase" to describe this process. The term *fission* is used in nuclear physics to describe the breaking apart of nuclear particles. It

is not used to describe changes of state of matter. Specific heat is the amount of energy in calories required to raise one gram of a substance by 1°C. Equilibrium is the state of a system or body at rest or lacking acceleration which results when all the forces acting upon it are equal to zero and the sum of all of the torques equals zero. In chemistry, it is the state of a reaction when all the products and reactants are balanced.

64. **(E)** A simple cubic crystal is the only unit cell mentioned that has, on average, one atom per unit cell. A simple cubic unit cell has one atom in each of the eight corners of the unit cell, but only one-eighth of each of those atoms is ascribed to that particular unit cell. A face-centered unit cell has four atoms per unit cell; while a body-centered unit cell has two atoms per unit cell.

65. **(E)** The alimentary canal is also known as the gastrointestinal (GI) tract and includes the mouth, pharynx, esophagus, stomach, small intestine, and large intestine.

66. **(D)** Proteins are catalysts in the laboratory, so the formation of proteins in the laboratory under conditions presumed to be representative of early earth history is key evidence of the evolution of life on earth. Stanley Miller provided support for Oparin's hypotheses in experiments in which he succeeded in producing amino acids by exposing simple inorganic molecules to electrical charges similar to lightning. Sidney Fox conducted experiments that proved ultraviolet light may induce the formation of dipeptides from amino acids. He also showed that polyphosphoric acid could increase the yield of these polymers, a process that simulates the modern role of ATP in protein synthesis. Researcher Cyril Ponnamperuma demonstrated that small amounts of guanine formed from the thermal polymerization of amino acids.

67. **(C)** This is known as incomplete dominance. Neither white nor red is dominant over the other.

68. **(B)** RW is a symbol for genotype. In this case, the RW genotype produces a pink phenotype. R and W represent the alleles for red and white, respectively.

69. **(B)** Both parents have two alleles that are the same, thus they have homozygous genotypes for color.

70. **(D)** While (A), (B), and (C) could have been true, a red snapdragon could have been produced by any of those choices. However, a white snapdragon cannot produce a red snapdragon as an offspring even if paired with a red snapdragon.

71. **(E)**   If two of the heterozygous offspring of an incomplete dominant trait are bred, the Punnett square would be

	R	W
R	RR	RW
W	RW	WW

The phenotypic ratio of the offspring then is one-fourth red, one-half pink, and one-fourth white, a 1:2:1 ratio—1 red: 2 pink: 1 white.

72. **(D)**   A habitat refers to the physical place where an organism lives. A species' habitat must include all the factors that will support its life and repro- duction.

73. **(A)**   Nickel has an unpaired electron in its d-orbital, which induces a magnetic field and causes it to be attracted to another magnetic field. Zinc chloride does not have such an unpaired electron and is not attracted to a magnet.

74. **(C)**   The heat absorbed by the water equals the mass of the water mul- tiplied by the specific heat of water times the increase in temperature change. The 840 J added to the water is enough heat to raise the temperature of 20 g of water by 10°C.

75. **(B)**   A light-year is a distance, not a speed or velocity. It is also not a time measurement. A light-year represents the measurement of the distance to one celestial body from another celestial body, measured as a multiple or frac- tion of the distance light travels in one year. It is equal to $(3.0 \times 10^8$ m/s$)(3.6 \times 10^3$ s/hr$)(2.4 \times 10^1$ hr/day$)(3.65 \times 10^2$ days/yr$)(1$ yr$) = 95 \times 10^{14}$ m $= 9.5 \times 10^{15}$ m $= 9.5 \times 10^{12}$ km $= 9,500,000,000,000$ km or 9.5 trillion kilometers.

76. **(D)**   Since the half-life of C 14 is 5,730 years, that means it takes 5,730 years for half the C 14 to decay to C 12. Since the end sample has ¼ C 12, we see that two half-life periods would have occurred. The first would have decayed the sample to half of each type, and the second time period would degrade the half sample to a quarter sample. Two half-life periods is a total of 11,460 years.

77. **(D)**   An example of igneous rock is granite. Marble is a metamorphic rock, while limestone, cement, and sandstone are all sedimentary rocks.

78. **(B)** Although it appears that galaxies are moving apart, Hubble's law explains that this apparent motion is the expansion of the space between them, not the motion of the galaxies themselves. Hubble's law states that the redshift in light coming from a distant galaxy is directly and linearly proportional to its distance from Earth.

79. **(D)** There is no epistematic region in plant roots. Roots have four major structural regions that run vertically from bottom to top. The root cap is composed of dead, thick-walled cells and covers the tip of the root, protecting it as the root pushes through soil. The meristematic region is just above the root cap. It consists of undifferentiated cells that undergo mitosis, providing the cells that grow to form the elongation region. In the elongation region, cells differentiate, large vacuoles are formed, and cells grow. As the cells differentiate into various root tissues, they become part of the maturation region.

80. **(B)** Gregor Mendel determined that one gene is sometimes dominant over another gene for the same trait (i.e., it expressed itself over the other). This is known as the law of dominance, Mendel's second law of inheritance.

81. **(B)** Electrons have very small mass, much less than either protons or neutrons. They are found orbiting in a cloud surrounding the nucleus. Electrons are negatively charged. An ion is an atom with a greater or fewer number of electrons than the standard atom for the element, causing a charge of positive or negative due to the unequal number of protons and electrons. An atom's valence number is the number of electrons in its highest (not lowest) energy level.

82. **(B)** Astrophysicists speculate that just 1/100 of a second after the big bang, the entire universe was filled with elementary particles (i.e., electrons, protons, positrons, nutrinos, photons, etc.). At 1 second, the temperature was 10^{10} K, which was still too hot for neutrons and protons to stay together in the nuclei by the strong nuclear force. After about 3 minutes, it had cooled to about 10^9 K. Electrons and positrons were annihilated, generating photons, neutrinos, anti-neutrinos, and a small number of neutrons and protons. The universe was now as hot and dense as the core of a star undergoing nuclear fusion. However, it wasn't until 300,000 years later that the nuclei could hold on to the electrons, clearing the vast fog. The process then continued to cool, coalesce, and expand through fusion, forming stars and galaxies in the visible universe. Fission does not occur until much later in stellar evolution. Spontaneous generation, disproven by Pasteur, has nothing to do with the evolution of stars. Combustion is common in various exothermic processes in a general way. Stellar explosions indicative of the latter stages of stellar evolution generally occur toward the end of a star's life, not at the origination.

83. **(A)** The answer is that entropy increases as a natural process goes from one equilibrium state to another. This is the only direction that heat flow will go in an irreversible process.

84. **(D)** Using Ohm's law, $V = IR$, solve for $R = V / I$ with $V = 120$ V and $I = 10$ A. $R = 120$ V $/ 10$ A $= 12$ V $/$ A or 12 ohms. All of the other answers are results of erroneous calculations or misapplications of Ohm's law.

85. **(B)** Stomata are openings in the leaf surface that allow for exchange of water and gases.

86. **(C)** The individual we recognize as an adult fern is actually the mature sporophyte.

87. **(A)** Hydrogen gas is the least polar because it is bonded to itself as a di-atomic molecule. Therefore, there is no difference in electronegativity between the two atoms in the bond, and it is entirely nonpolar.

88. **(E)** Both a gas and plasma have no defined shape or volume. A solid has a definite shape and volume. A liquid holds the shape of its container and thus has a definite volume. A plastic is not a state of matter and is confused with the fourth state of matter, plasma.

89. **(B)** Conditions such as temperature, pH, water balance, and sugar levels must be monitored and controlled in order to keep them within the accepted ranges that will not inhibit life. Cells and living organisms have homeostatic mechanisms that serve to keep body conditions within normal ranges.

90. **(B)** The cerebrum controls sensory and motor responses, memory, speech, and intelligence factors. It does not control involuntary muscles.

91. **(C)** Fog consists of a visible collection of minute water droplets suspended in the atmosphere near the Earth's surface. It occurs when atmospheric humidity combines with a warm layer of air that is transported over a cold body of water or land surface.

92. **(E)** Due to the high specific heat capacity of water, land surfaces will heat up more rapidly than water surfaces. Since warmer air is less dense than cooler air, this uneven heating along coastal areas causes vertical expansion of the isobaric field over the land and compression of the field over the water. This forms an elevated area of high pressure over the land and an elevated area of low pressure over the water. The pressure gradient force acts on the air

and moves it from higher pressure to lower pressure. The net movement of air toward the low pressure aloft induces an area of high pressure on the water surface, while the net movement of air away from the high pressure aloft induces an area of low pressure on the land surface. The pressure gradient force now begins to move the surface air from the higher pressure on the water surface towards the lower pressure on the land surface. It is this surface flow of air that is the sea (or lake) breeze. The greater the contrast is between water temperature and land temperature, the stronger the breeze. At night, the land will cool faster than the adjacent water, reversing the process and forming a land breeze from the land towards the water.

93. **(D)**   The electrical properties of cardiac muscle tissue cause the beating of the heart muscle that results in the pumping of blood through the body.

94. **(C)**   Ingested food does not pass through the salivary glands. The saliva secreted from these glands enters the digestive tract and helps digest the food.

95. **(C)**   Carrying capacity (designated by K) is the number of organisms that can be supported within a particular ecosystem.

96. **(D)**   Quarks, bosons, neutrinos, and positrons are all subatomic particles. An electron is an atomic particle that represents the negatively charged part of an atom.

97. **(A)**   Digestive enzymes are released by the pancreas and gall bladder into the small intestine.

98. **(A)**   Insects have spiracles that allow for gas exchange.

99. **(A)**   Over 70 percent of Earth's surface is covered by water. The great majority of Earth's photosynthesis takes place near the surface of the oceans with 70 percent of the entire amount of it taking place in the euphotic zone to a depth of 100 m. Many people mistakenly think that the tropical rainforests and deciduous forests are responsible for most of the production of oxygen during photosynthesis, but this is not so. The tundra and deserts are even more obviously incorrect because the amount of plant life in these biomes is very sparse.

100. **(C)**   A replacement reaction occurs when a compound is broken down into its components and recombined with another reactant—as shown by the equation $AB + C \rightarrow AC + B$. The reaction $A + B \rightarrow AB$ represents a combination reaction; $AB \rightarrow A + B$ and $AB + CD \rightarrow A + B + C + D$ are both decomposition reactions; and $A + C \rightarrow AC + B$ is not a possible reaction since it is not

with the first law of thermodynamics, which states that matter cannot be created or destroyed in a chemical reaction. Since B was not a reactant, it cannot be a product.

101. **(D)** Ecology is literally "the study of" (ology) a "place to live" (eco).

102. **(E)** Each species is a distinct group of individuals that are able to mate and produce viable offspring.

103. **(B)** Einstein's energy equation, $E = mc^2$, is based on the premise that the speed of light for all observers is constant, and that energy is directly proportional to mass. As energy increases, so does its mass. The speed of light is considered constant; the mass and energy values must increase or decrease directly and proportionately.

104. **(D)** Plants that produce their own food through photosynthesis are known as autotrophs. (Mushrooms are fungi; they do not produce their own food.)

105. **(A)** The speed of light is the same in all directions. In a vacuum, the speed of light remains constant. The speed of light in a liquid is slower than in air. The speed of light is the same on the moon as it is on the Earth.

106. **(B)** The principle of supererogation is completely fictitious, so this is the correct answer. The principle of original horizontality states that if rock layers are not laid horizontally, then something forced the structures to move. The principle of lateral continuity means that sediments are originally deposited in layers that extend laterally in all directions and eventually thin out. The principle of fossil succession says that if rocks are undisturbed, the oldest layers of rock should be on the bottom and will have older fossils in them. The principle of uniformitarianism states that present geological events explain former ones. It is popularly stated as the principle that "the present is the key to the past."

107. **(A)** A redshift in the electromagnetic spectrum of the light from a faraway star means that the star is moving away from the observer. In the 1920s, Edwin Hubble (1889–1953) observed that galaxies around the Milky Way were moving away from us because of this redshift, and those further away are moving away from us even more rapidly; it is not moving toward us. The redshift does not indicate that a star is ready to explode, is a dwarf star, or is a giant nova.

108. **(C)** These eras are parts of the Phanerozoic Eon and represent the past 570 million years. Cenozoic represents "recent life," Mesozoic represents

"middle life," and Paleozoic represents "old life." There were complex life-forms during all three of these eras.

109. **(A)**   Parasitism is symbiosis in which one species benefits, but the other is harmed.

110. **(B)**   An axis is defined as a line connecting two poles. Earth has an axis connecting the North Pole and the South Pole. The other choices are incorrect.

111. **(D)**   There are estimated to be about 100 billion stars in the universe. To count to a billion, if a person counted one number per second, it would take over 34 years. To then count to 100 billion would take $34 \times 100 = 3,400$ years! In other words, a billion is a huge number.

112. **(B)**   The astronaut will feel as if he is being pushed forward toward the front of the spacecraft. The others are incorrect directions of motion. There is a negative acceleration (deceleration) and thus a negative force occurring since the vehicle is slowing down.

113. **(C)**   Blue-green algae is a prokaryotic organism in the Kingdom Monera. Prokaryotes have no nucleus-or-membrane-bound organelles.

114. **(B)**   The celestial sphere is an imaginary sphere centered on and surrounding Earth upon which the background stars are projected. The sun, moon, planets, and other celestial bodies seem to move relative to this background of fixed stars. It is a model used to describe positions and motions of astronomical bodies. A geodesic dome is not an astronomical tool, but is simply an architectural structure. A stellar ball is a made-up term. The Cartesian coordinate system is a mathematical system used to plot points on an x-y graph. The equatorial coordinate system is another mathematical system used to plot specific celestial bodies in the sky using time and angular coordinates of right ascension and declination. It relates the stars to their apparent motion in the sky along the celestial sphere relative to the celestial equator. It is used to make measurements within the celestial sphere, but is not actually the sphere itself.

115. **(B)**   The "greenhouse effect" is the result of radiation being blocked from leaving the atmosphere because of the ozone layer. Depletion of the ozone layer would impact the "greenhouse effect," not cause it. The "greenhouse effect" is also caused mainly by other atmospheric gases such as water vapor and carbon dioxide. This depletion will increase radiation because the hole in the ozone layer will get larger. Acid rain is primarily caused by oxides of sulfur and nitrogen due to pollution. Photochemical reactions involving oxides of nitrogen and chloro-

fluorocarbons play a major role in ozone destruction. These chemicals react with ozone and lead to a net decrease in ozone concentration in the stratosphere. Since ozone is a strong absorber of incoming ultraviolet (UV) radiation, any decrease in ozone concentration will increase the amount of UV radiation reaching the surface. This will increase the risk of skin cancer from exposure to the sun significantly. With this in mind, it is easy so see why (D) is incorrect. However, the ozone depletion has no impact on global warming directly.

116. **(C)**   The pressure gradient force plays no significant role in vertical air circulations. Since temperature decreases with height, as the valley air warms during the day, it becomes less dense than the air along the adjacent hillsides and begins to flow up the surrounding slopes. At night, air in the hills cools faster than the air in the valleys. Gravity pulls the cooler, denser air down the hillsides into the valleys. It is low pressure near the top of the mountain that forces breezes up from the valley, so (E) is wrong.

117. **(A)**   Only the size of the atom increases as you move down and to the left in the periodic table.

118. **(C)**   The greater the force necessary to change its state of motion. Newton's first law of motion states that an object in motion will stay in motion and an object at rest will stay at rest until acted upon by an outside force. Since Newton's second law of motion states that Force = (mass)(acceleration), then in order to change its motion, as the object increases in mass, more force will be necessary to alter its acceleration. Its position may be changed slightly with the same amount of force as might be applied to a smaller object, so changing its position is not the correct answer. Greater force may not change its shape at all, and will not change its density.

119. **(A)**   The top of the sine wave is the crest. The bottom is the trough. The amplitude represents the height of the wave. The period is the wave's cycle length. The frequency is the number of cycles per second.

120. **(D)**   The water molecules, which are the medium, are not carried, but the wave peaks do move toward shore. Answer (A) erroneously states the opposite of what is mentioned in the question. Although the ocean is somewhat mixed each day, this mixing is due to turbulence and currents, not waves. Similarly, debris washes ashore by turbulence and currents and not wave action. Waves also do not move swimmers, nor water; the waves travel through the water and the swimmer will bob up and down but will not be carried by the wave. Again, currents and turbulence are responsible for moving both the water and swimmers.

Practice Test 2

CLEP Natural Sciences

This test is also on CD-ROM in our special interactive
CLEP Natural Sciences TestWare®

(Answer sheets appear in the back of this book.)

TIME: 90 Minutes
120 Questions

DIRECTIONS: Each of the following group of questions consists
of five lettered terms followed by a list of numbered phrases or
sentences. For each numbered phrase or sentence, select the one
choice that is most clearly related to it. Each choice may be used
once, more than once, or not at all.

Questions 1-5 _____

(A) Ordovician

(D) Silurian

(B) Cambrian

(E) Permian

(C) Precambrian

_____ 1. Fossilized exoskeletons, explosion of evolution into multitudes of
phyla

_____ 2. Fossilized burrows indicate development of multicellular animals
with only soft parts

_____ 3. Mass extinctions followed by diversification of species that survived
extinctions

_____ 4. Development of land plants

_____ 5. New species developed through adaptive radiation

Questions 6–10 _____

    (A) Primary oocytes

    (B) Cleavage

    (C) Secondary spermatocytes

    (D) Oogenesis

    (E) Polar body

_____   6. Present in reproductive organs at birth

_____   7. Division of the zygote into multiple cells

_____   8. Haploid cells that will develop into male gametes

_____   9. Infertile cell resulting from meiosis II in females

_____   10. Develop into spermatid

Questions 11–14 _____

    (A) Alpha decay   (D) Neutron capture

    (B) Beta (β-) decay   (E) Gamma radiation

    (C) Positron decay

_____   11. The nuclear reaction that turns a proton into a neutron

_____   12. The emission of very high energy photons

_____   13. The nuclear reaction that gives off the nucleus of a helium atom

_____   14. The nuclear reaction that turns a neutron into a proton

Questions 15–18 _____

    (A) $Ag^+ + I^- \rightarrow AgI$

    (B) $HC_2H_3O_2 + OH^- \rightarrow C_2H_3O_2^- + H_2O$

    (C) $NaCl\ (l) \rightarrow Na\ (l) + Cl_2\ (g)$

    (D) $Mg + O_2 \rightarrow MgO$

    (E) $Fe_2^+ + 8H^+ + MnO_4^- \rightarrow Fe^{3+} + Mn^{2+} + 4H_2O$

_____ 15. Two electrons are transferred in this reaction.

_____ 16. This reaction results in a basic solution.

_____ 17. This reaction yields a cloudy product.

_____ 18. This reaction takes place in an electrolytic cell with the input of electrical energy.

Questions 19–23 _____

    (A) Limiting factors   (D) Density

    (B) Law of minimums   (E) Law of tolerance

    (C) Homeostasis

_____ 19. Biotic and abiotic influences that cause a disturbance in an ecosystem that affects the population growth rate

_____ 20. Dynamic balance achieved within an ecosystem functioning at its optimum level

_____ 21. The tendency for the resource in shortest supply to limit the population growth

_____ 22. Population growth is limited by having more of a substance than is required

_____ 23. Number of organisms per area

DIRECTIONS: Each of the questions or incomplete statements below is followed by five possible answers or completions. Select the best choice in each case and fill in the corresponding oval on the answer sheet.

24. Which of the following is within the phylum Chordata?

    (A) Crabs   (D) Mollusks

    (B) Flat worms   (E) Perch

    (C) Nematodes

25. Which of the following organs does NOT function as an organ of the immune system to defend the body from infection?

    (A) Tonsils

    (B) Lymph nodes

    (C) Spinal cord

    (D) Spleen

    (E) Thymus

26. Which of the following is NOT included in Oparin's hypothesis?

    (A) H_2O existed only in the form of ice.

    (B) The young Earth had very little oxygen present in the atmosphere.

    (C) The Earth is more than four billion years old.

    (D) Heat energy was abundantly available because of the Earth's cooling.

    (E) Large organic molecules capable of dividing and absorption (co-acervates) became plentiful resulting in eventual evolution of early life.

27. Both London, England, and Hudson Bay, Canada, are on the same north latitude, yet London's winters average 35°F warmer. What could account for this difference?

    (A) England is an island.

    (B) The waters of the Gulf Stream wash the English coast.

    (C) Latitude is not a factor in determining temperature.

(D) Warm winds from France moderate the weather in England.

(E) The waters of the Gulf Stream wash the Canadian coast.

28. Which of the following is a true statement regarding fundamental atomic particles?

(A) There are five different types of quarks.

(B) Each quark is called a *flavor*.

(C) The five flavors of quarks are *up*, *down*, *strange*, *ceiling*, and *floor*.

(D) The basic combination structure of three quarks for a proton is one *up* quark, one *down* quark, and one *strange* quark.

(E) The structure of the atom is nearly solved, since quarks are the most fundamental property that exists.

29. Which of the following best explains why solid copper is a strong conductor, but solid copper sulfate is NOT?

(A) The sulfate blocks the flow of electrons.

(B) The unpaired electrons in copper's outer shell allow electricity to flow through the atom.

(C) The d-level electrons in metallic bonds are delocalized.

(D) Any compound with sulfur would not conduct electricity.

(E) The copper is more diluted in copper sulfate.

30. Members of which of the following categories are most closely related?

(A) Phylum   (D) Class

(B) Genus   (E) Order

(C) Kingdom

31. After a forest fire, a meadow community develops and is later replaced by a temperate forest community. This process is called

(A) commensalism   (D) climaxing

(B) succession   (E) mutualism

(C) dynamic equilibrium

32. If the nucleus of an oxygen isotope (with 8 protons and 8 neutrons) was split exactly in two, what would the new element(s) consist of (neglect consideration of any energy that would be involved)?

   (A) Two oxygen atoms   (D) Two neon atoms

   (B) Two beryllium atoms   (E) One oxygen ion

   (C) Two helium atoms

33. Given the order of magnitude of the four fundamental forces, what is their order from weakest to strongest?

   (A) Gravity, strong nuclear, weak nuclear, electromagnetic

   (B) Gravity, weak nuclear, electromagnetic, strong nuclear

   (C) Strong nuclear, electromagnetic, weak nuclear, gravity

   (D) Strong nuclear, weak nuclear, gravity, electromagnetic

   (E) Electromagnetic, gravity, strong nuclear, weak nuclear

34. Which of the following kingdoms contains photosynthetic organisms?

   (A) Monera   (D) Fungi

   (B) Protista   (E) Chordata

   (C) Animalia

35. A cup of water is placed in a microwave. The timer is set for four minutes, which is plenty of time for it to come to a boil. A second cup is then placed in the same microwave containing a piece of a chocolate bar. It melts in less than a minute. The difference in the amount of time required to melt the chocolate versus boiling the water can be BEST explained by which physical characteristic?

   (A) ΔT

   (B) British thermal unit (Btu)

   (C) Specific heat

   (D) Kelvin temperature

   (E) Temperature inversion

36. Which layer of the atmosphere is closest to the surface of Earth?

    (A) Exosphere   (D) Stratosphere

    (B) Thermosphere   (E) Troposphere

    (C) Mesosphere

37. Thermodynamics deals with the study of which of the following systems which can be observed and measured in experiments?

    (A) Large scale response

    (B) Small scale response

    (C) Small scale and large scale responses

    (D) Flow between small scale and large scale responses

    (E) Large scale to small scale responses

38. Which of the following cell organelles is known as the cell's "power-house" because it produces energy for the cell's use?

    (A) Nucleus

    (B) Mitochondrion

    (C) Smooth endoplasmic reticulum

    (D) Ribosome

    (E) Cell membrane

39. Which of the following factors exerts the most influence over limiting cell size?

    (A) A rigid cell wall

    (B) The ratio of surface area to volume of cytoplasm

    (C) Replication of mitochondria

    (D) The chemical composition of the cytoplasm

    (E) The chemical composition of the cell membrane

40.   The cause of Earth's magnetic field is

(A) enormous currents

(B) space satellites

(C) still a mystery from deep in Earth's core

(D) found in the Earth's crust

(E) huge amounts of iron, nickel, and cobalt

41.   Which of the following explains why a sound wave has a higher pitch than the original source?

(A) The source is standing still.

(B) The source is moving forward.

(C) The source is moving away.

(D) The source is going up and down.

(E) The source has a higher amplitude than the resultant wave.

42.   When water pressure is equal inside and outside the cell, it is said to be

(A) hydrostatic

(B) diffuse

(C) isohydri

(D) isotonic

(E) hydrophobic

43.   When astronauts sleep aboard the space shuttle, they strap themselves to a wall or a bunk. If one of the thruster rockets were fired, resulting in a change of shuttle velocity and acceleration, any unstrapped sleeping astronaut would be injured by slamming into a shuttle wall. The sleeping astronauts would need to be strapped down because

(A) their bodies have inertia

(B) gravity is not strong enough to keep them from touching their beds

(C) the body functions need to be constantly monitored

(D) astronauts cannot sleep while floating in free space

(E) their bodies need a reaction force

44. Which of the following organelles is found in plants only and help provide rigidity to cells?

   (A) Microtubules

   (B) Cell walls

   (C) Microfilaments

   (D) Centrioles

   (E) Mitochondria

45. Which of the following statements about enzymes is NOT true?

   (A) High temperatures destroy most enzymes.

   (B) Enzymes only function within living things.

   (C) An enzyme is unaffected by the reactions it catalyzes, so it can be used over and over again.

   (D) Enzymes are usually very specific to certain reactions.

   (E) Some enzymes contain a non-protein component that is essential to their function.

46. Which of the following pairs of matter and antimatter are related correctly?

   (A) Proton and antiproton

   (B) Electron and antielectron

   (C) Neutron and neutrino

   (D) Positron and negitron

   (E) Neutrino and quark

47. The astronomical unit or AU is

   (A) the radius of the Moon

   (B) the average distance of Earth from the Sun

   (C) the force that the Sun exerts on a planet

   (D) a recently discovered satellite of Jupiter

   (E) a quantum measurement of the energy released by a falling asteroid

48. Scurvy is a disease caused by a lack of Vitamin C, in which the body is unable to build enough collagen (a major component of connective tissue). The most plausible explanation for this malfunction is

    (A) Vitamin C is an amino acid component of collagen

    (B) Vitamin C is a coenzyme required in the synthesis of collagen

    (C) Vitamin C destroys collagen

    (D) Vitamin C is produced by collagen

    (E) Vitamin C is not related to collagen

49. An ion that attaches to an enzyme to become better able to catalyze a reaction is known as

    (A) a protein   (D) a prosthetic group

    (B) an inorganic cofactor   (E) a vitamin

    (C) a coenzyme

50. When a stream full of sediments flows out of a narrow mountain canyon and widens into a stream channel, losing velocity and forming large fan-shaped deposits, it is called a(n)

    (A) delta   (D) topset bed

    (B) tributary   (E) meandering stream

    (C) alluvial fan

51. A thermodynamic process that does not involve heat transfer is called a(n)

    (A) equilibrium process   (D) cooled-state process

    (B) net-sum process   (E) steady-state process

    (C) adiabatic process

52. Monotremes are mammals that lay eggs. The feature of egg laying in this case most likely suggests

    (A) a common ancestry with birds

    (B) a convergent evolution of analogous traits

(C) a common ancestry with reptiles

(D) an evolution of homologous traits

(E) a mutational trait

53. Which of the following gases would be expected to show the greatest deviation from ideal behavior?

(A) H_2 (D) O_2

(B) H_2S (E) CH_4

(C) H_2O

54. If you were aboard a spacecraft that is traveling away from Earth at 9.8 m/s^2, you would feel the same force as if you were standing on Earth's surface. This is a representation of

(A) Einstein's equivalence principle

(B) a total inaccuracy

(C) the results of the Michelson-Morley experiment

(D) the relationships associated with light, mass, and energy in Einstein's general theory of relativity

(E) the Doppler effect

55. The synthesis of ATP molecules to store energy is an example of

(A) anabolism   (D) lysis

(B) catabolism   (E) inhibition

(C) enzyme response

56. Energy transformations that occur as chemicals are broken apart or synthesized within the cell are collectively known as

(A) catabolism   (D) synthesis

(B) anabolism   (E) lysis

(C) metabolism

57. Archimedes' principle says that an object is buoyed up by a force that is equal to the

    (A) weight of the fluid displaced

    (B) volume of the fluid displaced

    (C) mass of the fluid displaced

    (D) mass of the object

    (E) inverse squared of the density of the fluid

58. When determining the molar volume of a gas by collecting the gas over water, which of the following laws must be considered to take into account the pressure exerted by water vapor in the collection bottle?

    (A) Boyle's law   (D) Henry's law

    (B) Charles's law   (E) Pascal's law

    (C) Dalton's law

59. Which of the following is NOT true of an electromagnet?

    (A) When electricity flows through a wire, the wire becomes a magnet.

    (B) An electromagnet is a permanent magnet.

    (C) The strength of an electromagnet is limited and cannot be increased easily.

    (D) Both (B) and (C)

    (E) (A), (B), and (C)

60. Two-thirds of all known active volcanoes have occurred in the

    (A) Atlantic Ocean   (D) Baltic Sea

    (B) Pacific Ocean   (E) Indian Ocean

    (C) Gulf of Mexico

61. Which of the following types of waves are longitudinal?

    (A) The direct wave and the reflected wave from a radio station

    (B) P-waves from an earthquake

    (C) Electromagnetic (EM) waves in a vacuum

(D) Gravitation waves on a dwarf star

(E) Ocean waves

62. A solid object with a specific gravity greater than 1 will typically do which of the following, based on this parameter alone?

(A) Sink in liquid water

(B) Float in liquid water

(C) Completely and immediately dissolve in liquid water

(D) Increase the temperature of the water

(E) Mix evenly and stay mixed in liquid water

63. The continuous cycle of the alternating rise and fall of the sea level, observed along the coastlines and bodies of water connected to the sea, is called

(A) the tide

(B) moon exercises

(C) sun exercises

(D) a tidal wave

(E) a tsunami

Questions 64–68

In this illustration "T" stands for tall and "t" for short.

	T	T
t	Tt	Tt
t	Tt	Tt

64. The illustration above is called

(A) a Mendelian diagram

(B) a genotype

(C) a phenotype

(D) a phenogram

(E) a Punnett square

65.   What is the genotype of each of the parents?

(A) TT and tt   (D) tt

(B) Tt   (E) Tt and TT

(C) TT

66.   The gametes for this cross will have which possible genes?

(A) T, T   (D) t, t

(B) T, t   (E) XY

(C) TT, tt

67.   What will be the phenotypic ratios of the offspring in this cross?

(A) 4 tall: 0 short   (D) 3 Tt: 1 tt

(B) 2 tall: 2 short   (E) XY

(C) 4 Tt: 0 tt

68.   If two of the offspring are crossed, what will the phenotypic ratio of the next generation be?

(A) 4 Tt: 0tt   (D) 3 tall: 1 short

(B) 1 tt: 2 Tt; 1 TT   (E) XY

(C) 4 tall: 0 short

69.   Suppose you are in a spacecraft that is flying through space at a speed that makes the clocks on board seem, as seen from Earth, like they are going half as fast from their point of reference. You measure a friend's mass on Earth and your own before you leave as 70 kg. Assuming you did not gain or lose any mass, what will your mass be on board the spacecraft?

(A) 35 kg

(B) 70 kg

(C) 140 kg

(D) 210 kg

(E) 420 kg

70. The parallax of a star is

    (A) its temperature divided by its mass

    (B) its mass divided by its temperature

    (C) the angle through which the star appears to move in the course of half a year

    (D) the angle through which the star appears to move in the course of a year

    (E) the luminosity of the star in angstrom units

71. Which kingdom has members that were most likely to have evolved earlier than members of any other kingdom?

    (A) Kingdom Protista   (D) Kingdom Animalia

    (B) Kingdom Plantae   (E) Kingdom Fungi

    (C) Kingdom Monera

72. In mechanics, there are three fundamental quantities that can be measured. All mechanical measurements can be reduced to a combination of these three quantities. What are they?

    (A) Weights, distances, and motions

    (B) Solids, liquids, and gasses

    (C) Heights, lengths, and widths

    (D) Length, mass, and time

    (E) Space, time, and matter

73. Which of the following demonstrates the highest melting point?

    (A) Hydrogen gas

    (B) Butane

    (C) KI

    (D) SiC

    (E) H_2O

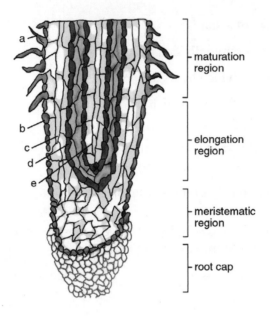

Root Cross-section

Questions 74–78 _____

Match the tissue type (all are types of primary root tissue) labeled a–e on the diagram (and corresponding to answer choices A–E), with the correct name given in the following five numbered questions.

(A) a   (D) d

(B) b   (E) e

(C) c

_____ 74. Vascular cylinder

_____ 75. Epidermis

_____ 76. Root hairs

_____ 77. Endodermis

_____ 78. Cortex

79. Astronomers call the visible surface of the sun the

    (A) photosphere   (D) flare

    (B) plasma   (E) corona

    (C) sunspot

80. The weight of an object depends on the

    (A) size of the object and its volume

    (B) mass of an object and its density

    (C) mass of an object and the gravitational force pulling on it

    (D) density of an object and the amount of force it exerts upward against gravity

    (E) type of material in the object and how much pressure is exerted on it

81. A bilayer of phospholipids with protein globules interspersed is characteristic of which of the following organelles?

    (A) Cell (or plasma) membrane

    (B) Mitochondria

    (C) Lysosome

    (D) Chromatin

    (E) Ribosome

82. As light from a star moves outward into space, its energy covers larger and larger areas. The brightness of the star decreases proportionately to the square of its distance from the source. This means that if the distance is quadrupled, the brightness will decrease by a factor of

    (A) 2   (D) 16

    (B) 4   (E) 32

    (C) 8

83. The iron-containing molecule that carries oxygen within red blood cells throughout the body via the circulatory system is the

    (A) lymphocyte   (D) hemoglobin

    (B) erythrocyte   (E) carbohydrate

    (C) gamma globulin

84. An unknown plant found in the forest has five petals on its flower and a tap root system. Which of the following is most likely true?

    (A) The stem has random arrangements of vascular bundles.

    (B) The plant's seed has only one cotyledon.

    (C) The leaves of the plant have parallel veins.

    (D) The leaves of the plant have networked veins.

    (E) The flowers have no seeds.

85. Which of the following is a characteristic of light?

    (A) Light behaves as a particle.

    (B) Light behaves as a wave.

    (C) Light speeds up and slows down as it moves through a medium.

    (D) Light moves in a medium called luminiferous ether.

    (E) Both (A) and (B) are correct.

86. Why do we see lightning before we hear thunder?

    (A) The lightning occurs closer than the thunder.

    (B) Lightning is composed of multiple strokes.

    (C) Thunder occurs higher in the clouds.

    (D) Because of the differences between the speeds of light and sound

    (E) Because the sound is slowed down by the liquid drops during the rainstorm associated with the event

87. Temporary movement of a species from one range to another, then back to the original range, is known as

    (A) immigration   (D) dispersion

    (B) migration   (E) removal

    (C) emigration

88. Given that a substance has a mass of 6.00 grams, an energy source raises
     the temperature by 2.345°C and transfers 12 calories of energy to it. If
     the substance does not melt, thaw, freeze, boil, or condense, what is its
     specific heat?

     (A) 2.0 cal/g/°C   (D) 2.56 cal/g/°C

     (B) 8.52 cal/g/°C   (E) .39 cal/g/°C

     (C) 1.17 cal/g/°C

89. You have just experienced weightless flight on a zero gravity plane,
     which travels in parabolic motion at approximately 600 miles per hour
     over the Atlantic Ocean. As the plane dives toward the Earth, you floated
     in the plane's fuselage. Inside the aircraft, you experienced the same ab-
     sence of gravity that an astronaut does who is flying in the space shuttle
     as it orbits Earth. This is a representation of

     (A) Einstein's equivalence principle

     (B) a total inaccuracy

     (C) the results of the Michelson-Morley experiment

     (D) the relationships associated with light, mass, and energy in Ein-
          stein's general theory of relativity

     (E) the relationships associated with velocity due to gravity in Ein-
          stein's special theory of relativity

90. How is the relative strength of a thunderstorm updraft estimated?

     (A) By the intensity of the lightning

     (B) By the height of the cloud base

     (C) By the speed of the wind gusts measured at the surface

     (D) By the size of the precipitation particles (raindrops or hailstones)

     (E) By the speed of the rain droplets as they fall to the surface

91. Plants reproduce through alternation in generations. The diploid genera-
     tion that produces male and female gametophytes is known as the

     (A) zygotic generation   (D) second generation

     (B) sporophyte generation   (E) first generation

     (C) gametophyte generation

92. Suppose that an isotope of carbon has 6 electrons and 6 neutrons. What is its approximate atomic mass?

(A) 6   (D) 24

(B) 12   (E) 36

(C) 18

93. Which of the following demonstrates the greatest increase between the atom's second and third ionization energies?

(A) He   (D) Al

(B) Na   (E) N

(C) Mg

94. A particular plant has individuals that are either male or female. A male individual of this plant may have all of the following EXCEPT

(A) a filament   (D) pollen grains

(B) an anther   (E) tube nuclei

(C) a stigma

95. Since galaxies, planets and stars are bound together by gravity, we don't expand locally even though the universe does. This is because gravity is reduced as the distances are squared. Since this is so, which of the following best explains what the universe is expanding into?

(A) No one knows because it is too big to see its boundaries.

(B) It appears that the farther we look out into the universe, the more "stuff" we see. There is no end to the matter in the universe.

(C) Most cosmologists are becoming convinced that the universe has a limit akin to that of a big sphere. It appears to be infinite because of the curve of space.

(D) Nothing. Since the universe is infinite, nothing exists outside of it. As it expands, it is still infinite, just bigger.

(E) The universe is in danger of expanding into a black hole that will eventually pull the entire universe into it.

96. Which of the following structural layers of the Earth is liquid?

    (A) crust   (D) lithosphere

    (B) mantle   (E) asthenosphere

    (C) core

97. The law of segregation states that

    (A) one gene is usually dominant over the other (expresses itself over the other)

    (B) genes are inherited via a process of multiple alleles

    (C) genes are separated in gamete formation and randomly brought to-gether in fertilization

    (D) gamete formation causes mutation in genetic material of both parents

    (E) mutation of genes is inevitable

98. What is the Celsius equivalent of 54.5°F?

    (A) 22.5°C   (D) 62.3°C

    (B) 12.5°C   (E) 45.0°C

    (C) 66.1°C

99. Two carbon rods are put into a solution of $CuSO_4$. The electrodes are connected to a power source, which is turned on for 10 minutes. Which of the following will occur?

    (A) The mass of the cathode will increase.

    (B) The mass of the anode will increase.

    (C) Neither electrodes will change in mass.

    (D) A gas will be produced at the cathode.

    (E) No gas will be produced at either electrode.

100. Which of the following are not involved in the immune system?

    (A) Antibodies   (D) Epithelial cells

    (B) Stem cells   (E) B cells

    (C) T cells

101. Diamondback rattlesnakes fill a niche in a chaparral biome. Which of the following characteristics does NOT directly contribute to the viability of the snake in its niche?

    (A) Pond water temperature

    (B) Population of hawks

    (C) Population of mice

    (D) Average daily temperature

    (E) Average yearly rainfall

102. To be considered a mineral, the substance must never have been a part of a living organism and must be found in

    (A) rock

    (B) ore

    (C) nature

    (D) sand

    (E) water

103. Which of the following is NOT a trait of an animal?

    (A) Animal cells have organized nuclei and membrane-bound organelles.

    (B) Animal cells do not have cell walls or plastids.

    (C) Animals are only capable of asexual reproduction.

    (D) Animals develop from embryonic stages.

    (E) Animals are heterotrophic (they do not produce their own food).

104. Plants and animals obtain usable nitrogen through the action of

    (A) respiration

    (B) nitrogen fixation by bacteria and lightning

    (C) nitrogen processing in the atmosphere

    (D) digestion

    (E) photosynthesis

105. Why does a cement floor feel cooler to the touch than a wooden floor?

(A) Because the cement floor never absorbs enough heat to reach room temperature.

(B) Because the heat conductivity of cement is higher than wood, heat flows more readily through your fingers.

(C) Because the heat conductivity of cement is higher than wood, heat flows more readily into your fingers.

(D) Because the heat conductivity of wood is higher than cement, heat flows more readily from your fingers.

(E) Because the heat conductivity of wood is higher than cement, heat flows more readily into your fingers.

106. As you move across a row in the periodic table, which of the following traits does NOT increase?

(A) Atomic radius   (D) Ionization energy

(B) Electronegativity   (E) Acidity of the oxides

(C) Electron affinity

107. If Star X appears to be 2.5 times as bright as Star Y, then the two stars differ in magnitude by

(A) 0   (D) 0.5

(B) 1   (E) 5

(C) 2.5

108. Which of the following is NOT a step in the carbon cycle?

(A) Carbon is taken in by plants and used to form carbohydrates through photosynthesis.

(B) Carbon is dissolved out of the air into ocean water, combined with calcium to form calcium carbonate, and used by mollusks to form their shells.

(C) Carbon is taken in by animal respiration and used to form carbohydrates.

(D) Detritus feeders return carbon to elemental form.

(E) Burning fossil fuels releases carbon dioxide into the atmosphere where it can be used by plants.

109. The stomach secretes all of the following EXCEPT

    (A) digestive enzymes   (D) acetic acid

    (B) hydrochloric acid   (E) mucous

    (C) gastric juices

110. Minerals are identified and classified by all of the following measurable physical properties EXCEPT for

    (A) firmness   (D) luster

    (B) cleavage   (E) color

    (C) fracture

111. The organelle of a cell that engages in both passive and active transport is the

    (A) rough endoplasmic reticulum

    (B) smooth endoplasmic reticulum

    (C) Golgi complex

    (D) cell wall

    (E) cell (plasma) membrane

112. The path of the Sun across the celestial sphere is called the

    (A) ecliptic   (D) solstice

    (B) celestial equator   (E) orbital path

    (C) equinox

113. Which of the following statements is true?

    (A) A niche only includes the physical features of an organism's habitat.

    (B) An organism's habitat must include all the biotic and abiotic factors that will support its life and reproduction.

    (C) A niche refers to the biotic features of an organism's habitat.

    (D) An organism's habitat includes only biotic factors such as weather, temperature, etc.

    (E) An organism's niche does not include its habitat.

114. Compare the bond angles in CH_4 versus XeF_4.

    (A) Both have the same bond angles.

    (B) CH_4 demonstrates 109.5°; XeF_4 demonstrates 90°.

    (C) CH_4 demonstrates 109.5°; XeF_4 demonstrates 120°.

    (D) CH_4 demonstrates 90°; XeF_4 demonstrates 120°.

    (E) CH_4 demonstrates 90°; XeF_4 demonstrates 109.5°.

115. It takes a certain amount of energy to change a sample of liquid to its gaseous state, if it is assumed that the substance can exist in both states. The quantity varies for different substances and is called the

    (A) heat of fusion   (D) heat of vaporization

    (B) heat index   (E) specific heat

    (C) heat wave constant

116. A pond ecosystem has sharp boundaries at the shorelines. The sharp boundary of an ecosystem is known as a(n)

    (A) closed community   (D) borderline

    (B) open community   (E) system

    (C) ecotone

117. The fossil of a fish skeleton is found in a limestone bed. The fish most likely belonged to the class

    (A) Chondrichthyes   (D) Aves

    (B) Reptilia   (E) Amphibia

    (C) Osteichthyes

118. Which one of the following statements about cells is NOT true?

    (A) All living things are made up of one or more cells.

    (B) Cells may be seen with a microscope.

    (C) Cells are the basic units of life.

    (D) All cells come from pre-existing cells.

    (E) All cells have cell walls.

119. When refraction occurs, part of a wave

    (A) is bent more than another part

    (B) slows down before another part

    (C) is pushed to one side

    (D) is closer together than it appears to be

    (E) reflects back to the source

120. A bottle with a message is tossed into the ocean off the shore of Siberia in the Sea of Okhotsk. Where can it be expected to wash ashore?

    (A) Australia

    (B) Western North America

    (C) The Sea of Japan

    (D) Eastern Mexico

    (E) Western South America

Practice Test 2

CLEP Natural Sciences

Answer Key

1. (B)	25. (C)	49. (D)	73. (D)	97. (C)
2. (C)	26. (A)	50. (C)	74. (E)	98. (B)
3. (A)	27. (B)	51. (C)	75. (B)	99. (A)
4. (A)	28. (B)	52. (B)	76. (A)	100. (D)
5. (D)	29. (C)	53. (B)	77. (D)	101. (A)
6. (A)	30. (B)	54. (A)	78. (C)	102. (C)
7. (B)	31. (B)	55. (A)	79. (A)	103. (C)
8. (C)	32. (B)	56. (C)	80. (C)	104. (B)
9. (E)	33. (C)	57. (A)	81. (A)	105. (B)
10. (C)	34. (B)	58. (C)	82. (D)	106. (A)
11. (C)	35. (C)	59. (D)	83. (D)	107. (B)
12. (E)	36. (E)	60. (B)	84. (D)	108. (A)
13. (A)	37. (A)	61. (B)	85. (E)	109. (D)
14. (B)	38. (B)	62. (A)	86. (D)	110. (A)
15. (D)	39. (B)	63. (A)	87. (B)	111. (E)
16. (B)	40. (C)	64. (E)	88. (B)	112. (A)
17. (A)	41. (B)	65. (A)	89. (A)	113. (B)
18. (C)	42. (D)	66. (B)	90. (D)	114. (B)
19. (A)	43. (A)	67. (A)	91. (B)	115. (D)
20. (C)	44. (B)	68. (D)	92. (B)	116. (C)
21. (B)	45. (B)	69. (B)	93. (C)	117. (C)
22. (E)	46. (A)	70. (C)	94. (C)	118. (E)
23. (D)	47. (B)	71. (C)	95. (D)	119. (B)
24. (E)	48. (B)	72. (D)	96. (C)	120. (B)

Detailed Explanations of Answers

Practice Test 2

1. **(B)** During the Cambrian period (the first period of the Paleozoic era), which began about 570 million years ago, the fossil record begins to show multicellular organisms with hard parts, namely exoskeletons. The fossil record at this time includes fossil representations from all modern-day (and some extinct) phyla. This sudden appearance of multitudes of differentiated animal forms is known as the Cambrian explosion.

2. **(C)** Fossilized burrows from multicellular organisms begin to appear in the geological record approximately 700 million years ago during the Precambrian period. These multicellular animals had only soft parts—no hard parts that could be fossilized.

3. **(A)** The Ordovician period was marked by vast extinctions followed by diversification among species that survived past the Cambrian extinctions.

4. **(A)** The Ordovician is also known for the development of land plants.

5. **(D)** Adaptive radiation is the mechanism credited with the development of new species in the Silurian period, from 440 to 410 million years ago.

6. **(A)** Primary oocytes are typically present in great numbers in the female's ovaries at birth.

7. **(B)** All multicellular organisms that reproduce sexually begin life as a zygote. The zygote then undergoes a series of cell divisions known as cleavage. Cleavage is the division of the zygote cell.

8. **(C)** The primary spermatocytes then undergo meiosis I forming secondary spermatocytes with a single chromosome set. The secondary spermatocytes go through meiosis II, forming spermatid that are haploid. These spermatid then develop into the sperm cells.

9. **(E)** Primary oocytes undergo meiosis I forming one secondary oocyte and one smaller polar body. Both the secondary oocyte and the polar body

undergo meiosis II—the polar body producing two polar bodies that are not functional cells, the oocyte producing one more polar body and one haploid egg cell.

10. **(C)** The secondary spermatocytes go through meiosis II, forming spermatid that are haploid.

11. **(C)** Positron decay results in the departure of a subatomic particle that carries away a positive charge and results in a proton being turned into a neutron. As a result, the mass number remains the same, but the atomic number decreases by 1.

12. **(E)** Gamma radiation is composed of photons of very short wavelength and high energy. Gamma radiation usually accompanies other types of radioactive decay and is the vehicle by which energy is carried away from the atom.

13. **(A)** Alpha decay results in a bundle of nuclear material leaving the atom. This is a very stable bundle of material that consists of two protons and two neutrons—equivalent to the nucleus of a helium atom.

14. **(B)** Beta decay is the opposite of positron decay and results in an electron carrying a negative charge away from the atom and ultimately turning a neutron into a proton. The overall mass number stays the same, but the atomic number increases by 1.

15. **(D)** Two electrons are transferred per atom in the oxidation-reduction reaction between magnesium and oxygen. Magnesium is oxidized by losing two electrons, and oxygen is reduced.

16. **(B)** The titration of acetic acid by a strong base results in the production of water and the acetate ion, which is a weak base—thereby leaving the solution basic.

17. **(A)** A cloudy product results in the formation of silver iodide (AgI) precipitate.

18. **(C)** In an electrolytic cell, melted sodium chloride will react by having the sodium ions move toward the cathode and the chloride ion move toward the anode. Sodium metal will be formed at the cathode, and chloride gas will be formed at the anode.

19. **(A)** The balance of the ecosystem can be destroyed by the removal, or decrease, of a single factor or by the addition, or increase, of a factor.

20. **(C)**   Homeostasis is a dynamic balance that is achieved within an ecosystem that is functioning at its optimum level.

21. **(B)**   The law of minimums (also known as the Liebig-Blackman Law of Limits) states that the resource in shortest supply in an ecosystem will limit population growth.

22. **(E)**   The law of tolerance (or Shelford's law) states that population growth may be limited by having more of an element (such as heat or water) than it can tolerate.

23. **(D)**   The number of individuals of a particular species that live in a particular area is known as the population density (number of organisms per area).

24. **(E)**   Chordates include all organisms with spinal cords and vertebrae. The items A–D are all invertebrates. A perch is a vertebrate and thus within the phylum Chordata.

25. **(C)**   The spinal cord is not directly involved with immunity. The organs of the immune system in humans and other higher invertebrates include the lymph nodes, spleen, thymus, and tonsils.

26. **(A)**   Oparin's hypothesis included the idea that most water on the Earth was in the form of steam, not ice. Oparin proposed that the Earth was approximately 4.6 billion years old and that there was a reducing atmosphere, meaning there was very little oxygen present. Instead, there was an abundance of ammonia, hydrogen, methane, and steam (H_2O). The Earth was in the process of cooling down, so there was a great deal of heat energy available, as well as a pattern of recurring violent lightening storms providing another source of energy. During this cooling of the Earth, much of the steam surrounding the earth would condense, forming hot seas. In the presence of abundant energy, the synthesis of simple organic molecules from the available chemicals became possible. These organic substances then collected in the hot, turbulent seas (sometimes referred to as the "primordial soup"). As the concentration of organic molecules became very high, they began forming into larger, charged, complex molecules. Oparin called these highly absorptive molecules coacervates. Coacervates were also able to divide.

27. **(B)**   The Gulf Stream consists of warm equatorial currents that raise the temperature of the winds that pass over England, thus warming the land. Being an island does not make England warmer. Latitude does affect temperature; the higher the latitude, the greater the sun's angle and the cooler the air. The winds

that affect England do not come from France. Gulf Stream winds do not affect the Canadian coast.

28. **(B)** Answer (A) is one quark type too few; there are six of them. *Ceiling* and *floor* are not quark types. The six quark types are *up*, *down*, *strange*, *charm*, *bottom*, and *top* (or *beauty* and *truth* to European physicists). The three-quark combination for a proton is two *up* quarks and one *down* quark. The proton doesn't include a *strange* quark.

29. **(C)** The delocalized electrons in copper and other transition metals create an "electron sea," which is fundamental to the construction of the metallic attraction that holds solid copper together.

30. **(B)** The order of classification from least specific to most specific is kingdom, phylum, class, order, family, genus, and species. Of those listed, genus is the most specific with members most closely related to each other.

31. **(B)** When one community completely replaces another over time in a given area, it is known as succession.

32. **(B)** The two oxygen atoms would produce two atoms of beryllium, each with four protons and four neutrons. The reaction doesn't form the same element since each of the resulting atoms contains only four protons, which identifies the element. Since the atom was split, it is no longer oxygen because each separate atom has four protons, not eight. Helium contains two protons, and neon contains ten.

33. **(C)** The strongest of the fundamental forces is the strong nuclear force that impacts objects at a range of about 10^{-15} meters. Then comes the electromagnetic force, which influences objects at an infinite range throughout the universe. After that, the weak nuclear force impacts objects that are in the same range as those impacted by the strong force. Gravity is the weakest of the four, but affects everything in the universe as well.

34. **(B)** Photosynthetic organisms are found in the Kingdom Plantae and the Kingdom Protista. Chordata is a phyla, not a kingdom.

35. **(C)** Although ΔT is a description of the change in temperature, it does not explain anything about why the water takes longer to boil than the piece of chocolate will melt. A Btu is a unit of heat transfer that is quoted a lot in heating and cooling systems. It certainly is used to measure specific heat in units of Btu's per pounds per degree Fahrenheit (Btu/lb/°F), but this is a unit of measure, not a physical property of matter. Specific heat is the measurable ability of a substance to retain or lose heat. It is measured as the amount of heat required

to raise the temperature of a gram of a substance by 1°C. Kelvin temperature is simply a measuring convention that relates all bodies to an absolute scale of heat transfer measurement, where zero is the temperature at which molecular motion ceases.

36. **(E)** The order of the layers of Earth from closest to farthest away is troposphere, stratosphere, mesosphere, thermosphere, and exosphere.

37. **(A)** Thermodynamics deals only in the large-scale responses of a system. It does not involve small-scale measurements, either alone or in combination with large-scale responses.

38. **(B)** Mitochondria are called the cell's "powerhouses," being the center of cellular respiration. [Cellular respiration is the process of breaking up covalent bonds within sugar molecules with the intake of oxygen and release of energy in the form of ATP (adenosine tri-phosphate) molecules. ATP is the energy form used by all cell processes.] Mitochondria (singular of mitochondrion) are found wherever energy is needed within the cell, and are more numerous in cells that require more energy (muscle, etc.).

39. **(B)** The size of cells is limited by the ratio of its volume to its surface area. A cell will only remain stable if the surface area of the plasma membrane maintains a balance with the volume of cytoplasm.

40. **(C)** Earth acts through its center as a large magnet. Scientists are not sure what produces the enormous magnetic currents that are deep within the Earth and responsible for Earth's magnetic field. There is not enough magnetic material within the crust or mantle to explain the magnetic force of Earth based solely on the natural magnets. Turbulent motion in the upper core's electrically conductive fluid is suspected to be responsible for the magnetism, but a reasonable explanation is still lacking because of the complexity of how it operates, according to scientists who study it.

41. **(B)** When the pitch of a sound wave gets higher, that means that the wave is oscillating faster. This will happen when the source is moving toward the listener. If the source were moving away, the pitch would get lower. If the source were standing still, there would be no change in pitch. Moving the source up and down will not change its pitch. The amplitude of a wave affects the volume, but not the pitch.

42. **(D)** When the water pressure inside and outside the cell is equal, it is said to be in an isotonic (or isomotic) state. Water will pass through the membrane by osmosis from an area of higher concentration to an area of lower

concentration (thus higher to lower water pressure) in order to produce isotonic conditions.

43. **(A)**   According to Newton's first law of motion, the sleeping astronauts would continue their motion in a straight line if the shuttle suddenly changed velocity due to the firing of its thrusters. If the shuttle slowed down, the astronauts would move forward relative to the walls. This is all due to the fact that the astronauts have mass, or inertia. Gravity is so weak that it is negligible on the astronauts. They can be monitored by battery-driven devices that allow them to move around. They can certainly sleep without being strapped in. Bodies do not need a reaction force in order to sleep.

44. **(B)**   While microtubules, microfilaments, and centrioles all provide structure to cells, cell walls are only found in plants. Mitochondria are found in both plant and animal cells, and are not used for structure, but for the processing of energy.

45. **(B)**   Enzymes catalyze reactions in both living and nonliving environments.

46. **(A)**   The proton's nemesis particle is the antiproton, which has the same mass but carries a negative charge. There is no such thing as an *antielectron*; the electron's antimatter is the *positron*. A *neutrino* is an extremely small elementary particle with no charge, that is created by certain types of radioactive decay. There is no such thing as a "negitron." (It is spelled incorrectly.) However, Carl D. Anderson, who discovered the *positron,* did once consider changing the name of the electron to the "*negatron,*" so that the term *electron* could be used as a term for a generically charged particle, either positive or negative. That did not happen, of course. That answer is also incorrect if the sequence of matter and antimatter is considered, since the *positron* is the antimatter, and the matter would be the (correctly spelled) *negatron*. The neutrino and quark are both subatomic particles, not matter and antimatter.

47. **(B)**   The AU is defined as the average distance of Earth from the Sun, which is approximately 150 million kilometers or 93 million miles.

48. **(B)**   Vitamins are organic cofactors or coenzymes that are required by some enzymatic reactions. In this case, it is the coenzyme required for the process of synthesizing collagen.

49. **(D)**   Prosthetic groups, which may be ions or non-protein molecules, are similar to cofactors in that they facilitate the enzyme reaction. However,

prosthetic groups are tightly attached by covalent bonds to the enzyme, rather than being separate atoms or molecules.

50. **(C)** An alluvial fan results when fast-moving mountain canyons transport large amounts of material out of the mountain into a slower moving stream channel, where it is deposited into the bottom in a fan-shaped area. It differs from a delta in that its source is a canyon, whereas deltas are deposited at the base of a river into a lake or ocean. The tributary is the name of a smaller channel of water that feeds into a larger body of water. Topset beds are a type of delta sediment with coarse materials. A meandering stream is a single-channel stream that flows with a snake-like or serpentine pattern.

51. **(C)** *Adiabatic* comes from the Latin word meaning "does not pass through." In an adiabatic process involving a fluid, heat does not pass through the fluid. When heat passes between objects in a thermodynamic relationship, we call it a diabatic process, because there is a heat transfer. A common and practical example of an adiabatic situation is the effects of a thermal window pane. The air between the two panes of glass disallows the transfer of heat through the inside glass to the outer glass on a cold winter day.

52. **(B)** The egg-laying trait of monotremes is most likely an example of convergent evolution of that trait that is analogous to reptiles and birds. Analogous traits are an example of convergent evolution in which similar traits evolve in species without related ancestries.

53. **(B)** The ideal gas law assumes that there is no intermolecular attraction and that the volume of the gas molecules is insignificant relative to the space between the molecules. Therefore, gases that are large molecules and/or demonstrate strong intermolecular attraction are likely to be non-ideal gases. Hydrogen sulfide is both the largest gas molecule of the options and shows very strong intermolecular attraction, because of the difference in electronegativity between hydrogen and sulfur. Water vapor also shows strong intermolecular attraction, but it is a much smaller molecule.

54. **(A)** Einstein's equivalence theory explains how a person acting as an observer in a spacecraft enclosed in a completely sealed, opaque chamber perceives the forces acting upon that spacecraft as if the person were experiencing the gravitational pull of Earth. This experience acts according to the equation, Force = (mass)(acceleration) or $F = ma$. The Michelson-Morley experiment shows that the speed of light is the same in all directions, and has nothing to do with special relativity described here. Einstein's general theory of relativity involving the speed of light is not addressed in this question. This problem also has nothing to do with the Doppler effect.

55. **(A)** The process whereby cells build molecules and store energy (in the form of chemical bonds) is called anabolism.

56. **(C)** Cellular metabolism is a general term that includes all types of energy transformation processes, including photosynthesis, respiration, growth, movement, etc. These energy transformations occur as chemicals that are broken apart (catabolism) or synthesized within the cell (anabolism).

57. **(A)** Although (C) is technically correct, since on Earth mass and weight are the same value, the principle as expressed by Archimedes was stated in terms of weight of the object in a fluid.

58. **(C)** If the collection vessel is exposed to the surface of water, as it usually is when collecting a gas in the laboratory, then water evaporates from the surface and combines with the collected gas. Therefore, to be accurate in calculating how many moles of gas are produced in the reaction, Dalton's law must be used to account for the moles of water vapor also in the collection vessel. Dalton's law states that the total pressure exerted by a mixture of gases equals the sum of the partial pressures of each component in the mixture.

59. **(D)** An electromagnet is not a permanent magnet; it ceases to be a magnet when the electricity ceases to flow through the wire. The strength of an electromagnet can be increased easily by increasing the number of coils in the wire. Since (D) allows the choice of (B), which states that an electromagnet is permanent, and (C) which means that the strength of a magnet is limited, (D) includes both incorrect answers, making it the correct answer. The first answer is a true statement; therefore, it is not the correct answer. Answer (E) includes answer (A), so it should not be selected.

60. **(B)** About 500 volcanoes are known to have been active, with two-thirds of them in the Pacific Ocean.

61. **(B)** P-waves, also called push waves, travel out directly from the epicenter of an earthquake and form longitudinal waves. The other answers represent transverse waves. Gravity is not a wave; it is a force.

62. **(A)** Based on specific gravity alone, an object that is denser than water will sink. A substance will not dissolve in water or increase water temperature based upon its specific gravity, though it may do so because of other properties. The ability of a substance to mix with water is not due to its specific gravity.

63. **(A)** The tide is the continuous cycle of an alternatively rising and falling sea level along the coastlines and in bodies of water connected to the sea. The moon is the single greatest influence on the tides.

64. **(E)**   The illustration is called a Punnett square.

65. **(A)**   The genotypes of the parents are TT and tt.

66. **(B)**   Every gamete will have either the T gene or the t gene.

67. **(A)**   All offspring will have a genotype Tt and a dominant gene for tallness (T), so all will have a phenotype of tall. Thus. the ratio is 4 tall; 0 short.

68. **(D)**   The genotype ratio will be 1 TT: 2 Tt: 1 tt. Since T (tall) is dominant to t (short), only one out of four will be short. The phenotypic ratio will be 3 tall; 1 short.

69. **(B)**   The mass of the object does not change because it is measured independently of the force of gravity on Earth or acceleration of the spacecraft. This is what differentiates mass from weight.

70. **(C)**   The angle through which the star appears to move in the course of half a year is called the parallax. The time involved is based on measuring the angle of observation from both extremes of Earth's orbit around the Sun, which is at a maximum separation every half year.

71. **(C)**   Kingdom Monera contains prokaryotic cells, which are considered to be the first to evolve.

72. **(D)**   Lengths have to do with intervals of space, measured in three dimensions. The standard of measurement in physics is the meter. Mass is the amount of substance that an object contains and is measured in grams or kilograms. Time is a measurement of duration that we measure in seconds. The system of units most commonly used by scientists is the m-k-s system; astrophysics measures in centimeters, grams and seconds, known as the c-g-s system.

73. **(D)**   The highest melting point will be demonstrated by the crystal that has the strongest forces holding it in the crystalline structure. In this case, SiC is held together with network covalent attractions, which are stronger than ionic and polar intermolecular attractions.

74. **(E)**   In the center of the root is the vascular cylinder (e), including xylem and phloem tissue.

75. **(B)**   The primary tissues include the outermost layer, the epidermis (b). The epidermis is one cell layer thick, and serves to protect the internal root tissue and absorb nutrients and water.

76. **(A)**   In the maturation region, the epidermis produces root hairs (a), extensions of the cells that reach between soil particles and retrieve water and minerals.

77. **(D)**   Inside the cortex is a ring of endodermis (d), a single layer of cells that are tightly connected, so no substances can pass between cells. This feature allows the endodermis to act as a filter; all substances entering the vascular tissues from the root must pass through these cells.

78. **(C)**   Inside the epidermis is a ring known as the cortex (c), made of large parenchyma cells. Parenchyma cells are present in many tissues of plants; they are thin-walled cells loosely packed to allow for flow of gases and mineral uptake.

79. **(A)**   The photosphere is what we observe on the Sun's surface. Plasma is the state of matter engulfing the Sun's interior, and represents the fourth state of matter. A sunspot and a flare are local phenomena occurring on the Sun's surface. The corona is the outside ring of the Sun's surface which is visible during an eclipse.

80. **(C)**   Considering the size of an object does not describe it quantitatively. Mass is correct but density represents mass per unit volume, which is not needed to find weight. The force it exerts is not upward, but downward toward the Earth by gravity. Weight and mass are both able to be determined independently of the type of material it contains. The amount of pressure exerted on an object does not determine its weight, but rather the amount of gravity exerted does.

81. **(A)**   The cell membrane is composed of a double layer (bilayer) of phospholipids with protein globules imbedded within the layers. The construction of the membrane allows it to aid cell function by permitting entrance and exit of molecules as needed by the cell.

82. **(D)**   If the distance from the source of energy doubles, the brightness reduces by a factor of x^2. Square the distance four times to get 4^2 or 16. So the star is 16 times dimmer at 4 times the distance away.

83. **(D)**   Oxygen is carried by hemoglobin molecules (that contain iron) in red blood cells. Lymphocytes and erythrocytes are types of blood cells; carbohydrates are sugar molecules; and gamma globulins are protein molecules found in the blood.

84. **(D)**   Dicots (plants with two cotyledons in each seed) have taproot systems and flowers with petals in multiples of four or five. The leaves of a dicot

will have networked or branching veins, and the vascular bundles within the stem will be arranged in rings.

85. **(E)** Light behaves as both a particle and a wave. The speed of light is a constant value of 3.0×10^8 m/s or 183,310 mi/s. Prior to Einstein's theories, answer (D) was the common scientific theory that Einstein helped to disprove.

86. **(D)** Lightning heats the air to several thousand degrees in only a fraction of a second. This causes the air to expand rapidly. Surrounding air rushes in to fill the space left by the expanding heated air. It is the air rushing in which creates the sonic boom we know as thunder. By now, it should be evident that lightning and thunder originate at essentially the same location. In addition, the energy released by the lightning creates the noise associated with the event. Some thunder rumbles for a very long time. There may actually be no rain at all when the lightning strikes; the sound would speed up if it travels through a liquid, not slow down. Light travels at 3×10^8 m/s; sound travels at a speed of 343 m/s in air, which completely explains why we see the lightning before hearing the thunder.

87. **(B)** Temporary movement into a new range and back again is known as migration.

88. **(B)** To calculate the specific heat, we need to determine the amount of calories transferred per degree Celsius. However, since we have 6 grams of the substance, we must divide the 12 calories by 6 grams, which comes out to 2 calories per gram (rounded to three significant digits). We then divide by the temperature of 2.345°C to get the specific heat of 8.52 cal/g/°C. We would erroneously get (A) if we neglect to divide by the increase in temperature. Answer (C) is reached erroneously by dividing the temperature by the calories per gram. Choices (D) and (E) are inaccurately reached if we neglect to divide the calories.

89. **(A)** Einstein's equivalence theory explains how a person acting as an observer in a spacecraft enclosed in a chamber that is completely sealed and opaque perceives the forces acting upon that spacecraft in the same manner as if the person were experiencing the gravitational pull of Earth according to the equation, Force = (mass)(acceleration) or $F = ma$. In this case, the absence of gravity is due to the distance above Earth that the space shuttle is orbiting. The Michelson-Morley experiment shows that the speed of light is the same in all directions and has nothing to do with special relativity as described here. Einstein's general theory of relativity involving the speed of light is expressed in the equation $E = mc^2$, which again is not addressed in this question. Although

answer (E) mentions special relativity, it does so in terms of velocity rather than acceleration, which is erroneous.

90. **(D)**   The intensity of the lightning is determined by complex processes which electrify the cloud. The updraft is only indirectly associated with this. The height of the cloud base is determined by the vertical temperature and dew point lapse rates in the atmosphere. This height can be estimated well before a thunderstorm ever forms and is not dependent on the updraft. Wind gusts at the surface are mainly caused by the downdraft. The speed of rain droplets is dependent on gravity and is unaffected by updraft. It is the strength of the updraft that determines how large individual precipitation elements will grow before they can no longer remain suspended in the cloud. Thus, stronger updrafts produce larger raindrops (or hailstones) than do weaker ones.

91. **(B)**   The reproductive organs of the sporophyte generation produce gametophytes through the process of meiosis. Gametophytes may be male or female and are haploid. Either can be considered first or second generations. Zygotes are produced when the spore fertilizes the egg.

92. **(B)**   Since an atom of carbon must have six protons, by definition, in order to be carbon, then the atomic mass of the isotope is the number of protons and neutrons in its nucleus (6 + 6 = 12).

93. **(C)**   Magnesium demonstrates the greatest difference between its second and third ionization energies because it has two electrons in its outer shell. To remove the third would require breaking into the inner, more tightly held, second shell—which requires considerably more energy.

94. **(C)**   The male structure is the stamen, consisting of the anther atop a long, hollow filament. The anther has four lobes and contains the cells (microspore mother cells) that become pollen. Some mature pollen grains are conveyed (usually by wind, birds, or insects) to a flower of a compatible species where they stick to the stigma. The stigma produces chemicals that stimulate the pollen to burrow into the style, forming a hollow pollen tube. This tube is produced by the tube nucleus that has developed from a portion of the pollen grain. The pollen tube extends down toward the ovary.

95. **(D)**   The universe is infinite; there is nothing outside of it. When infinity expands, it is still infinity, just bigger. Our telescopes are able to see to the ends of the perceived universe. We don't see more matter at the ends of the universe. We see space expanding and matter ending. There is no evidence that the universe is spherical or that it will be sucked into a huge black hole. But it sure makes for a great sci-fi movie!

96. **(C)** The core is speculated to contain a liquid center within the inner core. The other layers of Earth are all solid.

97. **(C)** The first law of Mendelian genetics is the law of segregation, stating that traits are expressed from a pair of genes in the individual, one of which came from each parent. The genes are separated in gamete formation, and then randomly brought together in fertilization.

98. **(B)** To convert from Celsius to Fahrenheit, use the formula $C = 5/9 \, (F - 32)$. Plugging in the numbers will yield $C = 5/9 \, (54.5 - 32) = 5/9 \, (22.5) = 12.5°C$. Errors common in the other answers are because of either using the wrong formula, or incorrectly manipulating the numbers mathematically.

99. **(A)** The mass of the cathode will increase because the copper ions in solution will gain electrons and precipitate solid copper onto the cathode.

100. **(D)** Epithelial (skin) cells have no direct function in immunity. Cells involved in immunity are called lymphocytes and begin in bone marrow as stem cells. There are two classes of lymphocytes, B cells and T cells. B cells emerge from the bone marrow, mature, and produce antibodies into the bloodstream that find and attach themselves to foreign antigens (toxins, bacteria, foreign cells, etc.). The attachment of an antibody to an antigen marks the pair for destruction. T cells mature in the thymus gland. Some T cells patrol the blood for antigens like B cells, but T cells are also equipped to destroy antigens themselves. T cells also regulate the body's immune responses.

101. **(A)** All of the items except pond water temperature will directly affect the snake's niche. Hawks are predators of snakes, preventing the snake population from being overgrown. Mice are the main food source, so without them the snakes will suffer. Daily temperature and yearly rainfall amounts determine the types of plants that will grow and provide shade and camouflage, as well as the body temperature of the snake (needs warm climate). An organism's niche is the role it plays within the ecosystem. It includes its physical requirements (such as light and water) and its biological activities (how it reproduces, how it acquires food, etc.). In most cases, the most important aspect of an organism's niche is its place in the food chain.

102. **(C)** To be considered a mineral, the substance must never have been part of a living organism and must be found in nature. Minerals are the most common form of solid material found in Earth's crust.

103. **(C)**   All of the choices are true except (C). Animal species are capable of sexual reproduction, though some are also capable of asexual reproduction (i.e., hydra).

104. **(B)**   Neither plants nor animals are able to use nitrogen directly from the air. Instead, a process known as nitrogen fixation makes nitrogen available for absorption by the roots of plants. Nitrogen fixation is the process of combining it with either hydrogen or oxygen. Nitrogen fixation is accomplished in one of two ways—either by nitrogen fixing bacteria or by the action of lightning.

105. **(B)**   The conductivity of the cement allows heat from your fingers to flow to it more than the wood does. This heat flow feels as if the cement is cooler than the wood, even though both floors may be the same temperature.

106. **(A)**   Moving to the right on the periodic table across a row, each new element experiences a greater pull between the nucleus and the ever-increasing number of electrons, which pulls in the outer shell of electrons and decreases the atomic radius.

107. **(B)**   A decrease of one unit in magnitude corresponds to an increase of brightness by a factor of 2.5. Since Star X appears to be 2.5 times as bright as Star Y, their magnitudes differ by a value of 1 unit.

108. **(A)**   Animal respiration releases carbon dioxide back into the atmosphere in large quantities; it does not take in carbon dioxide for use. Most of the carbon within organisms is derived from the production of carbohydrates in plants through photosynthesis. Carbon is also dissolved directly into the oceans, where it is combined with calcium to form calcium carbonate—used by mollusks to form their shells. Detritus feeders include worms, mites, insects, and crustaceans that feed on dead organic matter, returning the carbon to the cycle through chemical breakdown and respiration. Organic matter that is left to decay may under conditions of heat and pressure be transformed into coal, oil, or natural gas—the fossil fuels. When fossil fuels are burned for energy, the combustion process releases carbon dioxide back into the atmosphere, where it is available to plants for photosynthesis.

109. **(D)**   The stomach does not secrete acetic acid.

110. **(A)**   Firmness is not a measureable physical property of minerals, so it is the correct answer to this question. Hardness is another one not listed in this question. The others are all identifiable properties of minerals.

111. **(E)**   The selective permeability of the cell membrane serves to manage the concentration of substances within the cell, preserving its health. There are two methods by which substances can cross the cell membrane: passive transport and active transport.

112. **(A)**   The ecliptic is the apparent annual path "through the planets and stars" that the Sun follows. The celestial equator is the imaginary line surrounding Earth that extends the equator up into the heavens. The equinox is not an astronomical boundary, but represents the time of year when the amount of daylight and nightlight are equal in spring and fall. The solstice is the same calendar demarcation in winter and summer, when the shortest and longest daylight occurs at the start of these seasons, and Earth is closest and farthest from the Sun during its annual trajectory. An orbital path is simply that—the generic name for the path that a satellite, either natural or artificial, takes as it travels around another celestial body.

113. **(B)**   A species' (and thus an organism's) habitat must include all the factors that will support its life and reproduction. These factors may be biotic (i.e., living—food source, predators, etc.) and abiotic (i.e., nonliving—weather, temperature, soil features, etc.).

114. **(B)** CH_4 demonstrates 109.5° between the C-H bonds, while XeF_4 demonstrates 90° angles between its Xe-F bonds. Even though the formulas are similar, the different geometry is a result of the larger size of the Xe atom and the highly electronegative F atoms creating an "expanded octet." Two other pairs of unbonded electron pairs around Xenon also take up space, forcing the bonds to fluorine to be closer together than the C-H bonds in methane.

115. **(D)**   Heat of vaporization (H), or enthalpy, is the amount of energy needed to turn a given quantity of a substance into a gas. Heat of fusion is the change of a solid to a liquid or vice versa. A heat index has nothing to do with changes of state. It is a measure of the amount of heat in a particular environmental area. A heat wave constant is a fictitious term. Specific heat is the amount of heat energy necessary to raise 1g of a substance by 1°C.

116. **(C)**   The sharp boundary of a community is called an ecotone.

117. **(C)**   Bony fish belong to the class Osteichthyes. Since soft tissues would not fossilize well, it would be unlikely to find a fossil of a cartilaginous (nonbony) fish (Chondrichthyes). Reptilia, Aves, and Amphibia are not classes of fish.

118. **(E)**   Only plant cells have cell walls, while all cells have a cell/plasma membrane. The rest of the choices are tenets of cell theory.

119. **(B)**   Refraction is the bending of waves toward the direction of the slower wave velocity. One part of the wave slows down before another part. One part of the wave does not bend more than another part; it is not pushed to one side but goes through the medium equally. It is also not closer together at one part than another. The last answer explains reflection, not refraction.

120. **(B)**   The bottle will drift eastward until it will ride the Kuroshio current to the North Pacific Drift and wash ashore on the western side of North America.

Practice Test 3

CLEP Natural Sciences

(Answer sheets appear in the back of this book.)

TIME: 90 Minutes
120 Questions

DIRECTIONS: Each of the following group of questions consists of five lettered terms followed by a list of numbered phrases or sentences. For each numbered phrase or sentence, select the one choice that is most clearly related to it. Each choice may be used once, more than once, or not at all.

Questions 1–5

(A) Carrying capacity

(B) Density independent factors

(C) Range

(D) Competition

(E) Emigration

_____ 1. Abiotic limiting factors

_____ 2. Total area occupied by a particular species

_____ 3. Permanent one-way movement out of the original range

_____ 4. The state that organisms with overlapping niches are in when resources are in short supply

_____ 5. Maximum population level in which population will continue to thrive

Questions 6–8 _____

(A) Releaser   (D) Reflex

(B) Instinct   (E) Fixed action pattern

(C) Stimulus

____ 6. Highly stereotyped innate behavior

____ 7. Instinctive movement in response to a stimulus

____ 8. Unlearned series of actions that are a pre-programmed response to a particular stimulus (a releaser or sign stimulus)

Questions 9–13 _____

(A) Differential reproduction

(B) Mutation

(C) Gene migration

(D) Hardy-Weinberg Equilibrium

(E) Allopatric speciation

____ 9. Accidental change in genetic material

____ 10. The best adapted individuals are the most likely individuals to reproduce viable offspring

____ 11. In a population that is in equilibrium with its environment, gene frequencies and geneotype ratios remain constant

____ 12. The evolution of two separate species due to two populations being geographically isolated from each other

____ 13. The infiltration of a previously isolated group by a member of an adjacent population, resulting in the increase of genetic possibilities

Questions 14–16 _____

    (A) Savanna   (D) Desert

    (B) Tropical rainforest   (E) Tundra

    (C) Taiga

_____ 14. Extreme cold, low precipitation, modified grassland, permafrost

_____ 15. Extreme hot or cold, sparse vegetation, very low precipitation, reptiles

_____ 16. Warm temperatures, moderate precipitation, grassland

Questions 17–21 _____

    (A) Centriole   (D) Endocytic vesicle

    (B) Free ribosomes   (E) Nucleus

    (C) Lysosomes

_____ 17. Digestive organelles that also serve to break up dead cell material

_____ 18. Site of protein synthesis

_____ 19. Membrane sac that transports large molecules through the cell membrane

_____ 20. Site of reproduction

_____ 21. Pinwheel arrangement of microtubules that form structural skeleton

Questions 22–26 _____

    (A) Connective tissue   (D) Adipose tissue

    (B) Epithelial tissue   (E) Blood tissue

    (C) Cartilage tissue

_____ 22. Covers the outside of internal organs

_____ 23. Lines the interior of internal organs

_____ 24. Reduces friction between bones

_____ 25. Insulates and cushions

_____ 26. Fights infection, transports waste

Questions 27–30 _____

    (A) $N_2 (g) + 3H_2 (g) \rightarrow 2NH_3 (g)$

    (B) $AgI \rightarrow Ag^+ + I^-, \Delta H = -15 \text{ kJ/mol}$

    (C) $H_2C_2O_4 + MnO_4^- + H_2SO_4 \rightarrow MnSO_4 + CO_2 + H_2O$

    (D) $NaSCN \rightarrow Na^+ + SCN^-, \Delta H = 345 \text{ kJ/mol}$

    (E) $C_4H_{10} + O_2 \rightarrow CO_2 + H_2O$

_____ 27. Increasing the temperature will increase the solubility of the ion in solution for this reaction.

_____ 28. Decreasing the temperature will increase the solubility of the ion in solution for this reaction.

_____ 29. This reaction is considered a combustion reaction.

_____ 30. Adding acid to this reaction will cause it to go forward.

Questions 31–35 _____

    (A) Stem   (D) Lateral bud

    (B) Node   (E) Shoot apex

    (C) Internode

____ 31. Supports leaves so they are exposed to sunlight

____ 32. Food and water transport organ

____ 33. Meristem tissue in region of elongation at the top of plant

____ 34. Young leaves

____ 35. Location on the stem where new leaves sprout

Questions 36–40 _____

    (A) H   (D) Th

    (B) F   (E) Ar

    (C) Na

____ 36. The most electronegative element

____ 37. The element that combines with hydrogen to form a halide

____ 38. The most abundant element in the universe

____ 39. The element whose most abundant naturally occurring isotopes are radioactive

____ 40. The element that has a full outer shell

Questions 41–44 _____

    (A) KI   (D) $Fe(NO_3)_3$

    (B) H_2O_2 (E) Mg

    (C) NaOH

_____ 41. Reaction of this substance with a strong acid would produce hydrogen gas.

_____ 42. Heating this substance produces a gas.

_____ 43. Combining a solution of this substance with a solution of lead nitrate will produce a yellow precipitate.

_____ 44. Mixing this with KSCN will produce a blood-red solution.

DIRECTIONS: Each of the questions or incomplete statements below is followed by five possible answers or completions. Select the best choice in each case and fill in the corresponding oval on the answer sheet.

---

45. In the 1700s, the French scientist Lamarck proposed the idea that animals develop characteristics over the course of their lives that help them adapt to changes in their environment. For instance, Lamarck suggested that giraffes developed long necks over their lifespan in order to enable them to reach food on high tree branches. This now discredited theory (which was replaced by Darwin's model of natural selection) is known as the theory of

    (A) acquired characteristics   (D) special isolation

    (B) natural selection   (E) genetic mutation

    (C) genetic drift

46. The names of the layers of the Earth include all of the following EXCEPT

    (A) asthenosphere   (D) hydrosphere

    (B) lithosphere   (E) solid iron core

(C)   mantle

47.   A toddler pushes a wagon across a room with a constant force of 100N. If the wagon is pushed 10 meters, how much work does the toddler do?

(A)   10 Joules   (D)   1,000 Joules

(B)   100 Joules   (E)   10,000 Joules

(C)   110 Joules

48.   Kepler's second law says, essentially, that

(A)   force equals mass times acceleration

(B)   the square of the period is proportional to the cube of the semi-major axis

(C)   the orbits of the planets are ellipses with the Sun as one focus

(D)   the line from the Sun to a planet sweeps equal areas in equal times

(E)   the force of gravity is inversely proportional to the square of the distance between the center of the planets

49.   Photosynthesis would NOT proceed without which of the following that allow moisture and gases to pass in and out of a leaf?

(A)   Surface hairs   (D)   Epidermal cells

(B)   Stomata   (E)   Mesoderm cells

(C)   Cuticles

50.   Streptococcus pyogenes is a bacterium that causes strep throat infection. Penicillin is an effective antibiotic against Streptococcus pyogenes. However, when antibiotics are used incorrectly, some bacteria may survive. Surviving bacteria will have a higher level of resistance to the antibiotic. Since the living resistant bacteria will then reproduce, the antibiotic resistance will be magnified in subsequent generations. This development of strains of antibiotic-resistant bacteria is an example of

(A)   genetic drift   (D)   genetic equilibrium

(B)   natural selection   (E)   acquired characteristics

(C)   mutation

51. In which of the following media will a sound wave travel the fastest?

(A) Outer space   (D) Air

(B) A cold fluid   (E) Steel

(C) A hot fluid

52. A type of geological anticline that contains a round or oval upward bulge of rock layers is called a

(A) dome   (D) fault

(B) basin   (E) fold

(C) dip

53. Which unit of temperature is stated correctly and used to measure absolute zero?

(A) Degrees Fahrenheit   (D) Degrees Kelvin

(B) Degrees Celsius   (E) Degrees Rankine

(C) Degrees Centigrade

54. Which of the following planets has no natural satellites?

(A) Mars   (D) Venus

(B) Earth   (E) Saturn

(C) Jupiter

55. Which of the following is an explanation of how altruistic traits evolve?

(A) Presence of an altruistic trait in an individual decreases its fitness to survive.

(B) Kin selection in mating would accomplish the proliferation of altruistic traits.

(C) Genetic drift would account for the development of altruistic traits.

(D) Species that experience adaptive radiation also develop altruism.

(E) Natural selection favors the altruistic individual.

56. Which system is only found in vertebrates?

    (A) Gas exchange (respiratory) system

    (B) Circulatory

    (C) Musculoskeletal system

    (D) Nervous system

    (E) Digestive system

Questions 57–60 _____

Match the following sets of thermodynamic parameters.

(A) H_2O (D) Pb

(B) $C_{12}H_{26}$ (E) SiO

(C) PbS

57. To melt this substance, polar intermolecular attractions must be overcome.

58. To melt this substance, metallic attractions must be overcome.

59. To melt this substance, network covalent attractions must be overcome.

60. To melt this substance, ionic attractions must be overcome.

61. If a frame of reference is accelerating or decelerating, light rays

    (A) travel in straight lines

    (B) follow the shortest possible path

    (C) travel in curved paths

    (D) are attracted by gravitational fields

    (E) reflect off objects in no apparent pattern

62. Convert 0.00000435 g into scientific notation.

    (A) 43.5×10^{-7} g   (D) 4.35×10^{6} g

    (B) 4.35×10^{-6} kg   (E) $.435 \times 10^{-5}$ g

    (C) 4.35×10^{-6} g

63. Which of the following statements is true?

(A) One of the main things Einstein proved is that there is an absolute time standard.

(B) You can synchronize two clocks so that two observers in two different places will see both clocks exactly in agreement to each other within 1 billionth of a second.

(C) Distance and time are directly related to each other.

(D) There is a luminiferous ether that light passes through that explains the relationship of light and time dilation.

(E) Energy, mass, and light are not related.

64. Which of the following has the highest bond order?

(A) Carbon tetrachloride   (D) Hydrogen gas

(B) Carbon dioxide   (E) Water

(C) Carbonate anion

65. The father of our modern taxonomic key was

(A) Carolus Linneaus   (D) Gregor Mendel

(B) Robert Hooke   (E) Joseph Priestly

(C) Charles Darwin

66. The term *Homo sapiens* is an example of

(A) family and phylum names

(B) a class name

(C) a taxonomic key

(D) binomial nomenclature

(E) a species name

67. Which of the following planets is closer to the Sun than Earth?

(A) Mars   (D) Jupiter

(B) Saturn   (E) Uranus

(C) Venus

68. Which of the following statements about photosynthesis is NOT true?

    (A) Photosynthesis occurs through numerous small steps.

    (B) Photosynthesis can be summarized by the equation
    $6CO_2 + 6H_2O + \text{light energy} \rightarrow C_6H_{12}O_6 + 6O_2.$

    (C) Chlorophyll is not harmed or used up by the photosynthetic process.

    (D) Photosynthesis occurs in green plants and algae.

    (E) Chlorophyll speeds the photosynthetic process, but it is not required for photosynthesis to occur.

69. Which of the following statements is NOT true of glycolysis?

    (A) Glycolysis breaks down glucose into smaller molecules.

    (B) Glycolysis only occurs in plant cells.

    (C) The process of respiration always begins with glycolysis.

    (D) Glycolysis occurs in the cytoplasm of all living cells.

    (E) Glycolysis yields energy.

70. When measuring the flow of heat in a system, a natural process that starts at one equilibrium state and flows to another while being impacted by the entropy of the system plus the environment, what will entropy do to create an irreversible process?

    (A) Increase

    (B) Decrease

    (C) Remain static

    (D) Fluctuate between increases and decreases in a random pattern

    (E) Increase steadily and then drop off, similarly to the conservation of momentum in a closed system

71. A sample of butane was completely combusted at STP. How many moles of butane were burned if 44.8 liters of carbon dioxide were produced as a result?

    (A) 0.5 moles   (D) 2.0 moles

    (B) 1.0 moles   (E) 2.5 moles

    (C) 1.5 moles

72. What is the most likely outcome when the gene frequency within a given population remains constant?

(A) The rate of evolution within the population will increase.

(B) Expression of dominant traits will increase within the population.

(C) Evolution will not take place within this population.

(D) There will be an increase in the recessive traits within the population.

(E) Natural selection of the dominant species will occur.

73. The leaves of an Easter Lily have parallel veins. Which of the following is most likely false?

(A) An Easter Lily has seeds with double cotyledons.

(B) An Easter Lily has vascular bundles arranged randomly in its stem.

(C) The roots of the Easter Lily are fibrous.

(D) The flower of the lily has three petals.

(E) An Easter Lily grows from a monocot seed.

74. Which of the following is a length of DNA (with corresponding histones) that is responsible for the production of a particular protein that causes a particular trait to be expressed in an organism? Each consists of about four nucleosomes of a chromosome.

(A) Chromosome   (D) Gene

(B) Mutation   (E) Autosome

(C) Genome

75. Weathering is the wearing away of rocks and is a never-ending process. Chemical weathering, which is more active in warm and humid climates, consists of

(A) the oxidation of iron in the rocks

(B) decay, alteration, and leaching

(C) the faulting and fracture of rocks

(D) breaking down of rock by biological activity

(E) Both (A) and (B)

76. In 2001, the International Astronomical Union (IAU) came up with a new definition for Pluto, in which it was reclassified as a dwarf planet. The definition was modified in 2006 as "a celestial body that (a) is in orbit around the Sun, (b) has sufficient mass for its self-gravity to overcome rigid body forces, so that it assumes a hydrostatic equilibrium (nearly round) shape, (c) has not cleared the neighborhood around its orbit, and which of the following?

    (A) Contains traces of water on its surface

    (B) Shows potential for future space exploration to its surface

    (C) Is not a satellite

    (D) Has an axis of inclination less than 60 degrees to the ecliptic

    (E) Rotates on its axis in a counterclockwise direction

77. How does DNA produce particular genetic traits?

    (A) Through DNA replication

    (B) Through protein synthesis

    (C) Through genetic imprinting

    (D) Through genetic maintenance

    (E) Through cloning

78. Structural genes are responsible for coding the proteins necessary to

    (A) develop the organization of body structure

    (B) determine the timing of eye formation

    (C) synthesize epithelial tissue

    (D) determine the sequence of neural development

    (E) form zygotes

79. If two stars have the same luminosity, but different brightnesses,

    (A) the dimmer star is closer

    (B) the brighter star is closer

    (C) the stars are the same distance away

    (D) the stars are standard candles

    (E) there is no way to know which is closer or farther away

80.   What are the two components of acceleration?

(A) Angular momentum and inertia

(B) Velocity over time and direction

(C) Downward pull and upward thrust

(D) Speed and distance

(E) Force and mass

81.   Icy worlds that measure a few kilometers across are

(A) meteroids   (D) asteroids

(B) meteors   (E) plutoids

(C) comets

82.   Which of the following is NOT true of viruses?

(A) Viruses often kill their host cell.

(B) Viruses consist of a protein capsule, DNA, RNA, and sometimes enzymes.

(C) Viruses cannot carry on metabolic functions without a host organism.

(D) Viruses have the ability to reproduce themselves.

(E) Scientists have agreed that viruses are the smallest living organisms.

83.   Which of the following describes a system in which entropy has decreased or is decreasing?

(A) A broken window   (D) Lukewarm water

(B) A nuclear explosion   (E) Cell division

(C) A messy bedroom

84.   The Sun's galactic motion in the Milky Way can be described as

(A) radial motion towards the center of the galaxy

(B) radial motion away from the center of the galaxy

(C) motion along a very elongated ellipse

(D) motion in a circular orbit

(E) spiral motion away from the epicenter

85. A single DNA strand had the sequence GATACCA. Which of the following would complement that DNA strand?

(A) GATACCA

(B) CTATGGT

(C) ACCATAG

(D) CUAUCCU

(E) UCCUAUC

86. Hurricanes, cyclones, and typhoons occur over

(A) land

(B) water

(C) land during the day

(D) water and land

(E) arid zones

87. In order of increasing distance from the Sun, the terrestrial planets are

(A) Mars, Venus, Earth, and Mercury

(B) Mercury, Venus, Earth, and Mars

(C) Jupiter, Saturn, Uranus, and Neptune

(D) Mercury, Venus, Mars, and Earth

(E) Neptune, Jupiter, Uranus, and Mars

88. Absolute temperature is best described as a measure of the

(A) speed of molecules

(B) pressure between molecules

(C) number of molecules

(D) average translational kinetic energy of molecules

(E) hottest temperature possible for a specific molecule

89. If a star has a parallax of 0.1 seconds, its distance is how many parsecs?

(A) 2

(B) 1

(C) ½

(D) 10

(E) 0.1

90. The crust of the Earth is composed of a thin layer of rocks covering the surface. Rocks are defined as aggregates or collections of

(A) symmetry

(D) clastics

(B) fossils

(E) macerals

(C) minerals

91. Scientists divide the history of Earth into eras. Which of the following arranges these eras into their proper sequence from oldest to most recent?

(A) Cenozoic, Mesozoic, Paleozoic, Precambrian

(B) Precambrian, Paleozoic, Mesozoic, Cenozoic

(C) Mesozoic, Cenozoic, Paleozoic, Precambrian

(D) Paleozoic, Precambrian, Cenozoic, Mesozoic

(E) Precambrian, Cenozoic, Paleozoic, Mesozoic

Questions 92–95 _____

In snapdragons, a red flower crossed with a white flower produces a pink flower. In this illustration, R represents red and W white. The Punnett square for a cross between a white snapdragon and a red snapdragon is shown here:

	R	R
W	RW	RW
W	RW	RW

92. The cross illustrated in this Punnett square is an example of

(A) a sex-linked trait

(D) a dihybrid cross

(B) multiple alleles

(E) complete dominance

(C) incomplete dominance

93. The symbol RW represents which of the following?

   (A) The allele for red   (D) The allele for white

   (B) The genotype for pink   (E) The genotype for white

   (C) The phenotype for pink

94. In this cross, both parents have genotypes that are

   (A) heterozygous for color   (D) dominant for pink

   (B) homozygous for color   (E) dominant for white

   (C) recessive for pink

95. Which of the following statements about this cross must be true?

   (A) Both parents of the red snapdragon must have had the genotype
        RR.

   (B) One of the parents of the red snapdragon must have had the geno-
        type RR.

   (C) Both parents of the red snapdragon must have been pink.

   (D) Neither parent of the red snapdragon could be white.

   (E) One parent of the red snapdragon must have been white.

96. Multiple sclerosis is a disease that destroys the myelin sheath around
     nerve bodies. Which of the following would NOT be an effect of losing
     the myelin sheath?

   (A) Nerve tissue loses its white color.

   (B) Nerve impulses are impaired.

   (C) Sensory input is increased.

   (D) Senses such as sight may be adversely affected.

   (E) Control of muscle function may be lost.

97. For a gas, a useful state variable is the enthalpy H, which is defined to be

(A) the sum of the internal energy E plus the difference between the pressure p and volume V of the gas: $H = E + p - V$

(B) the sum of the external energy E plus the product of the pressure p and volume V of the gas: $H = E + p*V$

(C) the product of the internal energy E and the product of the pressure p and volume V of the gas: $H = E * (p*V)$

(D) the difference of the internal energy E minus the product of the pressure p and volume V of the gas: $H = E - p* V$

(E) the difference of the pressure p and volume V of the gas minus the external energy E: $H = E - p* V$

98. If two heterozygous offspring of a variety of plant expressing an incomplete dominant trait such as Red, White, and Pink in snapdragon flowers are crossed, what will be the ratio of the phenotypes in the offspring?

(A) 0 red: 4 pink: 0 white   (D) 2 red: 0 pink: 2 white

(B) 2 red: 2 pink: 0 white   (E) 1 red: 2 pink: 1 white

(C) 1 red: 1 pink: 1 white

99. The warmest place in the atmosphere is near the ground because the

(A) ground is under the ozone layer

(B) ground can store heat

(C) ground is covered by ice in some regions

(D) Earth is both land and water

(E) Sun's rays are warmest near the ground

100. Which of the following statements about magnets is false?

(A) Magnets are materials that will attract items made of iron, cobalt, and nickel.

(B) Natural magnets found in the ground are called lodestones.

(C) Magnetized atoms group together in domains, or large clusters, which line up with north-seeking poles at one end and south-seeking poles at the other.

(D) The older theory, which said that magnetism was due to molecules behaving as tiny magnets with all north-seeking poles facing in one direction and south-seeking poles facing in the other, is not currently held as true by most scientists.

(E) Earth does not behave as a huge magnet because it is not a magnet.

101. Which of the following embryonic membranes is matched correctly with its function?

(A) Yolk sac—heart protection

(B) Allantois—gas exchange

(C) Chorion—food storage

(D) Amnion—energy transfer

(E) Peritoneum—cushions the embryo

102. The standard system of measurement in physics is the

(A) *mks* system, in fundamental units of distance, mass, and time

(B) *kgs* system, in fundamental units of length, width, and height

(C) *cms* system, in fundamental units of distance, volume, and time

(D) *mgs* system, in fundamental units of distance, mass, and time

(E) *lwh* system, in fundamental units of length, width, and height

103. Using the acceleration formula, $x = x_0 + v_0 t + \frac{1}{2} at^2$, how far will a braking car go before stopping if it goes from 20 m/s to a full stop, decelerating at a rate of 5 m/s^2?

(A) 120 meters

(B) 80 meters

(C) 70 meters

(D) 40 meters

(E) 100 meters

104. The sky is blue because

    (A) outer space is blue

    (B) it is a reflection of the blue bodies of water on the surface

    (C) sunlight is scattered by the atmosphere before it reaches Earth

    (D) the sun emits most of the light in the blue portion of the spectrum

    (E) the distance of the mesosphere from the Earth's surface makes it appear blue to our eyes

105. Heat transfer occurs

    (A) from an object of a lower temperature to one of a higher temperature

    (B) from an object of a higher temperature to one of a lower temperature

    (C) when electrons bump into each other

    (D) when the temperature rises

    (E) only when objects come in contact with each other

106. What is the hottest possible temperature in the universe?

    (A) + 35,900,000 °R

    (B) + 35,900,000 °C

    (C) + 35,900,000 °F

    (D) + 35,900,000 K

    (E) There is no upper limit to a possible hottest temperature in the universe, just as there is no coldest possible temperature.

107. All of the following are major structural regions of roots EXCEPT the

    (A) meristematic region   (D) epistematic region

    (B) elongation region   (E) maturation region

    (C) root cap

108. Bernoulli's principle states that

    (A) internal fluid pressure decreases as fluid speed increases

(B) as the volume of a gas increases at constant temperature, the pressure increases

(C) an object in air is buoyed up by a force equal to the weight of the air displaced

(D) internal fluid pressure increases as fluid speed increases

(E) a fluid in a container expands when cooled and contracts when heated

109. When a yellow pea plant is crossed with a green pea plant, all the offspring are yellow. The law that best explains this is the

(A) law of intolerance

(B) law of dominance

(C) law of interference

(D) law of relative genes

(E) law of codominance

110. We can determine the temperature of a star by

(A) measuring its spectrum

(B) measuring the Doppler shift of its spectral lines

(C) measuring its distance and apparent magnitude

(D) obtaining the chemical composition

(E) measuring its brightness

111. Which of the following would be a reason for temperature changes as you travel up through the atmosphere?

(A) Distance from the sun decreases

(B) Weather disruptions cause mixing of the temperatures

(C) Presence of ozone

(D) Presence of man

(E) Changes in composition

112. Traits that are produced by the expression of more than one set of genes are known as

    (A) polygenic traits

    (B) autosomal traits

    (C) sex-limited traits

    (D) monohybrid traits

    (E) dihybrid traits

113. Use this table to answer the following question.

Substance	S° (J/ K mol)
C_2H_2 (g)	249.0
CO_2 (g)	213.6
H_2O (l)	69.96
O_2 (g)	205.0

The numeric value for the standard change in entropy for the combustion of C_2H_2 (g) is closest to

    (A) −267 J/mol K

    (B) +267 J/mol K

    (C) −497 J/mol K

    (D) +497 J/mol K

    (E) −763 J/mol K

114. Specific heat is related to the amount of heat

    (A) contained by a specific object

    (B) contained by one molecule

    (C) transferred by one molecule

    (D) needed to change the temperature of 1 g of a substance by 1°C

    (E) that a specific material contains when heated for a specific period of time

115. The process of genetic inheritance was first investigated and explained by

    (A) Robert Hooke

    (B) Dmitri Mendeleev

    (C) Theodor Schwann

    (D) Matthias Schleiden

    (E) Gregor Mendel

116. The biogeography of a tropical island is affected by numerous factors, including which of the following?

    (A) Volcanic activity and prevailing winds

    (B) Distance from other land masses

    (C) Human, insect, and plant populations

    (D) Only (A) and (C)

    (E) (A), (B), and (C)

117. The ability of a body to change shape when a force is applied and then return to its original shape when that force is removed is called

    (A) elasticity   (D) flexibility

    (B) compression   (E) rigidity

    (C) spring force

118. The modern synthesis concept of evolution stresses that

    (A) evolution represents gradual change in traits across populations

    (B) evolution is only seen on the species level

    (C) evolution may occur in bursts over a short period of time

    (D) evolution represents the presence of acquired characteristics in individuals

    (E) evolution occurs through only one mechanistic process

119. The name of the original supercontinental land mass that existed in geological time nearly 250 million years ago before the continents divided was called

    (A) Paleozoa   (D) Protozoa

    (B) Precambrian   (E) Continental Drift

    (C) Pangea

120. The ratio of the speed of light in a vacuum to its speed in a given material is called the index of

    (A) reflection   (D) resonance

    (B) refraction   (E) resolution

    (C) reflux

Practice Test 3

CLEP Natural Sciences

Answer Key

1. (B)	25. (D)	49. (B)	73. (A)	97. (B)
2. (C)	26. (E)	50. (B)	74. (D)	98. (E)
3. (E)	27. (D)	51. (E)	75. (E)	99. (B)
4. (D)	28. (B)	52. (A)	76. (C)	100. (E)
5. (A)	29. (E)	53. (E)	77. (B)	101. (B)
6. (B)	30. (C)	54. (D)	78. (C)	102. (A)
7. (D)	31. (A)	55. (B)	79. (B)	103. (D)
8. (E)	32. (A)	56. (C)	80. (B)	104. (C)
9. (B)	33. (E)	57. (A)	81. (C)	105. (B)
10. (A)	34. (D)	58. (D)	82. (E)	106. (E)
11. (D)	35. (B)	59. (E)	83. (E)	107. (D)
12. (E)	36. (B)	60. (C)	84. (D)	108. (B)
13. (C)	37. (C)	61. (B)	85. (B)	109. (B)
14. (E)	38. (A)	62. (C)	86. (D)	110. (A)
15. (D)	39. (D)	63. (C)	87. (B)	111. (E)
16. (A)	40. (E)	64. (B)	88. (D)	112. (A)
17. (C)	41. (E)	65. (A)	89. (D)	113. (A)
18. (B)	42. (B)	66. (D)	90. (C)	114. (D)
19. (D)	43. (A)	67. (C)	91. (B)	115. (E)
20. (E)	44. (D)	68. (E)	92. (C)	116. (E)
21. (A)	45. (A)	69. (B)	93. (B)	117. (A)
22. (A)	46. (D)	70. (A)	94. (B)	118. (A)
23. (B)	47. (D)	71. (A)	95. (D)	119. (C)
24. (C)	48. (D)	72. (C)	96. (C)	120. (B)

Detailed Explanations of Answers

Practice Test 3

1. **(B)** Abiotic limiting factors (such as pollution, drought, etc.) are also known as density independent factors—they are independent of population density.

2. **(C)** Populations have a particular geographic area with suitable conditions; this total area occupied by a species is known as the range.

3. **(E)** Emigration is a permanent one-way movement of a species out of its original range into another.

4. **(D)** Two or more different species that live within the same area and overlap niches are said to be in competition if the resource they both require is in limited supply.

5. **(A)** Within a given area, the maximum level the population may reach where it will continue to thrive is known as the carrying capacity.

6. **(B)** Innate behaviors are the actions in animals we call instincts. Innate behaviors are highly stereotyped—they are similar actions performed by many individuals.

7. **(D)** A reflex is an instinctive movement of a body part in response to a stimulus.

8. **(E)** A fixed action pattern is the most complex of stereotyped behaviors. It is a pre-programmed response to a particular stimulus known as a *releaser* or a *sign stimulus*. FAPs include courtship behaviors, circadian rhythms, and feeding of young. Organisms automatically perform FAPs without any prior experience (they are not learned).

9. **(B)** A mutation is an accidental change of the DNA sequence of a gene that results in creating a change of trait that is not found in the parent.

10. **(A)**   Differential reproduction proposes that those individuals within a population that are most adapted to the environment are also the most likely individuals to reproduce viable offspring.

11. **(D)**   The Hardy-Weinberg law of equilibrium states that where random mating is occurring within a population that is in equilibrium with its environment, the gene frequencies and genotype ratios will remain constant from generation to generation. The Hardy-Weinberg law is a mathematical formula that shows why recessive genes do not disappear over time from a population.

12. **(E)**   Allopatric speciation occurs when two populations are geographically isolated from each. Over time this results in the production of two separate species.

13. **(C)**   When an individual from an adjacent population of the same species immigrates and breeds with a member of a previously locally isolated group, it results in a change of the gene pool, known as gene migration.

14. **(E)**   Tundra has extreme cold temperatures, low precipitation, modified grassland, perma-frost, a short growing season, and some plants and animals.

15. **(D)**   Desert has extreme hot or cold temperatures, with very low precipitation, sandy or rocky terrain, sparse vegetation (mainly succulents), small animals, rodents, and reptiles.

16. **(A)**   Savanna is a warm climate with moderate precipitation, grassland, and light seasonal rains.

17. **(C)**   Lysosomes are membrane-bound organelles that contain digestive enzymes that digest dead or unused material within the cell or materials absorbed by the cell for use.

18. **(B)**   Free ribosomes are the sites of protein synthesis within cells. Free ribosomes float unattached within the cytoplasm. They contain RNA that is specific to their function (ribosomal RNA or rRNA) in protein formation.

19. **(D)**   Endocytic vesicles are formed when the plasma membrane of a cell encloses a molecule outside the membrane and then releases a membrane-bound sack containing the desired molecule into the cytoplasm. This process allows the cell to absorb molecules that are larger in size than would be able to pass through the cell membrane.

20. **(E)**   The nucleus contains the chromosomes, and is the site of reproduction through mitosis and meiosis.

21. **(A)**   Centrioles are tubes constructed of a geometrical arrangement of microtubules in a pinwheel shape. Their function includes the formation of new microtubules, but is primarily to form the structural skeleton around which cells split during mitosis and meiosis.

22. **(A)**   Connective tissue covers internal organs and comprises ligaments and tendons. This tissue holds tissues and organs together, stabilizing the body structure.

23. **(B)**   Epithelial tissue covers the body (skin) and lines internal organs. It protects the body and its organs, and is responsible for secretion of oils, sweat, and other substances as part of the excretory system.

24. **(C)**   Found at the end of bones and in the ears and nose, cartilage tissue reduces friction between bones, while supporting and connecting them.

25. **(D)**   Adipose tissue is found beneath the skin and around organs providing cushioning, insulation, and fat storage.

26. **(E)**   Blood tissue exists within the blood vessels and heart, and is essential for carrying oxygen to cells, fighting infection, and carrying nutrients and waste to and from cells. Blood also has clotting capabilities that preserve the body's functions in case of injury.

27. **(D)**   Solubility increases when the temperature is raised in endothermic solution reactions. According to Le Chatelier's principle, the reaction will respond by using the heat and dissolving more into solution.

28. **(B)**   Solubility decreases when the temperature is raised in an exothermic solution reaction.

29. **(E)**   The oxidation of butane to form carbon dioxide and water is considered a combustion reaction.

30. **(C)**   Adding an acid to this reaction will prompt a forward reaction as a result of Le Chatelier's principle. The reaction will respond by using up the acid, which is chemically the same as adding sulfuric acid.

31. **(A)**   The stem supports the leaves, so that they are exposed to sunlight.

32. **(A)** The stem is also the main organ for transporting food and water to and from the leaves. In some cases the stem also is used to store food; for instance, a potato is a tuber (stem) that stores starch.

33. **(E)** The shoot apex is composed of meristem tissue and is the region where elongation of the stem occurs.

34. **(D)** New leaves begin as lateral buds, which can be seen on growing plants.

35. **(B)** Nodes are the locations along the stem where new leaves sprout, and the space between nodes is the internode.

36. **(B)** Flourine is the most electronegative element. Its tendency to gain an electron to have a full set of *p*-orbitals, combined with the small atomic radius which puts the outer electrons close to the positively charged nucleus, make fluorine highly electronegative.

37. **(C)** Sodium, along with other alkaline metals, will combine with hydrogen to form halide compounds. Halides are unique in that they are the only time that hydrogen atoms take a negative oxidation state.

38. **(A)** Hydrogen is the most abundant element in the universe; oxygen is the most abundant element on the Earth.

39. **(D)** Thorium (Th) is the heaviest element, and the only one whose most abundant naturally occurring isotopes are radioactive. While the others have naturally occurring isotopes that are radioactive, such isotopes occur with very low frequency.

40. **(E)** Argon, as an inert gas, has a full set of *p*-orbitals and *s*-orbitals at $n = 3$.

41. **(E)** Magnesium is an active metal that will release its electrons to protons to produce hydrogen gas. The other metals that are options are bound up in ionic attractions and have already released control of their electrons.

42. **(B)** Heating hydrogen peroxide will increase the rate at which it decomposes into oxygen gas and water.

43. **(A)** Potassium iodide will dissolve and yield soluble iodide ions, which will combine with lead ions in solution to form the yellow precipitate lead iodide.

44. **(D)** The combination of the thiocyanate ion with the soluble iron (III) ion yields blood-red iron (III) thiocyanate, a coordination compound.

45. **(A)** Lamarck's theory of acquired characteristics was later discredited, but it led scientists to think about possible alternatives to explain the origins of biological life.

46. **(D)** The hydrosphere is not a layer of Earth, but rather the name of the liquid water region of Earth's surface.

47. **(D)** The standard work equation, Work = (force)(distance) or $W = (f)(d)$, would be used, where W represents work, f represents force, and d represents distance. It would have the following values: $f = 100$ N, $d = 10$ m. So $W = (f)(d) = (100$ N$)(10$ m$) = 1000$ Nm. A Nm (Newton-meter) is a Joule, so 1,000 Nm = 1,000 Joules. The other answers would be wrong because of mathematical errors or not correctly defining force or distance in the work formula.

48. **(D)** Kepler's second law states that the line from the Sun to a planet sweeps equal areas in equal times. Choice (A) is Newton's second law, choice (B) is Kepler's third law, choice (C) is Kepler's first law, and choice (E) is Newton's gravitational law.

49. **(B)** Stomata are openings in the leaf surface that allow for exchange of water and gases. Epiderm and mesoderm are internal cells not related to gas exchange. The cuticle is a waxy covering that helps in water retention, while surface hairs increase surface area for water absorption.

50. **(B)** Natural selection occurs when the surviving species is the one that is most adapted to the environment (in this case, resistant to antibiotics). Clearly only the surviving competitors reproduce. Therefore, traits that provide the competitive edge will be represented most often in succeeding generations.

51. **(E)** Sound waves travel the fastest through a solid. Most of outer space is a vacuum, which would negate the propagation of sound. Sound moving through a fluid or air is slower than sound moving through steel.

52. **(A)** If it was a downward bulge formed by a syncline, it would be a basin. A dip is a measurement of the angle of declination, not a geological structure. It measures the angle formed between a plane of tilted rock and the horizontal plane. A fault is a fracture in the Earth where two planes that are separated move relative to each other. A fold is a compressionally deformed rock bed.

53. **(E)** Although Kelvin is also a measure of temperature used to determine absolute zero, it is incorrect because the nomenclature is wrong. The unit of temperature is not in units of degrees, but simply Kelvin. Absolute zero is the ideal temperature at which perfect crystalline substances may be reduced to a unique ground state. It is the temperature at which there is no molecular motion, measured as zero Kelvin, or zero degrees Rankine, which is equivalent to –273 degrees Celsius. The size of the Kelvin degree is the same as the size of the Celsius degree. Rankine degrees assign a different scale than Kelvin, resulting in significant value differences at extreme readings.

54. **(D)** Except for Mercury and Venus, all planets have natural satellites.

55. **(B)** Since the presence of altruistic traits may actually decrease the individual's fitness to survive, in order for the traits of altruism to evolve, it would be necessary for some other factor to influence the preservation and proliferation of those traits beyond natural selection. Kin selection would accomplish the proliferation of altruistic traits as species preferentially mate with close relatives, causing the altruistic traits to be magnified in the offspring.

56. **(C)** The musculoskeletal system provides the body with structure, stability, and the ability to move. By definition, the musculoskeletal system is unique to vertebrates, although some invertebrates (such as mollusks and insects) have external support structures (exoskeletons) and muscle.

57. **(A)** The crystal structure of frozen water, or ice, is held together from the polar intermolecular attractions between the slightly positive hydrogen side of the molecule *and* the slightly negative oxygen side of other water molecules.

58. **(D)** The crystal structure of solid metal is held together by metallic attractions, which must be overcome if the metal is to melt.

59. **(E)** The SiO crystal is held together with network covalent forces, which are the strongest of interatomic forces.

60. **(C)** PbS is held together with ionic attractions, which will need to be overcome in order to melt that substance.

61. **(B)** No matter whether a frame of reference is accelerating or decelerating, light rays always follow the shortest possible path between two points in space. Light rays can certainly be attracted by gravitational fields but not always.

62. **(C)** In answer (A), the decimal point is in the wrong location, because in *scientific notation*, the decimal point is always between the first and second significant digit. Answer (B) is incorrect because it labels the dimensions as kilograms instead of grams. We can verify this: $(4.35 \times 10^{-6} kg)(1.0 \times 10^3 g/1 kg)$ g $= 4.35 \times 10^{-3}$ g. But that equals 0.00435 g, which is off by a magnitude of 3. Answer (D) does not have a negative sign on the exponent; it represents the number $4.35 \times 1,000,000$ or 4,350,000 g. Answer (E) is wrong because of the location of the decimal point. It should be one digit to the right of the number to be in scientific notation, between the first and second digits.

63. **(C)** Distance and time are inextricably related. If two people are at all separated, then the light from two clocks in the same place will appear differently by 1 billionth of a second, because light from each object will arrive at each of their eyes at a different time. There is no luminiferous ether that light travels through in space. This is a theory that Einstein helped to disprove in the early 1900s. He did prove that energy, mass, and light are related through the equation $E = mc^2$.

64. **(B)** Carbon dioxide has a bond order of 2.0 (double bonds) between the carbon and the oxygen. Other than the carbonate ion, the other molecules have all single bonds. The carbonate ion demonstrates resonance, with a delocalized pair of electrons shared across three carbon-oxygen bonds, which results in a bond order of about 1.3.

65. **(A)** Our current taxonomic key is based on one first developed by Carolus Linneaus, who published his book *Systema Naturae* in 1735. Linneaus based his taxonomic keys on the morphological (outward anatomical) differences seen among species. Linneaus designed a system of classification for all known and unknown organisms according to their anatomical similarities and differences.

66. **(D)** The term *Homo sapiens* is an example of the two-word naming of species known as binomial nomenclature (literally meaning "two names" in Latin).

67. **(C)** Venus is closer to the Sun than Earth. The other planets on this list are farther from the Sun than Earth is.

68. **(E)** Though the process of photosynthesis actually occurs through numerous small steps, the entire process can be summed up with the following equation:

$$6CO_2 + 6H_2O + light\ energy \rightarrow C_6H_{12}O_6 + 6O_2$$

Chlorophyll is a green pigment that acts as the primary catalyst of photosynthesis. This unique pigment molecule has the ability of absorbing a photon of light. Chlorophyll is contained in the grana of the chloroplast. Photosynthesis can only occur where chlorophyll is present. Since it is a catalyst, it is not used up in the photosynthetic process, but must be present for the reactions to occur.

69. **(B)** Glycolysis is the reaction that breaks down glucose into smaller molecules and yields energy. Unlike photosynthesis (which only occurs in plant cells), respiration occurs in all cells. It is the first step in all respiration pathways and occurs in the cytoplasm of all living cells.

70. **(A)** Entropy increases as a natural process goes from one equilibrium state to another. This is the only direction that heat flow will go in an irreversible process. Stasis or decreases in entropy do not occur in natural processes when evaluated from a large-scale perspective.

71. **(A)** In the balanced reaction for the combustion of butane, four moles of carbon dioxide are produced for every mole of butane used up. 44.8 liters of gas represents 20 moles at STP, which therefore uses 0.5 mole of butane.

72. **(C)** Evolution of traits depends on the shifting of certain gene frequencies within a population. If gene frequencies remain constant, evolution does not occur.

73. **(A)** The seeds of Easter Lilies are monocotyledonous (single). They therefore also have leaves with parallel veins, flowers with petals in a multiple of three, a fibrous root system, and random arrangement of vascular bundles in their stems.

74. **(D)** A gene is the portion of DNA that produces a particular expressed trait. A gene is a portion of a chromosome. An organism's complete set of genes is its genome. A mutation is a mistake in gene coding.

75. **(E)** Chemical weathering is a complex process consisting of many factors. Faulting and fracturing are mechanical forms of weathering. Though they may assist in speeding up the chemical cycle, they are still grouped in the mechanical process. Breaking down rock through biological activity may lead to both mechanical and chemical weathering. However, it also is classified as a different group of weathering mechanism.

76. **(C)** The last part of the definition of dwarf planet is that it is not a satellite. The new name for these celestial bodies similar to Pluto is *dwarf planet* or

"plutoid." In July 2008, two other plutoids were identified besides Pluto: Eris, Pluto's twin planetoid, and Makemake, a new dwarf planet.

77. **(B)** The primary role of DNA in the cell is to control protein synthesis. Genetic traits are expressed and specialization of cells occurs as a result of the combination of proteins produced by the DNA of a cell.

78. **(C)** Structural genes are not involved in timing and development, but rather produce the actual proteins that form structures such as tissues and organs. Regulatory genes, on the other hand, determine functional or physiological events, such as growth. These specific genes control (regulate) when other genes are turned on or off, thus regulating when certain proteins that produce a specific trait will be synthesized.

79. **(B)** As light from a star is distributed outward from the source, its light energy per unit area decreases as it covers larger and larger areas in an inverse square relationship. Since it covers more area, its brightness dims exponentially. The luminosity is the sum of the total energy flowing through a unit area over the entire surface of the star per second. Since the luminosity of the two stars is equal, the only thing that needs to be observed and measured is the brightness. Since the brightness of the stars is proportional to its distance away, the brighter star would be closer. We know nothing about the intrinsic brightness of these two stars and there is no way to estimate their brightness based on some physical principle, which defines standard candles. We do know, however, which one is closer because of the relative brightness of each star, so (E) is incorrect.

80. **(B)** Angular momentum is a measure of angular velocity, not acceleration; inertia represents a state of motion, not a component of acceleration. Gravitational attraction and forces against gravity are forces involving acceleration respectively, but they don't represent the components of acceleration. Speed is a scalar related to velocity, while distance is an indirect second-tier component of acceleration. Force and mass are related to acceleration in Newton's second law of motion, $F = ma$, but are not components of acceleration per se.

81. **(C)** Meteoroids and meteors are generally smaller and not icy. Asteroids are generally large and rocky. Plutoids are descriptions of new "small solar-system bodies" into which Pluto has been reclassified along with other bodies.

82. **(E)** Viruses are the smallest organisms in the world, by far, but scientists disagree as to whether they are living organisms at all. Their structure consists of only a protein capsule, DNA, or RNA, and sometimes enzymes. They exist to merely reproduce themselves. Viruses do not have any organelles or metabolic capability of their own, so they survive and replicate by invading

a living cell of another organism and taking over its metabolic functions for its own use. The virus then utilizes the cell's mechanisms to reproduce itself, finally destroying the cell in the process. This invade-and-destruct operation of viruses causes the organism containing the infected cells to sicken and sometimes die as the virus overtakes more and more of its cells. Scientists do not agree as to whether viruses are actually "alive," since though they can reproduce themselves, they do not have the ability to conduct metabolic functions on their own.

83. **(E)** Of the examples given, the only process in which the available energy is increasing and disorder is being reduced is in the process of cell division. The broken window has an increase in disorder; energy was applied to the window that is no longer available, resulting in increasing entropy to the system. A nuclear explosion is a system in which energy is released in the form of heat and radioactivity, resulting in greater randomness or increased entropy. A messy room results from energy being used to bring about a more disordered system, increasing the entropy in the room. Lukewarm water is experiencing the reduction of available energy, as it moves from a more excited molecular state to a less excited state and results in increased entropy.

84. **(D)** The Sun's orbit in the Milky Way galaxy is nearly circular. This can be inferred from the fact that the Sun takes 230 million years to circle the galaxy once in a galactic year. The choices referring to radial motion towards the center of the galaxy and radial motion away from the center of the galaxy describe linear motion. Choice (C) refers to an extreme type of orbit, which doesn't really agree with the statement given in the text. Choice (E) describes a fictitious path.

85. **(B)** The complementary strand would be CTATGGT because guanine (G) pairs with cytosine (C), and thymine (T) pairs with adenine (A).

86. **(D)** Hurricanes, cyclones, and typhoons are regional names for the same meteorological events. They occur when the atmospheric conditions, tail movements, winds, and atmospheric pressure change severely. Although they pull billions of gallons of water from the ocean to generate their energy at any time of day or night, they can move over both water and land. Arid zones include deserts and dry regions, which normally do not experience hurricanes, though it is possible a hurricane could dump its moisture over one as it moves over land.

87. **(B)** Choice (A) erroneously transposes the order of Mercury and Mars. Choice (C) incorrectly lists the Jovian planets. Choice (D) transposes the order of Mars and Earth. Choice (E) erroneously lists the Jovian planets backwards.

88. **(D)** Though temperature is a measure of molecular motion, it does not measure the speed of the molecules in a strict sense. Nor does it measure the pressure between the molecules. Temperature also does not measure the number of molecules. It is nearly impossible to determine the hottest temperature for any molecule, let alone for specific ones.

89. **(D)** The distance in parsecs is equal to the inverse of a star's parallax in arcseconds; therefore, the correct answer is 10 parsecs. It is found by taking the reciprocal of the parallax value, so $0.1 = 1/10$, and the reciprocal would be $10/1$ or 10.

90. **(C)** All rocks are made up of minerals that are the building blocks of the crust of Earth. Symmetry is the geometric shape of the crystal lattice of a mineral. Fossils, clastics, and macerals are terms associated with sedimentary rock and do not universally apply to all types of rocks.

91. **(B)** The correct sequence from the oldest to youngest eras is Precambrian, Paleozoic, Mesozoic, Cenozoic.

92. **(C)** This is known as incomplete dominance. Neither white nor red is dominant over the other.

93. **(B)** RW is a symbol for genotype. In this case the RW genotype produces a pink phenotype. R and W represent the alleles for red and white, respectively.

94. **(B)** Both parents have two alleles that are the same; thus, they have homozygous genotypes for color.

95. **(D)** While A, B, and C could have been true, a red snapdragon could have been produced by any of those choices. However, a white snapdragon can not produce a red snapdragon as an offspring even if paired with a red.

96. **(C)** Sensory input depends on healthy function of nerves, which requires the myelin sheath to be intact. Sensory input would be impaired by the loss of the myelin sheath.

97. **(B)** The equation is written as $H = E + p* V$, where E is the external energy, p is the pressure, and V is the volume of the gas.

98. **(E)** If two of the heterozygous offspring of an incomplete dominant trait are crossed, each is RW and the Punnett square would be:

	R	W
R	RR	RW
W	RW	WW

The phenotypic ratio of the offspring then is one-fourth red, one-half pink, and one-fourth white, a 1 red: 2 pink: 1 white ratio.

99. **(B)**   The physical properties of the ground allow it to absorb heat. The troposphere is also under the ozone layer, yet it is colder than the ground. Ice is only covering certain parts of Earth where it affects the temperature of the surface. It doesn't affect the entire planet. Land and water have different rates of heating and cooling. (E) is wrong because not all of the answers are right.

100. **(E)**   Earth *does* behave as a huge magnet because it *is* a magnet.

101. **(B)**   The allantois appears in the third week of development and becomes part of the umbilical cord. It contains blood vessels that function to exchange gases and nutrients between the embryo and the mother. In reptilian egg-laying vertebrates, the allantois is a reservoir for wastes.

102. **(A)**   In answer (B), k would represent kilometers (length), which is not the fundamental measurement for length in physics because it would be way too long; grams are not units of width; and seconds are not units of height. Answer (C) is incorrect even though the c represents centimeters, which is a fundamental measurement of mass in astronomy (*cgs*), but meters are not a fundamental measurement for volume. Seconds (s) represent, correctly, a fundamental measurement of time. Answer (D) is incorrect because grams are too small a unit of measurement as the fundamental unit of mass, but not when combined with meters, but rather with centimeters. This would then make *cgs* the fundamental units of measurement in astronomy, with grams representing mass. The *lwh* system is not a "system of measurement" at all; it represents the three dimensions of length in a three-dimensional body.

103. **(D)**   Input values for the acceleration formula $x = x_0 + v_0 t + \frac{1}{2} at^2$ are $x_0 = 0$, $v_0 = 20$ m/s, and $t = 20$ m/s $/ 5$ m/s$^2 = 4$ s. Plugging these values into the formula, we find that the car will stop at a distance of $x = 0$ m $+ (20$ m/s$)(4$ s$) + \frac{1}{2}(-5$ s$^2)(4$ s$)^2 = 0$ m $+ 80$ m $- 40$ m $= 40$ m. Answer (A) would probably result from a miscalculation from a missing negative sign for deceleration resulting in adding 40 m instead of subtracting it. (B) was probably selected by those who only thought the acceleration portion of the equation needed to be solved

because both $x_0 = 0$ and $v_0 = 0$. (C) would probably result from forgetting to square the time in the acceleration portion of the equation, $\frac{1}{2} at^2$.

104. **(C)**   The sun emits energy throughout the entire electromagnetic spectrum, including all wavelengths of visible light. Bodies of water only appear to be reflected by the sky under certain conditions when a mirage forms. Not every day meets these conditions but the sky is usually blue. And since very little light reaches our eyes from stars other than the sun, outer space appears black, not blue. The distance of the surface to the mesosphere does not have anything to do with how we view its color. The atmosphere refracts light in the blue portion of the light spectrum so that the sky appears blue. Air molecules scatter the Sun's light in all directions. However, air is a selective scatterer, which scatters shorter wavelengths much more than longer ones. This causes more light from the shorter wavelength of the blue portion of the spectrum to be scattered to the Earth. This gives the sky its bluish appearance. At sunrise and sunset, though, the light must travel through much more of the atmosphere, due to its low angle of elevation. This causes most of the shorter wavelength blue portion of the spectrum to be scattered out before reaching Earth, leaving the longer wavelength red portion to be seen. This is what gives both sunrise and sunset a reddish appearance.

105. **(B)**   Heat transfer occurs by the collision of atoms, not just the electrons. While the temperature does rise during heat transfer, the heat source does maintain a simultaneous drop in temperature. Convection and radiation are forms of heat transfer that do not require contact.

106. **(E)**   There is no hottest possible temperature in the universe (that we know of).

107. **(D)**   There is no epistematic region in plant roots. Roots have four major structural regions that run vertically from bottom to top. The root cap is composed of dead, thick-walled cells and covers the tip of the root, protecting it as the root pushes through soil. The meristematic region is just above the root cap. It consists of undifferentiated cells that carry on mitosis, providing the cells that grow to form the elongation region. In the elongation region, cells differentiate, large vacuoles are formed, and cells grow. As the cells differentiate into various root tissues they become part of the maturation region.

108. **(B)**   The ideal gas law ($PV = nRT$) states that volume is directly proportional to pressure, so as volume increases, pressure increases. Answer (C) is a corollary of Archimedes' principle, not Bernoulli's principle. Fluids contract in cold air and expand in hot air, not vice versa.

109. **(B)**   Mendel determined that one gene is sometimes dominant over another gene for the same trait (that is, it expressed itself over the other). This is known as the law of dominance, Mendel's second law of inheritance.

110. **(A)**   The temperature of a star is determined from measuring its spectrum. The spectrum reveals information not just about the temperature, but composition and relative motion. Apparent magnitude (intrinsic brightness) is another property of the star and not directly related to its temperature.

111. **(E)**   Changes in composition in the atmosphere would cause different rates of heating. Changes in distance from the sun are insignificant versus the distance to the sun. Weather only affects the lowest atmospheric layer, the troposphere. Ozone is only found in one layer. Man does not significantly affect the atmosphere in its totality.

112. **(A)**   Traits, such as height and skin color, are produced from the expression of more than one set of genes and are known as polygenic traits. Monohybrid traits are those with matching alleles, while dihybrid have different alleles. Sex-limited traits would be those found on X or Y chromosomes only. Autosomal traits are determined by a single allele.

113. **(A)** $\Delta S^\circ_{reaction} = \Sigma S^\circ \text{ (products)} - \Sigma S^\circ \text{ (reactants)}$

$\Delta S^\circ_{reaction} = [(2 \times 213.6) + (70)] - [(249) + (2.5 \times 205)]$

$\Delta S^\circ_{reaction} = -264.3 \text{ J/K}$

114. **(D)**   It would be impossible to measure the amount of heat in one molecule, or the amount transferred by one molecule. The definition of specific heat is the amount of heat required to change the temperature of one gram of a substance by 1°C.

115. **(E)**   Gregor Mendel studied the relationships between traits expressed in parents and offspring, and the genes that caused the traits to be expressed. Robert Hooke, Theodor Schwann and Matthias Schleiden were all well known microbiologists (dealt with cells), and Dmitri Mendeleev is known for developing the periodic table of elements (chemistry).

116. **(E)**   Dispersal of species to an island is dependent on geographical as well as historical factors. Distance from other land masses is an important geographical factor. Prevailing winds and ocean currents are also geographical factors that will affect species introduction. Historical factors, such as climate shifts (for instance, the shift to an ice age), drought, volcanic action, plate shift-

ing, etc., will also affect which species are able to travel to a given island. In recent history dispersion has also occurred through human intervention and can be affected by such things as population increases and decreases among plants, animals, and humans.

117. **(A)**   Compression is a process that takes place with a gas, which has no defined shape. Spring force is not a physical property of a body. Flexibility is an indicator of the elasticity of a substance, but is not the physical parameter. Rigidity is the opposite or lack of elasticity; it defines the solid nature of an object.

118. **(A)**   The modern synthesis focused on the concept that evolution was a process of gradual adaptive change in traits across populations.

119. **(C)**   As a result of continental drift, the tectonic plates separated the once-united supercontinent into the seven continents that we observe today. The name was originated in 1920 by Alfred Wegener as part of the continental drift theory. Paleozoic and Precambrian are the names of geologic eras. Protozoa are one-celled organisms, and not a geological term.

120. **(B)**   The index of refraction defines the ratio of the speed of light in a vacuum to its speed in a given material.

Practice Test 1

CLEP Natural Sciences

Answer Sheet

1. Ⓐ Ⓑ Ⓒ Ⓓ Ⓔ
2. Ⓐ Ⓑ Ⓒ Ⓓ Ⓔ
3. Ⓐ Ⓑ Ⓒ Ⓓ Ⓔ
4. Ⓐ Ⓑ Ⓒ Ⓓ Ⓔ
5. Ⓐ Ⓑ Ⓒ Ⓓ Ⓔ
6. Ⓐ Ⓑ Ⓒ Ⓓ Ⓔ
7. Ⓐ Ⓑ Ⓒ Ⓓ Ⓔ
8. Ⓐ Ⓑ Ⓒ Ⓓ Ⓔ
9. Ⓐ Ⓑ Ⓒ Ⓓ Ⓔ
10. Ⓐ Ⓑ Ⓒ Ⓓ Ⓔ
11. Ⓐ Ⓑ Ⓒ Ⓓ Ⓔ
12. Ⓐ Ⓑ Ⓒ Ⓓ Ⓔ
13. Ⓐ Ⓑ Ⓒ Ⓓ Ⓔ
14. Ⓐ Ⓑ Ⓒ Ⓓ Ⓔ
15. Ⓐ Ⓑ Ⓒ Ⓓ Ⓔ
16. Ⓐ Ⓑ Ⓒ Ⓓ Ⓔ
17. Ⓐ Ⓑ Ⓒ Ⓓ Ⓔ
18. Ⓐ Ⓑ Ⓒ Ⓓ Ⓔ
19. Ⓐ Ⓑ Ⓒ Ⓓ Ⓔ
20. Ⓐ Ⓑ Ⓒ Ⓓ Ⓔ

21. Ⓐ Ⓑ Ⓒ Ⓓ Ⓔ
22. Ⓐ Ⓑ Ⓒ Ⓓ Ⓔ
23. Ⓐ Ⓑ Ⓒ Ⓓ Ⓔ
24. Ⓐ Ⓑ Ⓒ Ⓓ Ⓔ
25. Ⓐ Ⓑ Ⓒ Ⓓ Ⓔ
26. Ⓐ Ⓑ Ⓒ Ⓓ Ⓔ
27. Ⓐ Ⓑ Ⓒ Ⓓ Ⓔ
28. Ⓐ Ⓑ Ⓒ Ⓓ Ⓔ
29. Ⓐ Ⓑ Ⓒ Ⓓ Ⓔ
30. Ⓐ Ⓑ Ⓒ Ⓓ Ⓔ
31. Ⓐ Ⓑ Ⓒ Ⓓ Ⓔ
32. Ⓐ Ⓑ Ⓒ Ⓓ Ⓔ
33. Ⓐ Ⓑ Ⓒ Ⓓ Ⓔ
34. Ⓐ Ⓑ Ⓒ Ⓓ Ⓔ
35. Ⓐ Ⓑ Ⓒ Ⓓ Ⓔ
36. Ⓐ Ⓑ Ⓒ Ⓓ Ⓔ
37. Ⓐ Ⓑ Ⓒ Ⓓ Ⓔ
38. Ⓐ Ⓑ Ⓒ Ⓓ Ⓔ
39. Ⓐ Ⓑ Ⓒ Ⓓ Ⓔ
40. Ⓐ Ⓑ Ⓒ Ⓓ Ⓔ

41. Ⓐ Ⓑ Ⓒ Ⓓ Ⓔ
42. Ⓐ Ⓑ Ⓒ Ⓓ Ⓔ
43. Ⓐ Ⓑ Ⓒ Ⓓ Ⓔ
44. Ⓐ Ⓑ Ⓒ Ⓓ Ⓔ
45. Ⓐ Ⓑ Ⓒ Ⓓ Ⓔ
46. Ⓐ Ⓑ Ⓒ Ⓓ Ⓔ
47. Ⓐ Ⓑ Ⓒ Ⓓ Ⓔ
48. Ⓐ Ⓑ Ⓒ Ⓓ Ⓔ
49. Ⓐ Ⓑ Ⓒ Ⓓ Ⓔ
50. Ⓐ Ⓑ Ⓒ Ⓓ Ⓔ
51. Ⓐ Ⓑ Ⓒ Ⓓ Ⓔ
52. Ⓐ Ⓑ Ⓒ Ⓓ Ⓔ
53. Ⓐ Ⓑ Ⓒ Ⓓ Ⓔ
54. Ⓐ Ⓑ Ⓒ Ⓓ Ⓔ
55. Ⓐ Ⓑ Ⓒ Ⓓ Ⓔ
56. Ⓐ Ⓑ Ⓒ Ⓓ Ⓔ
57. Ⓐ Ⓑ Ⓒ Ⓓ Ⓔ
58. Ⓐ Ⓑ Ⓒ Ⓓ Ⓔ
59. Ⓐ Ⓑ Ⓒ Ⓓ Ⓔ
60. Ⓐ Ⓑ Ⓒ Ⓓ Ⓔ

Practice Test 1

CLEP Natural Sciences

Answer Sheet

61. Ⓐ Ⓑ Ⓒ Ⓓ Ⓔ
62. Ⓐ Ⓑ Ⓒ Ⓓ Ⓔ
63. Ⓐ Ⓑ Ⓒ Ⓓ Ⓔ
64. Ⓐ Ⓑ Ⓒ Ⓓ Ⓔ
65. Ⓐ Ⓑ Ⓒ Ⓓ Ⓔ
66. Ⓐ Ⓑ Ⓒ Ⓓ Ⓔ
67. Ⓐ Ⓑ Ⓒ Ⓓ Ⓔ
68. Ⓐ Ⓑ Ⓒ Ⓓ Ⓔ
69. Ⓐ Ⓑ Ⓒ Ⓓ Ⓔ
70. Ⓐ Ⓑ Ⓒ Ⓓ Ⓔ
71. Ⓐ Ⓑ Ⓒ Ⓓ Ⓔ
72. Ⓐ Ⓑ Ⓒ Ⓓ Ⓔ
73. Ⓐ Ⓑ Ⓒ Ⓓ Ⓔ
74. Ⓐ Ⓑ Ⓒ Ⓓ Ⓔ
75. Ⓐ Ⓑ Ⓒ Ⓓ Ⓔ
76. Ⓐ Ⓑ Ⓒ Ⓓ Ⓔ
77. Ⓐ Ⓑ Ⓒ Ⓓ Ⓔ
78. Ⓐ Ⓑ Ⓒ Ⓓ Ⓔ
79. Ⓐ Ⓑ Ⓒ Ⓓ Ⓔ
80. Ⓐ Ⓑ Ⓒ Ⓓ Ⓔ

81. Ⓐ Ⓑ Ⓒ Ⓓ Ⓔ
82. Ⓐ Ⓑ Ⓒ Ⓓ Ⓔ
83. Ⓐ Ⓑ Ⓒ Ⓓ Ⓔ
84. Ⓐ Ⓑ Ⓒ Ⓓ Ⓔ
85. Ⓐ Ⓑ Ⓒ Ⓓ Ⓔ
86. Ⓐ Ⓑ Ⓒ Ⓓ Ⓔ
87. Ⓐ Ⓑ Ⓒ Ⓓ Ⓔ
88. Ⓐ Ⓑ Ⓒ Ⓓ Ⓔ
89. Ⓐ Ⓑ Ⓒ Ⓓ Ⓔ
90. Ⓐ Ⓑ Ⓒ Ⓓ Ⓔ
91. Ⓐ Ⓑ Ⓒ Ⓓ Ⓔ
92. Ⓐ Ⓑ Ⓒ Ⓓ Ⓔ
93. Ⓐ Ⓑ Ⓒ Ⓓ Ⓔ
94. Ⓐ Ⓑ Ⓒ Ⓓ Ⓔ
95. Ⓐ Ⓑ Ⓒ Ⓓ Ⓔ
96. Ⓐ Ⓑ Ⓒ Ⓓ Ⓔ
97. Ⓐ Ⓑ Ⓒ Ⓓ Ⓔ
98. Ⓐ Ⓑ Ⓒ Ⓓ Ⓔ
99. Ⓐ Ⓑ Ⓒ Ⓓ Ⓔ
100. Ⓐ Ⓑ Ⓒ Ⓓ Ⓔ

101. Ⓐ Ⓑ Ⓒ Ⓓ Ⓔ
102. Ⓐ Ⓑ Ⓒ Ⓓ Ⓔ
103. Ⓐ Ⓑ Ⓒ Ⓓ Ⓔ
104. Ⓐ Ⓑ Ⓒ Ⓓ Ⓔ
105. Ⓐ Ⓑ Ⓒ Ⓓ Ⓔ
106. Ⓐ Ⓑ Ⓒ Ⓓ Ⓔ
107. Ⓐ Ⓑ Ⓒ Ⓓ Ⓔ
108. Ⓐ Ⓑ Ⓒ Ⓓ Ⓔ
109. Ⓐ Ⓑ Ⓒ Ⓓ Ⓔ
110. Ⓐ Ⓑ Ⓒ Ⓓ Ⓔ
111. Ⓐ Ⓑ Ⓒ Ⓓ Ⓔ
112. Ⓐ Ⓑ Ⓒ Ⓓ Ⓔ
113. Ⓐ Ⓑ Ⓒ Ⓓ Ⓔ
114. Ⓐ Ⓑ Ⓒ Ⓓ Ⓔ
115. Ⓐ Ⓑ Ⓒ Ⓓ Ⓔ
116. Ⓐ Ⓑ Ⓒ Ⓓ Ⓔ
117. Ⓐ Ⓑ Ⓒ Ⓓ Ⓔ
118. Ⓐ Ⓑ Ⓒ Ⓓ Ⓔ
119. Ⓐ Ⓑ Ⓒ Ⓓ Ⓔ
120. Ⓐ Ⓑ Ⓒ Ⓓ Ⓔ

Practice Test 2
CLEP Natural Sciences

Answer Sheet

1. Ⓐ Ⓑ Ⓒ Ⓓ Ⓔ
2. Ⓐ Ⓑ Ⓒ Ⓓ Ⓔ
3. Ⓐ Ⓑ Ⓒ Ⓓ Ⓔ
4. Ⓐ Ⓑ Ⓒ Ⓓ Ⓔ
5. Ⓐ Ⓑ Ⓒ Ⓓ Ⓔ
6. Ⓐ Ⓑ Ⓒ Ⓓ Ⓔ
7. Ⓐ Ⓑ Ⓒ Ⓓ Ⓔ
8. Ⓐ Ⓑ Ⓒ Ⓓ Ⓔ
9. Ⓐ Ⓑ Ⓒ Ⓓ Ⓔ
10. Ⓐ Ⓑ Ⓒ Ⓓ Ⓔ
11. Ⓐ Ⓑ Ⓒ Ⓓ Ⓔ
12. Ⓐ Ⓑ Ⓒ Ⓓ Ⓔ
13. Ⓐ Ⓑ Ⓒ Ⓓ Ⓔ
14. Ⓐ Ⓑ Ⓒ Ⓓ Ⓔ
15. Ⓐ Ⓑ Ⓒ Ⓓ Ⓔ
16. Ⓐ Ⓑ Ⓒ Ⓓ Ⓔ
17. Ⓐ Ⓑ Ⓒ Ⓓ Ⓔ
18. Ⓐ Ⓑ Ⓒ Ⓓ Ⓔ
19. Ⓐ Ⓑ Ⓒ Ⓓ Ⓔ
20. Ⓐ Ⓑ Ⓒ Ⓓ Ⓔ

21. Ⓐ Ⓑ Ⓒ Ⓓ Ⓔ
22. Ⓐ Ⓑ Ⓒ Ⓓ Ⓔ
23. Ⓐ Ⓑ Ⓒ Ⓓ Ⓔ
24. Ⓐ Ⓑ Ⓒ Ⓓ Ⓔ
25. Ⓐ Ⓑ Ⓒ Ⓓ Ⓔ
26. Ⓐ Ⓑ Ⓒ Ⓓ Ⓔ
27. Ⓐ Ⓑ Ⓒ Ⓓ Ⓔ
28. Ⓐ Ⓑ Ⓒ Ⓓ Ⓔ
29. Ⓐ Ⓑ Ⓒ Ⓓ Ⓔ
30. Ⓐ Ⓑ Ⓒ Ⓓ Ⓔ
31. Ⓐ Ⓑ Ⓒ Ⓓ Ⓔ
32. Ⓐ Ⓑ Ⓒ Ⓓ Ⓔ
33. Ⓐ Ⓑ Ⓒ Ⓓ Ⓔ
34. Ⓐ Ⓑ Ⓒ Ⓓ Ⓔ
35. Ⓐ Ⓑ Ⓒ Ⓓ Ⓔ
36. Ⓐ Ⓑ Ⓒ Ⓓ Ⓔ
37. Ⓐ Ⓑ Ⓒ Ⓓ Ⓔ
38. Ⓐ Ⓑ Ⓒ Ⓓ Ⓔ
39. Ⓐ Ⓑ Ⓒ Ⓓ Ⓔ
40. Ⓐ Ⓑ Ⓒ Ⓓ Ⓔ

41. Ⓐ Ⓑ Ⓒ Ⓓ Ⓔ
42. Ⓐ Ⓑ Ⓒ Ⓓ Ⓔ
43. Ⓐ Ⓑ Ⓒ Ⓓ Ⓔ
44. Ⓐ Ⓑ Ⓒ Ⓓ Ⓔ
45. Ⓐ Ⓑ Ⓒ Ⓓ Ⓔ
46. Ⓐ Ⓑ Ⓒ Ⓓ Ⓔ
47. Ⓐ Ⓑ Ⓒ Ⓓ Ⓔ
48. Ⓐ Ⓑ Ⓒ Ⓓ Ⓔ
49. Ⓐ Ⓑ Ⓒ Ⓓ Ⓔ
50. Ⓐ Ⓑ Ⓒ Ⓓ Ⓔ
51. Ⓐ Ⓑ Ⓒ Ⓓ Ⓔ
52. Ⓐ Ⓑ Ⓒ Ⓓ Ⓔ
53. Ⓐ Ⓑ Ⓒ Ⓓ Ⓔ
54. Ⓐ Ⓑ Ⓒ Ⓓ Ⓔ
55. Ⓐ Ⓑ Ⓒ Ⓓ Ⓔ
56. Ⓐ Ⓑ Ⓒ Ⓓ Ⓔ
57. Ⓐ Ⓑ Ⓒ Ⓓ Ⓔ
58. Ⓐ Ⓑ Ⓒ Ⓓ Ⓔ
59. Ⓐ Ⓑ Ⓒ Ⓓ Ⓔ
60. Ⓐ Ⓑ Ⓒ Ⓓ Ⓔ

Practice Test 2

CLEP Natural Sciences

Answer Sheet

61. Ⓐ Ⓑ Ⓒ Ⓓ Ⓔ	81. Ⓐ Ⓑ Ⓒ Ⓓ Ⓔ	101. Ⓐ Ⓑ Ⓒ Ⓓ Ⓔ
62. Ⓐ Ⓑ Ⓒ Ⓓ Ⓔ	82. Ⓐ Ⓑ Ⓒ Ⓓ Ⓔ	102. Ⓐ Ⓑ Ⓒ Ⓓ Ⓔ
63. Ⓐ Ⓑ Ⓒ Ⓓ Ⓔ	83. Ⓐ Ⓑ Ⓒ Ⓓ Ⓔ	103. Ⓐ Ⓑ Ⓒ Ⓓ Ⓔ
64. Ⓐ Ⓑ Ⓒ Ⓓ Ⓔ	84. Ⓐ Ⓑ Ⓒ Ⓓ Ⓔ	104. Ⓐ Ⓑ Ⓒ Ⓓ Ⓔ
65. Ⓐ Ⓑ Ⓒ Ⓓ Ⓔ	85. Ⓐ Ⓑ Ⓒ Ⓓ Ⓔ	105. Ⓐ Ⓑ Ⓒ Ⓓ Ⓔ
66. Ⓐ Ⓑ Ⓒ Ⓓ Ⓔ	86. Ⓐ Ⓑ Ⓒ Ⓓ Ⓔ	106. Ⓐ Ⓑ Ⓒ Ⓓ Ⓔ
67. Ⓐ Ⓑ Ⓒ Ⓓ Ⓔ	87. Ⓐ Ⓑ Ⓒ Ⓓ Ⓔ	107. Ⓐ Ⓑ Ⓒ Ⓓ Ⓔ
68. Ⓐ Ⓑ Ⓒ Ⓓ Ⓔ	88. Ⓐ Ⓑ Ⓒ Ⓓ Ⓔ	108. Ⓐ Ⓑ Ⓒ Ⓓ Ⓔ
69. Ⓐ Ⓑ Ⓒ Ⓓ Ⓔ	89. Ⓐ Ⓑ Ⓒ Ⓓ Ⓔ	109. Ⓐ Ⓑ Ⓒ Ⓓ Ⓔ
70. Ⓐ Ⓑ Ⓒ Ⓓ Ⓔ	90. Ⓐ Ⓑ Ⓒ Ⓓ Ⓔ	110. Ⓐ Ⓑ Ⓒ Ⓓ Ⓔ
71. Ⓐ Ⓑ Ⓒ Ⓓ Ⓔ	91. Ⓐ Ⓑ Ⓒ Ⓓ Ⓔ	111. Ⓐ Ⓑ Ⓒ Ⓓ Ⓔ
72. Ⓐ Ⓑ Ⓒ Ⓓ Ⓔ	92. Ⓐ Ⓑ Ⓒ Ⓓ Ⓔ	112. Ⓐ Ⓑ Ⓒ Ⓓ Ⓔ
73. Ⓐ Ⓑ Ⓒ Ⓓ Ⓔ	93. Ⓐ Ⓑ Ⓒ Ⓓ Ⓔ	113. Ⓐ Ⓑ Ⓒ Ⓓ Ⓔ
74. Ⓐ Ⓑ Ⓒ Ⓓ Ⓔ	94. Ⓐ Ⓑ Ⓒ Ⓓ Ⓔ	114. Ⓐ Ⓑ Ⓒ Ⓓ Ⓔ
75. Ⓐ Ⓑ Ⓒ Ⓓ Ⓔ	95. Ⓐ Ⓑ Ⓒ Ⓓ Ⓔ	115. Ⓐ Ⓑ Ⓒ Ⓓ Ⓔ
76. Ⓐ Ⓑ Ⓒ Ⓓ Ⓔ	96. Ⓐ Ⓑ Ⓒ Ⓓ Ⓔ	116. Ⓐ Ⓑ Ⓒ Ⓓ Ⓔ
77. Ⓐ Ⓑ Ⓒ Ⓓ Ⓔ	97. Ⓐ Ⓑ Ⓒ Ⓓ Ⓔ	117. Ⓐ Ⓑ Ⓒ Ⓓ Ⓔ
78. Ⓐ Ⓑ Ⓒ Ⓓ Ⓔ	98. Ⓐ Ⓑ Ⓒ Ⓓ Ⓔ	118. Ⓐ Ⓑ Ⓒ Ⓓ Ⓔ
79. Ⓐ Ⓑ Ⓒ Ⓓ Ⓔ	99. Ⓐ Ⓑ Ⓒ Ⓓ Ⓔ	119. Ⓐ Ⓑ Ⓒ Ⓓ Ⓔ
80. Ⓐ Ⓑ Ⓒ Ⓓ Ⓔ	100. Ⓐ Ⓑ Ⓒ Ⓓ Ⓔ	120. Ⓐ Ⓑ Ⓒ Ⓓ Ⓔ

Practice Test 3

CLEP Natural Sciences

Answer Sheet

1. Ⓐ Ⓑ Ⓒ Ⓓ Ⓔ
2. Ⓐ Ⓑ Ⓒ Ⓓ Ⓔ
3. Ⓐ Ⓑ Ⓒ Ⓓ Ⓔ
4. Ⓐ Ⓑ Ⓒ Ⓓ Ⓔ
5. Ⓐ Ⓑ Ⓒ Ⓓ Ⓔ
6. Ⓐ Ⓑ Ⓒ Ⓓ Ⓔ
7. Ⓐ Ⓑ Ⓒ Ⓓ Ⓔ
8. Ⓐ Ⓑ Ⓒ Ⓓ Ⓔ
9. Ⓐ Ⓑ Ⓒ Ⓓ Ⓔ
10. Ⓐ Ⓑ Ⓒ Ⓓ Ⓔ
11. Ⓐ Ⓑ Ⓒ Ⓓ Ⓔ
12. Ⓐ Ⓑ Ⓒ Ⓓ Ⓔ
13. Ⓐ Ⓑ Ⓒ Ⓓ Ⓔ
14. Ⓐ Ⓑ Ⓒ Ⓓ Ⓔ
15. Ⓐ Ⓑ Ⓒ Ⓓ Ⓔ
16. Ⓐ Ⓑ Ⓒ Ⓓ Ⓔ
17. Ⓐ Ⓑ Ⓒ Ⓓ Ⓔ
18. Ⓐ Ⓑ Ⓒ Ⓓ Ⓔ
19. Ⓐ Ⓑ Ⓒ Ⓓ Ⓔ
20. Ⓐ Ⓑ Ⓒ Ⓓ Ⓔ

21. Ⓐ Ⓑ Ⓒ Ⓓ Ⓔ
22. Ⓐ Ⓑ Ⓒ Ⓓ Ⓔ
23. Ⓐ Ⓑ Ⓒ Ⓓ Ⓔ
24. Ⓐ Ⓑ Ⓒ Ⓓ Ⓔ
25. Ⓐ Ⓑ Ⓒ Ⓓ Ⓔ
26. Ⓐ Ⓑ Ⓒ Ⓓ Ⓔ
27. Ⓐ Ⓑ Ⓒ Ⓓ Ⓔ
28. Ⓐ Ⓑ Ⓒ Ⓓ Ⓔ
29. Ⓐ Ⓑ Ⓒ Ⓓ Ⓔ
30. Ⓐ Ⓑ Ⓒ Ⓓ Ⓔ
31. Ⓐ Ⓑ Ⓒ Ⓓ Ⓔ
32. Ⓐ Ⓑ Ⓒ Ⓓ Ⓔ
33. Ⓐ Ⓑ Ⓒ Ⓓ Ⓔ
34. Ⓐ Ⓑ Ⓒ Ⓓ Ⓔ
35. Ⓐ Ⓑ Ⓒ Ⓓ Ⓔ
36. Ⓐ Ⓑ Ⓒ Ⓓ Ⓔ
37. Ⓐ Ⓑ Ⓒ Ⓓ Ⓔ
38. Ⓐ Ⓑ Ⓒ Ⓓ Ⓔ
39. Ⓐ Ⓑ Ⓒ Ⓓ Ⓔ
40. Ⓐ Ⓑ Ⓒ Ⓓ Ⓔ

41. Ⓐ Ⓑ Ⓒ Ⓓ Ⓔ
42. Ⓐ Ⓑ Ⓒ Ⓓ Ⓔ
43. Ⓐ Ⓑ Ⓒ Ⓓ Ⓔ
44. Ⓐ Ⓑ Ⓒ Ⓓ Ⓔ
45. Ⓐ Ⓑ Ⓒ Ⓓ Ⓔ
46. Ⓐ Ⓑ Ⓒ Ⓓ Ⓔ
47. Ⓐ Ⓑ Ⓒ Ⓓ Ⓔ
48. Ⓐ Ⓑ Ⓒ Ⓓ Ⓔ
49. Ⓐ Ⓑ Ⓒ Ⓓ Ⓔ
50. Ⓐ Ⓑ Ⓒ Ⓓ Ⓔ
51. Ⓐ Ⓑ Ⓒ Ⓓ Ⓔ
52. Ⓐ Ⓑ Ⓒ Ⓓ Ⓔ
53. Ⓐ Ⓑ Ⓒ Ⓓ Ⓔ
54. Ⓐ Ⓑ Ⓒ Ⓓ Ⓔ
55. Ⓐ Ⓑ Ⓒ Ⓓ Ⓔ
56. Ⓐ Ⓑ Ⓒ Ⓓ Ⓔ
57. Ⓐ Ⓑ Ⓒ Ⓓ Ⓔ
58. Ⓐ Ⓑ Ⓒ Ⓓ Ⓔ
59. Ⓐ Ⓑ Ⓒ Ⓓ Ⓔ
60. Ⓐ Ⓑ Ⓒ Ⓓ Ⓔ

Practice Test 3

CLEP Natural Sciences

Answer Sheet

61. Ⓐ Ⓑ Ⓒ Ⓓ Ⓔ	81. Ⓐ Ⓑ Ⓒ Ⓓ Ⓔ	101. Ⓐ Ⓑ Ⓒ Ⓓ Ⓔ
62. Ⓐ Ⓑ Ⓒ Ⓓ Ⓔ	82. Ⓐ Ⓑ Ⓒ Ⓓ Ⓔ	102. Ⓐ Ⓑ Ⓒ Ⓓ Ⓔ
63. Ⓐ Ⓑ Ⓒ Ⓓ Ⓔ	83. Ⓐ Ⓑ Ⓒ Ⓓ Ⓔ	103. Ⓐ Ⓑ Ⓒ Ⓓ Ⓔ
64. Ⓐ Ⓑ Ⓒ Ⓓ Ⓔ	84. Ⓐ Ⓑ Ⓒ Ⓓ Ⓔ	104. Ⓐ Ⓑ Ⓒ Ⓓ Ⓔ
65. Ⓐ Ⓑ Ⓒ Ⓓ Ⓔ	85. Ⓐ Ⓑ Ⓒ Ⓓ Ⓔ	105. Ⓐ Ⓑ Ⓒ Ⓓ Ⓔ
66. Ⓐ Ⓑ Ⓒ Ⓓ Ⓔ	86. Ⓐ Ⓑ Ⓒ Ⓓ Ⓔ	106. Ⓐ Ⓑ Ⓒ Ⓓ Ⓔ
67. Ⓐ Ⓑ Ⓒ Ⓓ Ⓔ	87. Ⓐ Ⓑ Ⓒ Ⓓ Ⓔ	107. Ⓐ Ⓑ Ⓒ Ⓓ Ⓔ
68. Ⓐ Ⓑ Ⓒ Ⓓ Ⓔ	88. Ⓐ Ⓑ Ⓒ Ⓓ Ⓔ	108. Ⓐ Ⓑ Ⓒ Ⓓ Ⓔ
69. Ⓐ Ⓑ Ⓒ Ⓓ Ⓔ	89. Ⓐ Ⓑ Ⓒ Ⓓ Ⓔ	109. Ⓐ Ⓑ Ⓒ Ⓓ Ⓔ
70. Ⓐ Ⓑ Ⓒ Ⓓ Ⓔ	90. Ⓐ Ⓑ Ⓒ Ⓓ Ⓔ	110. Ⓐ Ⓑ Ⓒ Ⓓ Ⓔ
71. Ⓐ Ⓑ Ⓒ Ⓓ Ⓔ	91. Ⓐ Ⓑ Ⓒ Ⓓ Ⓔ	111. Ⓐ Ⓑ Ⓒ Ⓓ Ⓔ
72. Ⓐ Ⓑ Ⓒ Ⓓ Ⓔ	92. Ⓐ Ⓑ Ⓒ Ⓓ Ⓔ	112. Ⓐ Ⓑ Ⓒ Ⓓ Ⓔ
73. Ⓐ Ⓑ Ⓒ Ⓓ Ⓔ	93. Ⓐ Ⓑ Ⓒ Ⓓ Ⓔ	113. Ⓐ Ⓑ Ⓒ Ⓓ Ⓔ
74. Ⓐ Ⓑ Ⓒ Ⓓ Ⓔ	94. Ⓐ Ⓑ Ⓒ Ⓓ Ⓔ	114. Ⓐ Ⓑ Ⓒ Ⓓ Ⓔ
75. Ⓐ Ⓑ Ⓒ Ⓓ Ⓔ	95. Ⓐ Ⓑ Ⓒ Ⓓ Ⓔ	115. Ⓐ Ⓑ Ⓒ Ⓓ Ⓔ
76. Ⓐ Ⓑ Ⓒ Ⓓ Ⓔ	96. Ⓐ Ⓑ Ⓒ Ⓓ Ⓔ	116. Ⓐ Ⓑ Ⓒ Ⓓ Ⓔ
77. Ⓐ Ⓑ Ⓒ Ⓓ Ⓔ	97. Ⓐ Ⓑ Ⓒ Ⓓ Ⓔ	117. Ⓐ Ⓑ Ⓒ Ⓓ Ⓔ
78. Ⓐ Ⓑ Ⓒ Ⓓ Ⓔ	98. Ⓐ Ⓑ Ⓒ Ⓓ Ⓔ	118. Ⓐ Ⓑ Ⓒ Ⓓ Ⓔ
79. Ⓐ Ⓑ Ⓒ Ⓓ Ⓔ	99. Ⓐ Ⓑ Ⓒ Ⓓ Ⓔ	119. Ⓐ Ⓑ Ⓒ Ⓓ Ⓔ
80. Ⓐ Ⓑ Ⓒ Ⓓ Ⓔ	100. Ⓐ Ⓑ Ⓒ Ⓓ Ⓔ	120. Ⓐ Ⓑ Ⓒ Ⓓ Ⓔ

Index

H

I

INSTALLING REA's TestWare®

SYSTEM REQUIREMENTS

Pentium 75 MHz (300 MHz recommended) or a higher or compatible processor; Microsoft Windows 98 or later; 64 MB Available RAM; Internet Explorer 5.5 or higher

INSTALLATION

1. Insert the CLEP Natural Sciences TestWare® CD-ROM into the CD-ROM drive.
2. If the installation doesn't begin automatically, from the Start Menu choose the RUN command. When the RUN dialog box appears, type d:\setup (where *d* is the letter of your CD-ROM drive) at the prompt and click OK.
3. The installation process will begin. A dialog box proposing the directory "Program Files\REA\CLEP_NatSci" will appear. If the name and location are suitable, click OK. If you wish to specify a different name or location, type it in and click OK.
4. Start the CLEP Natural Sciences TestWare® application by double-clicking on the icon.

REA's CLEP Natural Sciences TestWare® is **EASY** to **LEARN AND USE**. To achieve maximum benefits, we recommend that you take a few minutes to go through the on-screen tutorial on your computer.

SSD ACCOMMODATIONS FOR STUDENTS WITH DISABILITIES

Many students qualify for extra time to take the CLEP Natural Sciences exam, and our TestWare® can be adapted to accommodate your time extension. This allows you to practice under the same extended-time accommodations that you will receive on the actual test day. To customize your TestWare® to suit the most common extensions, visit our website at *www.rea.com/ssd*.

TECHNICAL SUPPORT

REA's TestWare® is backed by customer and technical support. For questions about **installation or operation of your software**, contact us at:

Research & Education Association
Phone: (732) 819-8880 (9 a.m. to 5 p.m. ET, Monday–Friday)
Fax: (732) 819-8808
Website: www.rea.com
E-mail: info@rea.com

Note to Windows XP Users: In order for the TestWare® to function properly, please install and run the application under the same computer administrator-level user account. Installing the TestWare® as one user and running it as another could cause file-access path conflicts.